SPEAKING STONES

Contemporary Issues in the Middle East

SPEAKING STONES

Communiqués from the Intifada Underground

SHAUL MISHAL and REUBEN AHARONI

SYRACUSE UNIVERSITY PRESS

Copyright © 1994 by Syracuse University Press
Syracuse, New York 13244-5160

ALL RIGHTS RESERVED

First Edition 1994

94 95 96 97 98 99   6 5 4 3 2 1

The paper used in this publication meets the minimum
requirements of American National Standard for Information
Sciences—Permanence of Paper for Printed Library Materials,
ANSI Z39.48-1984. ∞™

Library of Congress Cataloging-in-Publication Data

Speaking stones : communiqués from the Intifada underground /
  [compiled, edited, and translated by] Shaul Mishal and Reuben
  Aharoni.
      p. cm.
    Includes bibliographical references and index.
    ISBN 0-8156-2606-1 (cloth). — ISBN 0-8156-2607-X (paper)
    1. Intifada, 1975- —Sources. 2. Ḥarakat al-Muqāwamah al-
Islāmīyah—History—Sources. 3. Palestinian Arabs—Politics and
government. I. Mishal, Shaul, 1945- . II. Aharoni, Re 'uven.
DS119.75.S68   1994
956.95'3044—dc20   93-38559

Manufactured in the United States of America

For Dan Horowitz
(1928–1991)

SHAUL MISHAL is an Associate Professor in the Department of Political Science at Tel Aviv University and is head of the Institute for Israeli Arab Studies at Beit Berl. He is the author of *West Bank/East Bank: The Palestinians in Jordan, 1949–1967* and *The PLO under ʿArafat: Between Gun and Olive Branch*.

REUBEN AHARONI is a Lecturer in the Department of Eretz Israel Studies, University of Haifa. A field research coordinator at the Institute of Israeli Arab Studies, he is the author (with Yitzhak Reiter) of *The Political Life of Arabs in Israel*.

CONTENTS

	Tables	xi
	Preface	xiii
	Acknowledgments	xvii
	Abbreviations	xix
1.	The Road to the Intifada	1
2.	Paper War: *The Intifada Leaflets*	25

Leaflets of the United National Command (UNC)

1.	In the wake of our people's glorious uprising	53
2.	O masses of our glorious people	55
3.	O masses of the magnificent Palestinian people	59
6.	O masses of our valiant people	64
10.	O proud struggling masses of our people	67
11.	Land Day Proclamation	72
12.	Qastel Proclamation	76
14.	Proclamation of the martyred commander... Abu Jihad	82
15.	The Workers Proclamation	87
16.	Palestine Proclamation [1]	93
18.	The Palestinian Child Proclamation	98
19.	The Detainees of the Uprising Proclamation	103
21.	The Blessed al-Aqsa [Mosque] Proclamation	108
23.	The Deportees Proclamation	113
24.	The Uprising Martyrs Behind Bars Proclamation	118

25.	The Martyrs of the Massacres Proclamation	123
26.	Palestine Proclamation [2]	130
27.	The National Council Proclamation	135
28.	The Independence Proclamation	140
29.	The Joy of the Independent Palestinian State Proclamation	146
30.	The Uprising Proclamation	151
36.	The Karameh Proclamation	157
41.	The Defiance and Continuity Proclamation	163
45.	The September and the Shahada Proclamation	169
48.	The Proclamation of Independence	175
55.	The Proclamation of Jerusalem, Eternal Capital of the Independent Palestinian State	181
68.	The Unity Around the PLO Proclamation	188
70.	The Building Proclamation	193

Leaflets of the Islamic Resistance Movement (Hamas)

1.	O *murabitun* on the soil of immaculate and beloved Palestine	201
2.	The Blessed Uprising	204
4.	O our Muslim people	208
6.	A general strike against the new American conspiracy	211
7.	March 7, a day of confrontation	214
8.	Al-Israʾ wal-Miʿraj escalation of the blessed resistance	216
11.	Call to students, teachers, responsible officials, and opinion molders among the public	221
13.	The massacres by the Nazi Jews are continuing	223
14.	I am at your command O Palestinian prisoner	225
16.	Tuesday, Ramadan 17, a day of remembrance of the great Battle of Badr	227
18.	O masses of Muslim *murabitun*	230
21.	The Battle of ʾUhud	232

22.	Saturday and Sunday, June 4, 5, will be days of confrontation and a general strike	234
28.	Islamic Palestine from the sea to the river	237
30.	In Memory of the massacre at Qibya and Kafr Qassim	241
31.	The martyr al-Qassam	245
32.	The partition of Palestine in 1947	249
33.	On December 25 (Qanun al-Awwal) of 1947	253
39.	The Month of Ramadan	257
45.	Knowledge and study are a sacred right	262
49.	The wretched Balfour Declaration	265
	Special Leaflet: Call to the 19th Palestinian National Council	269
	Special Leaflet: The distress of detainees from the Islamic Resistance Movement, Hamas, in Jewish prisons	274
71.	Praise be to God, prayer and peace to the leader of the *Mujahidun*	278
74.	Praise be to God, beloved of the believers	282
	The United National Command and Hamas: A Comparative View	287
	Glossary	293
	Selected Bibliography	295
	Index	299

TABLES

1. Types of Directives in UNC Leaflets by Periodic Distribution (absolute numbers) — 39
2. Types of Directives in Hamas Leaflets by Periodic Distribution (absolute numbers) — 40
3. Types of Directives Contained in UNC Leaflets by Periodic Distribution (in percentage) — 41
4. Types of Directives Contained in Hamas Leaflets by Periodic Distribution (in percentage) — 42
5. UNC and Hamas Leaflets: A Summary Presentation — 288

. . .
PREFACE

LATE JANUARY 1988, a Saturday morning, and the Gaza Strip is unresponsive to the Israeli occupation. The *Intifada* (uprising; literally, shaking off) is entering its fourth week. The streets are dotted with veiled women and youngsters, bare feet protruding from *galabiyyas,* athletic shoes from body-hugging jeans.

Miniature Palestinian flags hang from electricity poles. The streets are stone-strewn, noisy. Gaza is covered with soot from the smoke of burning tires. The air is saturated with tear gas.

It is a sad day in Gaza. The shops are closed, there are no cars in the streets, a general strike is underway. What does a woman about to give birth do, or a person about to die? Gaza is steeped in unquenchable fury and whispers of pain, vast hatred, fingers curling into fists, burning eyes. We are in the midst of a quarrel with no beginning and no end.

Hot winds blow at the approaches to the Shati refugee camp. I am with a friend, a press photographer. A soldier observes us from a lookout post on the roof of a building. The square is littered with the remnants of bonfires and overturned garbage cans. An officer in a jeep talks with soldiers who lean on a stone fence. Two little girls play at the entrance to a house. I greet them. Hearing my Arabic, two middle-aged men approach suspiciously. When they notice the "press" sticker (in English and Arabic) on the car windshield, they start a conversation. They tell us about the closing of the schools, the mass arrests carried out by night, the beatings, and the confiscation of local cars by the security forces for use in gaining entry to violent neighborhoods.

Others join in the conversation, and soon we are talking politics. "We want our own state. We want to live in peace with Israel. PLO or not, the main thing is that Israel leaves. You, the Israelis, are strong and we are weak. Why are you afraid of us? You have the atomic bomb. You have America, you have money and beautiful homes, you have education. What do you want from us?" The conversation breaks off. A furious youth who has emerged out of nowhere listens for a moment, then hisses the others silent. "Who are you? What are you doing here? Show me papers. He is a Jew, don't believe him." They begin to argue among themselves. My interlocutors quickly melt back into their homes, where they will undoubtedly settle the matter. I recall what the Israeli poet Natan Alterman said, that history is created in houses and in the marketplace; not in central committees of political parties or on the battlefield.

On my way back to the car, someone thrusts a wrinkled piece of paper into my hand. It is a clandestine printed leaflet. It says:

> O, all our people, men and women. O, our children: the Jews—brothers of the apes, assassins of the prophets, bloodsuckers, warmongers—are murdering you, depriving you of life after having plundered your homeland and your homes. Only Islam can break the Jews and destroy their dreams. Therefore, proclaim to them: Allah is great, Allah is greater than their army, Allah is greater than their airplanes and their weapons. When you struggle with them, take into account to request one of two bounties: martyrdom, or victory over them, and their defeat....
>
> To you our Muslim Palestinian people, Allah's blessing and protection! May Allah strengthen you and give you victory. Continue with your rejection and your struggle against the occupation methods, the dispossessions, deportations, prisons, tortures, travel restrictions, the dissemination of filth and pornography, the corruption and bribery, the improper and humiliating behavior, the heavy taxes, a life of suffering and of degradation to honor and to the houses of worship.

The name below these words was *Harakat al-muqawama al-Islamiyya*, the Islamic Resistance Movement—Hamas for short.

Gaza is not what is was. It is not responsive to closures, arrests, the hand that beats, or the raised club. I remembered the old Gaza. A city of packed marketplaces and hucksters on street corners, of children buzzing beelike around drivers to hawk their wares. Gaza with its hedges of sabra plants, its cafes, and its fish restaurants. Gaza that kept its fury on a low burner.

I cannot get Gaza out of my mind. The Intifada continues, and I find myself totally immersed in the events in the occupied territories. I look for a prop to lean on, a conceptual anchor that will enable me to come to grips with the sheer momentum of the events.

On my visits to Gaza and the West Bank, I discover the importance of these clandestine leaflets. Gradually, I come to realize that behind the youngsters and the stones and the barricades are words. They dictate the way of life and determine the boundaries of the permissible, they bring the people into the streets and instruct them what to do, when, and how. The population responds to the written directives and does not submit to the military pressures and economic sanctions. If one wants to know the why and wherefore of the Intifada's eruption, what the Palestinians think and what they are fighting for, how they operate and how they perceive Israel, the United States, and the Arab world, one should read the written words. The underground leaflets are the documents by which the Palestinians go forth and to which they return. This book is the result of that realization.

The book consists of two parts. The opening chapter deals with why and how the Intifada came about in late 1987 and what prevented its outbreak during the first twenty years of Israeli rule in the territories.

The second chapter is devoted to a content analysis of the leaflets in an effort to understand the forces that turned the wheels of the uprising: their goals, their modes of operation, and their success in obtaining the willing cooperation of all segments of the Palestinian population, despite the heavy pressures exerted by Israel.

The second part provides the reader with a selection of translated leaflets of the two leading bodies in the Intifada: The United National Command (UNC) (al-Qiyada al-wataniyya al-muwahada) and Hamas. Of all Intifada groups, these two have been able to ensure a considerable degree of obedience to their directives and to obtain broad compliance from the Palestinian population in the occupied territories.

The book includes 53 leaflets: 28 from the UNC and 25 from Hamas. Most of the leaflets are from the first year of the Intifada (December 1987–December 1988); the rest date from the second, the third, and the fourth year. These leaflets represent about a third of all the leaflets published and distributed by the two groups during the first four years— the formative period—of the Intifada. It is this formative period that redefined Palestinians' modes of political thinking, shaped patterns of collective response, and influenced individual behavior. Also during this period, the foundations for Palestinians' perceptions toward political developments and their views regarding a peace settlement with Israel were formulated.

Leaflets are presented chronologically according to their appearance in the field. Those selected for each year represent their contribution in highlighting issues of the Intifada, such as civil disobedience, self-reliance, forms of violence, institution building, and collective consciousness. In addition, the selected leaflets reflect Palestinian responses and interpretations of current events as perceived by the national and the religious camps.

An unmediated encounter with the leaflets will expose the reader to the ideological intensity, the political complexity, and the behavioral codes of the Palestinian uprising. In turn, this exposure should enable us to assess the various Palestinian perceptions of themselves and the ways in which they view their struggle and their future.

The historic Israeli-PLO agreement of September 1993 to establish a Palestinian Interim Self-Government Authority in the West Bank and the Gaza Strip will probably bring an end to the Intifada. Wounds, on both sides, may eventually heal. Willingness for political reconciliation will pave the road for mutual acceptance. Agreement over territorial compromises will increase the chances for peaceful coexistance and economic cooperation. The prose of reality will overcome the poetry of dogmatic ideologies.

Yet, for the coming years, the Intifada will remain in the hearts and the minds of the Palestinians. It will symbolize the heroic Palestinian response to the Israeli occupation. The Intifada will play a key role in shaping the collective memory of the Palestinians, their social consciousness, their political self-image, and their personal expectations. Above all, it will affect the attitudes and behavior of the Palestinians toward their political authorities and their future relations with Israel.

Reuben Aharoni, with intimate knowledge of Palestinian political realities and ideological diversities, provided me with invaluable insights and assisted in formulating my ideas regarding Palestinian perceptions and motives.

Shaul Mishal

Tel Aviv
October 1993

ACKNOWLEDGMENTS

MANY PEOPLE in different places and in different ways stand behind this book. David Apter and Ian Shapiro at Yale University, Avraham Sela at the Hebrew University of Jerusalem, and Asher Susser at the Moshe Dayan Center, Tel Aviv University, were kind enough to read drafts of the manuscript and to contribute useful comments. Moshe Semyonov and Yehouda Shenhav at Tel Aviv University were very helpful with their generous advice on how to approach quantitatively the vast amount of data contained in the leaflets, and Ran Hirshel, our energetic research assistant, demonstrated his skills in the process of carrying out the data analysis.

Mustafa Kabha and Tayyib Yunis, native Arabic speakers, and Ralph Mandel, an excellent English translator and editor, were with us at the crucial stage of the translation of the leaflets from Arabic to Hebrew and English. They drew up the first draft in both languages and continued to assist us with helpful advice. Without their help, this manuscript would be less coherent, more complicated, and perhaps unpublished.

Good fortune provided us with the help of Roslyn Langbart and Sylvia Weinberg, who bore the burden of typing patiently and efficiently.

We would have been unable to complete this volume had it not been for grants received from the Moshe Dayan Center for Middle Eastern and African Studies, the David Horowitz Institute for the Research of Developing Countries, and the Faculty of Social Science—all at Tel Aviv University.

ABBREVIATIONS

DFLP	Democratic Front for the Liberation of Palestine (al-Jabha al-dimuqratiyya li-tahrir filastin)
Fatah	Palestinian National Liberation Movement (Harakat al-tahrir al-watani al-filastini)
Hamas	Islamic Resistance Movement (Harakat al-muqawama al-Islamiyya)
NGC	National Guidance Committee (Lajnat al-tawjih al-watani)
PCP	Palestinian Communist Party (al-Hizb al-shuyuʿi al-filastini)
PFLP	Popular Front for the Liberation of Palestine (al-Jabha al-shaʿbiyya li-tahrir filastin)
PLO	Palestine Liberation Organization (Munazzamat al-tahrir al-filastiniyya)
PNC	Palestinian National Council (al-Majlis al-watani al-filastini)
UNC	United National Command [of the Uprising] (al-Qiyada al-wataniyya al-muwahada)
UNESCO	United Nations Educational, Scientific and Cultural Organization
UNRWA	United Nations Relief and Works Agency

SPEAKING STONES

1

• • •

THE ROAD TO THE INTIFADA

WHEN LEAFLETS AND POEMS guide people's routine, bring them into the streets and dictate the permissible and the forbidden, something serious is occurring. It happened to Zionism, it happened to national movements in Europe, in South America, and in Asia. It happened in Iran, and it has happened among the Palestinians in the West Bank and the Gaza Strip.

The Intifada did not spring from out of the blue. Since the Israeli conquest in 1967, the West Bank and Gaza had seen demonstrations, strikes, and violent riots against Israeli rule. But never before December 1987 had there been such a comprehensive, intense, and prolonged eruption against the occupation.

The Intifada inspired a new kind of Palestinian radicalism, a radicalism borne on young shoulders, a radicalism that conducts its dialogue with Israel and the local population via the stone, the slingshot, the petrol bomb, and the leaflet.

Demography, the economic situation, and the education received by the young generation have done their work. It was the convergence of the three processes, primarily during the latter part of the 1970s, that fostered a climate of political radicalism among Palestinian youth; and it was Israeli policy in the 1980s—which sought to purge the local Palestinian leadership of PLO supporters—that accelerated a process whereby the radical mood was transformed into militant action.

The Palestinians in the territories are largely a young people. In the first ten years of Israeli rule in the territories, the population of the West Bank and Gaza increased by almost 19 percent, and from 1977–1986, by 20 percent. In absolute figures, this means that from 1967–1977 the population of the West Bank grew by 110,000 (from 586,000 to 696,000), and of the Gaza Strip by 70,000 (from 381,000 in 1967 to 451,000 ten years later). In the period from 1977–1986, more than 140,000 persons were added to the population of the West Bank (from

696,000 to 836,000) and more than 94,000 in the Gaza Strip (from 451,000 to 545,000).[1]

The population growth increased the relative proportion of the young generation. Between 1977 and 1986, the 20–34 age group doubled in the West Bank, and in the Gaza Strip it grew by a third.[2] By the mid-1980s, half the Palestinian population in the West Bank and Gaza consisted of youngsters aged 14 or below, and a third of the population was in the 15–34 age group.[3]

The increase in the young population was paralleled by impressive strides in education. In 1970, about half the population aged 14 and above lacked formal education; by 1986 this figure had shrunk to less than half. At the beginning of 1970, only 1 percent of the adult population in the West Bank and Gaza had more than 13 years of schooling. Sixteen years later, the figure was 14 percent. In 1986, a quarter of the young people aged 18 and above in the West Bank and Gaza had more than 13 years of education, and nearly two-thirds of them had nine years or more.[4]

The following data, referring to men and women aged 18–24 in the West Bank of 1983, illustrate the rise in the educational level. Among men, only 1 percent were illiterate, 17 percent had completed six grades of elementary school, 43 percent had 12 years of education and had completed high school, and 23 percent had some form of higher education. Among the women, the illiteracy rate was 7.5 percent, 31 percent had six years of elementary school education, 14 percent had nine years, 34 percent had 12 years, and 13.5 percent had education beyond the high school level.[5]

The spread of higher education was an outcome of the establishment of academic institutions after 1967. At the time Israel entered the territories, they contained not a single university. Since the early 1970s, seven academic institutions opened their doors in the West Bank: Bir

---

1. Avraham Cohen, *Kalkalat ha-shtachim: ha-Gadah ha-Maʿravit ve-Retsuʿat ʿAzah, 1922–1980* (The economic development of the territories, 1922–1980) (Givat Haviva: Institute of Arabic Studies, 1986), 145–146; Stanley Miron, *ha-Shtachim ha-muchzaqim (demographyah, haskalah ve-kalkalah)* (The administered territories [Demography, education and economy]) (Ramat Gan: Yad Tabenkin, Mar. 1986), 3.

2. *Statistical Abstract of Israel 1987*, (Jerusalem: Central Bureau of Statistics, 1987), 38:702.

3. Meron Benvenisti, *1986 Report* (Washington, D.C.: American Enterprise Institute, The West Bank Data Base Project, 1986), 3.

4. *Statistical Abstract of Israel 1987*, 38:748–49.

5. Meron Benvenisti with Ziad Abu Ziad and Danny Rubinstein, *The West Bank Handbook* (Jerusalem: The Jerusalem Post, 1986), 69.

Zeit in 1972 and al-Najah in 1977 (both of which had previously been teachers' colleges); Bethlehem in 1973; Hebron, set up in 1971 as a college for Islamic studies, which became a university in 1980; Abu Dis, a college for scientific studies, in 1982; a college for religious studies in Beit Hanina in 1978; and a nurses' school in al-Bira, founded in 1979.

There are also six teachers' colleges in the West Bank: two sponsored by the United Nations Relief and Works Agency (UNRWA), three run by the government, and one private institution. In Gaza, on the other hand, there is only one university—the Islamic University, under the auspices of al-Azhar University in Egypt—and one teachers' college.[6]

The growth in the student population was unprecedented. In the mid-1970s, there were 1,086 students in the West Bank, and 7,500 in the early 1980s in the West Bank and Gaza combined. By the mid-1980s, there were 10,000 students in the West Bank, with an estimated 4,000 graduates each year: 2,000 from local universities and another 2,000 West Bank students completing their academic studies abroad.

The social volatility generated by the radical thrust was fueled by a growing gap between the more extended education available to the young generation and the limited availability of jobs commensurate with that education and the expectations it generated. There was a striking disparity between the increase in the number of university graduates and their inability to find suitable jobs in either the local or the Israeli labor markets. True, in the first decade of Israeli rule in the territories, both the West Bank and Gaza experienced high growth rates in terms of GNP and per capita consumption, thanks in large measure to the opening of the Israeli economy to workers from the territories. However, the local employment market relied predominantly on agriculture and menial labor. In the absence of changes in the economic infrastructure, employment opportunities commensurate with the education of the young generation did not develop.[7]

Only 15 percent of university graduates were able to find work suited to their qualifications. Others continued their studies or took blue-collar jobs that were far below their level of expectations and were irreconcilable with their self-image. Some drifted to Arab oil-exporting countries in search of employment, but the economic slowdown in those countries, beginning in 1983, reduced this form of emigration. According to Israeli Military Government figures for 1985, there were

---

6. Benvenisti, *1986 Report*, 209–10.
7. For more details, see Gad Gilbar, "Introduction", in Avraham Cohen, viii–ix.

4,000 unemployed university graduates in the West Bank. By the time the Intifada erupted, their number had risen to 8,000.[8]

High school graduates found themselves in the same boat. The majority remained unemployed or took jobs in Israel, usually in construction or the service sector. Both possibilities were incommensurate with their education and totally at variance with their expectations.[9]

The broadening of education among the Palestinian younger generation and the absence of suitable employment nourished a climate of political radicalism. The resultant gap—what sociologists call a disparity between high personal expectations in the employment sphere, generated by education, and opportunities in the economic market—fomented a desire for action geared to alter the existing order. In a situation where the potential economic loss was negligible, the benefit to be derived from changing that situation was perceived to be promising and attractive.

It was the Palestinian younger generation that agitated for change and directed its energies toward political activism, whether in the spirit of PLO secular nationalism or by endeavoring to remake the world in the image of Islam. While the Israeli authorities were tirelessly monitoring the activities of local figures and bodies suspected of supporting or cooperating with the PLO, Palestinian youth was engaged in community activity that grew exponentially. In time, this group would constitute the hard core of the Intifada.

Most of the activity revolved around the students and the local youth organizations. Student councils were established in all the institutions of higher education. In short order, these student bodies divided along ideological lines: supporters of Fatah, the Palestinian Left, and Muslim fundamentalists. Throughout the 1980s, the majority of the student councils were dominated by a coalition of Fatah and the Left.[10] With the exception of the religious universities in Hebron and Gaza, and the religious college in Beit Hanina, supporters of Fatah and Palestinian left-wing factions won majorities of over 60 percent in student council elections.

Like their counterparts in the Third World, Palestinian students possessed a highly developed national consciousness. They were aware of the importance of community activity in order to build a social and political infrastructure that could be used later either to achieve the

---

8. *Ha'aretz* (Tel Aviv), Apr. 26, 1988.
9. Numerical data on the problem are given in Miron, 5.
10. For more details, see Pinhas Inbari, *Meshulash ʿal ha-Yarden: ha-magaʿim ha-chasha'iyim bein Artsot-Habrit, Yarden ve-Ashaf* (Triangle on the Jordan: The secret contacts among U.S.A., Jordan and the PLO) (Jerusalem: Cana, 1982), 144.

PLO goal of national liberation or to establish a Muslim fundamentalist theocracy. Thus, besides the protest activity they initiated on campus, the students engaged in extensive community activity. At their insistence, West Bank universities required students to do community work before receiving their diploma. The students, in cooperation with women's organizations and trade unions, set up day creches and kindergartens, organized adult literacy courses, cleaned streets and cemeteries, and helped repair and expand homes in villages and refugee camps.

The students' projects were part of broader activity conducted by Lijan al-shabiba lil-ʿamal al-ijtimaʿi (Youth Committees for Social Activity)—known as al-Shabiba, founded in 1981 with the encouragement of Fatah. Their purpose was to carry out activity among broad sectors of the population, particularly the young. Al-Shabiba were active in urban neighborhoods and in refugee camps. Like the students, al-Shabiba activists helped the population deal with day-to-day problems. While al-Shabiba groups were gaining recruits among West Bank youth, Muslim organizations were in the ascendancy in the Gaza Strip. The most prominent was al-Mujammaʿ al-Islami (Islamic Association), founded in 1973. Identified with the Muslim Brothers movement, al-Mujammaʿ enjoyed considerable popularity among the students in the religious university of Gaza. Its activists worked with children and youth, organizing educational and sports activities. Their declared intention was to guide the young in the spirit of Islam and lay the ideological foundations for a Muslim state.

The activities initiated by the Palestinian youth had at least two immediate results. For the population at large, participating in community activities heightened the sense of self-reliance. While for the young activists, direct contact with the population supplied experience in dealing with daily problems. In the long run, the sustained interaction between the youngsters and the local population would erode the authority of local leaders, such as the *mukhtars,* who had acted as "go-betweens" for the population and the Israeli authorities. It would also undermine the effectiveness of the Military Government and the Civil Administration, providing the organizational basis for the Intifada.

The ability of Palestinian youth to gain the cooperation of broad sectors of the population, to the point of disrupting the day-to-day activities of the Israeli authorities, was not an inevitable outcome. It is difficult to imagine the Intifada without the youngsters first laying the groundwork among the local population. But it is equally insufficient to explain the sustainability and duration of the Intifada solely in terms of the youngsters' community activity. The key to the Intifada's resilience lies in the participation of the merchants and the white-collar group. The revolutionary fervor and style of action of the youngsters may have been in tune with the inner feelings of this class, but hardly with their wallets, their world view, or their way of life. They prefer caution to daring, measured steps over dramatic acts: "A bird in the hand is better than ten on the tree," says the Arab proverb.

If, nevertheless, the middle class became a full partner in the Intifada, the causes were twofold: one was the absence of an effective local leadership to shield them from the pressures exerted by the young radicals; and the second was the growing erosion in Jordan's standing in the West Bank, weakening its ability to offset radical influences. Both elements had existed in the period before the Lebanon War of 1982. Their subsequent disappearance created an institutional vacuum through which latent radicalism erupted in a manner that left both Israel and Jordan at a loss to contain or control events. As a result, what had seemed improbable from the point of view of the middle class in the pre-Intifada period assumed an aura of inevitability in the course of the uprising.

Jordan and the PLO: Coexistence Within a Prolonged Conflict

In the pre-Lebanon War era, both Jordan and the local leadership in the territories enjoyed political status and prestige enabling them to influence political developments in the West Bank. True, since 1967 the territories had undergone a veritable sea change. The heightened prestige of the PLO in the 1970s, in both the inter-Arab and the international arenas, generated a surge of national feeling among the Palestinians. These sentiments were channeled by the PLO into political activity in the West Bank and Gaza. In the mid-1970s, the PLO's efforts began to bear fruit. PLO influence was palpable in municipalities and in local bodies such as universities, student organizations, trade unions, charitable societies, and the press. In addition, new bodies were founded, such as youth organizations, which operated under PLO guidance.

Nevertheless, Jordan retained considerable political clout in the West Bank. The Hashemite Kingdom remained a political element to be reckoned with by the PLO. Relations between the PLO and Jordan were hardly fraternal or friendly. A deep conflict of interest divided them regarding the nature of the political settlement in the West Bank and Gaza. At the same time, the PLO was conscious of the possible adverse effects were it to exploit its success among the Palestinian population to spark an all-out confrontation with Jordan. Cooperation and coexistence with Amman was the order of the day.

The PLO had to take into account the categorical Israeli rejection of the idea of a Palestinian state in the West Bank and Gaza and espoused instead a political settlement with Jordanian participation. As long as this Israeli stand prevailed, the PLO could not rule out the possibility that its unwillingness to compromise was liable to vitiate its status among the Palestinians—who were anxious to see an end to the Israeli occupation—and push them into the arms of Jordan. It is here that one should look to understand the statement of Yasir Arafat's political adviser, Hani al-Hasan, that "no Palestinian strategist can afford to remove his eyes from Jordan for even a minute. The only Arab state able to replace us [as a party to a political settlement] is Jordan." Furthermore, "no Palestinian strategist can ignore the geographical fact that the Palestinian state-to-be will have two entrances: one from the East Bank and the second from Gaza. There can be no chance to ensure free access to the West Bank other than by having cooperative ties with Jordan."[11]

The day-to-day reality of the local Palestinian population added to the PLO's considerations in favor of cooperation and of keeping open channels of communication with Jordan. Ties with Jordan were a *sine qua non* for obtaining essential needs and services. These included: the export of agricultural produce and other goods via the Jordan River bridges; Amman's continued payment of salaries to civil servants who had served under Jordanian rule before the war of 1967; approval of development projects; exit permits and passports; matriculation certificates required for admittance to universities abroad; import and export licenses; and so forth. In none of these spheres could the PLO replace Jordan. The prolonged Israeli occupation and the growing Israeli-Jordanian interaction on routine matters, made the PLO increasingly inclined to accept the ties linking the residents of the territories to Jordan as a fact to be taken into account in its quest for political status in the territories. A head-on collision with Jordan would perhaps provide an outlet for revolutionary ardor; but it was inconsistent with the need to ensure the support of the population in the Israeli-held territories. Moreover, as the PLO moved toward a political process and sought ways to participate in negotiations that would assure it a territorial *quid pro quo* in the West Bank and Gaza, it was disposed to redefine its priorities in terms of the "here and now" reality rather than adhere to a dogmatic all-or-nothing approach. Dialogue and cooperation with Jordan became a key component in PLO policy toward the occupied territories.

11. *Filastin al-Thawra* (Beirut), Apr. 21, 1984.

A similar conclusion—that cooperation and dialogue were preferable to confrontation—had been reached in Amman. Jordan was intensely conscious of its profound differences with the PLO regarding the desired solution in the West Bank. PLO domination in the West Bank and the establishment of a PLO-led independent entity could threaten the very existence of the Hashemite Kingdom, in which Palestinians constituted approximately half of the population. One might argue that the logical course of action following from this premise entailed a head-on clash with the PLO similar to the civil war of 1970–1971. But other considerations were also at work: the political status acquired by the PLO in the Arab world and among the Palestinians since the mid-1970s; demographic trends in Jordan that favored the Palestinian side; the exposure of the Palestinian population on both banks of the Jordan to outside radical influences; and the constantly shifting alignments in the Arab world, which were not always to Jordan's advantage. Amman was disinclined to view the option of a frontal clash with the PLO as a preferable alternative to the existing political order. Such a confrontation could prove disastrously destabilizing for the regime, possibly even causing its collapse.

Recognizing the limitations of its power to neutralize the PLO in one swift blow as a political rival for West Bank hegemony, Jordan turned to flexible political methods. Amman's policy was guided by the principle that the less it infringed on Palestinian national symbols, the less friction would be generated with the PLO. A moderate level of friction would facilitate the continuation of Jordanian activity in the West Bank without the accompanying perception that such activity was detrimental to Palestinian national aspirations. Thus, in its public statements, Jordan endeavored to play down the importance of its disagreements with the Palestinians on the political future of the territories. Jordan continually declared that its political goals were identical with those of the Palestinians. It was careful not to challenge publicly resolutions of the highest inter-Arab forum, the Arab summit, which recognized the Palestinians as a separate entity with the right to establish their own sovereign state. As presented by Amman, any differences between the two sides were artificial and temporary, deriving less from a dispute over the Palestinians' right to self-determination than from choice of tactics.

Nowhere were Jordan's attempts to present a favorable approach toward PLO national aspirations more apparent than in the period following the 1973 Arab-Israeli war. In 1974, for example, Jordan endorsed the Rabat summit resolution that recognized the PLO as the sole legitimate representative of the Palestinian people. Jordan also supported the Rabat resolution stating that any territory in the West Bank and Gaza evacuated by Israel would be handed over to the PLO. In 1978, Jordan joined in a Baghdad summit resolution supporting the Palestinian right to a state. Jordan also conformed with the Baghdad summit resolution to form a joint committee with the PLO for distribution of $150 million annually to West Bank and Gaza local bodies.[12]

Jordan's public endorsement of the Arab summit resolutions concerning the Palestinian issue enabled Amman to retain its close ties with local institutions in the West Bank and to establish high-level government committees to deal with day-to-day matters. Amman also continued to pay the salaries of West Bank officials who had served in the Jordanian administration before 1967. Moreover, in 1979, Jordan issued new identity cards to residents of both the East and the West Bank, emphasizing the strong ties between the two areas. The PLO could hardly oppose such moves by Amman, and frequently accepted them as a necessary evil. With Israel breathing down the PLO's neck and the population fluctuating between identification with the PLO as the body expressing national aspirations, or with Jordan, the source for material needs, the PLO was reduced to making the best of a bad situation where Jordan's continued activity in the territories was concerned.

The Jordanian and PLO interest of preferring cooperation over confrontation spawned a pattern of relations most aptly described as coexistence within a prolonged conflict. Both sides were well aware of the gulf dividing them and the difficulty of reaching an agreement that would enable them to live side by side in political harmony. Yet, each side recognized its limitations to press for a solution of "one in place of the other." While both sides were clearly unwilling to accept each other fully, they were equally loath to adopt a position of total rejection. In the dusty reality of the Middle East arena, the price each side would pay in attempting to remove the other from the political stage was intolerable. Both therefore preferred to pursue a strategy that would mitigate the disadvantages of coexistence rather than strive for a new political order that excluded the other side. Underlying this pattern of relations was the sober perception that took root in both camps, holding that a clear decision in their protracted dispute was and remained wishful thinking; and that a mode of action based on a zero-sum perception was liable to end in tragedy: the assailant would become the assailed, the executioner, in Baudelaire's words, the condemned, and the wound—the dagger.

---

12. For more details, see Shaul Mishal, *The PLO under 'Arafat: Between Gun and Olive Branch* (New Haven: Yale Univ. Press, 1986), 169–71.

Hence, it was more promising for each side to concentrate on improving its positions and to beef up its bargaining ability vis-à-vis the other side, instead of pursuing an "all or nothing" policy to advance ultimate political goals.

The Jordan-PLO pattern of coexistence was hardly conducive to stability. Indeed, the dialogue and cooperation often seemed on the verge of collapse. Events that appeared to herald a change in the balance of forces between the two parties—the 1970–1971 civil war in Jordan, leading to the PLO's expulsion from the country; the resolutions of the 1974 Rabat summit conference, which gave an inter-Arab imprimatur to the PLO's standing in the West Bank and Gaza; the 1976 West Bank municipal elections, which brought to power pro-PLO leaders—these few examples are indicative of many others. Yet, each side feared to exploit its successes to take far-reaching steps that were liable to bring relations with the other side to a point of no return. After the civil war in Jordan, relations between Jordan and the PLO were renewed; after the Rabat summit, Arafat refrained from excoriating Jordan for its activity in the West Bank; and after the 1976 municipal elections, the PLO did not prevent the new mayors and other public figures in the West Bank from maintaining contacts with Jordan. Neither side contemplated seriously unleashing a confrontation that was liable to become an irreparable rift. Coexistence within a prolonged conflict was perceived by both sides as the lesser evil and as a situation preferable to any of the alternatives.

Coexistence and the Local Leadership

The pattern of coexistence worked out by Jordan and the PLO was profoundly influential in shaping the attitude of the Palestinian local leadership toward each of the two parties. As will be seen, the character of the relationship that developed between the West Bank and Jordan on the one hand and between the West Bank and the PLO on the other hand exercised a moderating influence on the stand of the Palestinian leadership in the territories toward Israel.

The state of coexistence between Jordan and the PLO spared the local leadership the need to choose between the two and enabled them to maintain ties with both sides alike. This was the case with both the traditional pro-Jordanian leaders, who dominated West Bank politics until the municipal elections of 1976, and the pro-PLO leaders who were victorious in those elections. Despite their pro-Jordanian leanings, the traditional leaders maintained contacts with the PLO, particularly after the latter began to evince an interest in a political settlement following the 1973 war. The same was true of the pro-PLO leaders centered in the National Guidance Committee (NGC), established in 1978. True, these leaders, especially the four mayors—Bassam al-Shakʿa in Nablus, Karim Khalaf in Ramallah, Fahd Qawasima in Hebron, and Muhammad Milhim in Halhul—identified strongly with the PLO and viewed the organization as an equal party in any future negotiations on the territories. Yet, they did not balk at dealing and cooperating with Amman on everyday affairs.

The conditions prevailing in the West Bank left the local leadership no real choice but to seek support from both Jordan and the PLO. The absence of a tradition of political independence in the West Bank, combined with the lack of a distinctive ideology and a self-sustaining economy, and the fact that the only common border with the Arab world was with Jordan, precluded the creation of an autonomous power base that might have impelled the West Bank leadership to pursue political initiatives beyond the parameters of Jordanian-PLO coexistence. An Israeli approach to the local leadership as a political partner for negotiations on a permanent settlement, if accompanied by far-reaching territorial concessions, might have created a convenient political climate to build such a power base. Without that willingness, it was unrealistic to expect the emergence of an independent power base in the West Bank.[13]

The coexistence between the PLO and Jordan, as well as the West Bank's economic dependence on Jordan, ideological allegiance with the PLO, and political reliance on both alike, created a situation in which any attempt by the local leadership to court one of the two parties at the expense of the other could jeopardize its very existence. Total submission to the PLO would trigger Jordan's wrath, undermining the local leadership's economic mainstay; while unequivocal affiliation with Jordan would have dragged the local leadership into a confrontation with the PLO, eroding its public standing.

As the local leadership became more aware that its bread was buttered by both Jordan and the PLO, it was increasingly disinclined to embark on a new path that could be perceived as a threat to either side's vital interests. The leadership scrupulously refrained from initiating or taking part in political activity beyond the day to day level—be it negotiations on a political settlement detached from the PLO, from Jordan, or from

13. On Israel's political stand regarding the leadership in the territories, see Shlomo Gazit, ha-Maqel ve ha-gezer: ha-mimshal ha-Yisraʾeli be-Yehudah ve-Shomron (The stick and the carrot: the Israeli administration in Judea and Samaria) (Tel Aviv: Zmora Bitan, 1985), 151–61, 335.

both; or full-scale civil disobedience against the Israeli authorities. Both types of activity conflicted with PLO and Jordanian interests. Civil disobedience, entailing a severance of contact with the Israelis, would lead to a forceful Israeli reaction. This, in turn, could harm the local institutions that assisted both Jordan and the PLO to tighten their grip on the Palestinian population. By the same token, talks by the local leadership with Israel on a political settlement would undercut the demand of both Jordan and the PLO to play a dominant role in decisions concerning the future of the territories.

During the first three years of the Israeli occupation, however, there was activity in both domains—attempts at civil disobedience, and feelers put out by local leaders for talks with Israel on a political settlement. Initiatives toward a political settlement were set in motion primarily by proponents of the Palestinian entity solution. Their activities took several forms. ʿAziz Shehada from Ramallah, Dr. Hamdi al-Taji al-Faruqi from al-Bira, and Muhammad Abu Shilbaya from Jerusalem were active mainly among the intelligentsia. They proposed negotiations with Israel for the establishment of a Palestinian state on the West Bank and the Gaza Strip as the prelude to a comprehensive settlement with the Arab states. Sheykh Muhammad ʿAli al-Jaʿbari, then mayor of Hebron, was more forthcoming. On several occasions during 1969 and 1970, he tried to lay the foundations for progress toward a direct settlement between Israel and the West Bank Palestinians. He suggested the formation of a political body based on the existing West Bank leadership, principally the mayors.[14]

These endeavors were paralleled by demonstrations and strikes against the Israeli authorities led by the Jordanian Communist party. Communist activists took the initiative in establishing Committees of National Solidarity in Nablus, Ramallah, and al-Bira that cooperated with members of radical groups such as the Baʿth and al-Qawmiyyun al-ʿArab (the Arab Nationalists). Behind the Communists' initiative lay the idea that the committees should engage in a political struggle against the Israeli authorities.[15] While the local leadership's attempts to forge a dialogue with Israel encountered fierce PLO opposition, the activity of protest and civil disobedience gained its support and encouragement. However, in the early 1970s, both modes of action gradually declined. The emerging coexistence between Jordan and the PLO encouraged the

---

14. On these attempts, see Elie Rekhess and Asher Susser, *Political Factors and Trends in the West Bank* (Tel Aviv: Occasional Papers, The Shiloah Center for Middle Eastern and African Studies, Tel Aviv University, 1974), 7–8, 11–13.

15. Ibid., 5–6.

leadership in the West Bank to move toward what can be termed controlled radicalism.

The ensuing activity was characterized by nonacceptance of the Israeli occupation but, at the same time, avoidance of a direct clash with the Israeli authorities. It did entail readiness for cooperation with Israel on daily matters. Such activity was pursued by pro-PLO and pro-Jordanian local leaders alike. The pro-Jordanians' moderate approach toward Israel was attended by declarations of support for the PLO as the embodiment of the Palestinians' national aspirations; while the radical stand of pro-PLO circles was tempered by pragmatism where contacts with Israel were concerned. Both camps denounced Israeli actions in the territories such as land expropriations, settlements, taxation, arrests, and house demolitions. Radical leaders organized strikes and mass demonstrations and voiced publicly their unequivocal support for the PLO as their sole representative in any political settlement. Nevertheless, the radicals, and certainly the more moderates, were careful not to strain their relations with Israel irrevocably. They maintained constant contact with the Military Government in order to ensure the continued operation of the local governments and of essential services in the realms of health, welfare, education, and commerce.

Local activity associated with controlled radicalism gained Jordan's acquiescence as well as PLO support. PLO backing for such activity was not self-evident. Although activity in the spirit of controlled radicalism helped the PLO maintain a political and economic infrastructure in the West Bank, it also entailed dependence on local institutions that derived their legitimacy from Israel. Against this background, one might argue that the PLO was willing to acquiesce in Israel's continued presence in the territories, assisting it to ensure normalization in day-to-day life.

Indeed, criticism along this line was leveled at Arafat by the left-wing factions within the PLO. Yet, the mainstream headed by Fatah preferred to support the pattern of controlled radicalism rather than back what it considered irresponsible radical activities against Israel. Arafat summoned all the rhetorical ability at his command to justify calculated radical actions. "The most important element in the Palestinian program is holding on to the land. Holding on to the land and not warfare alone. Warfare comes at a different level. If you only fight—that is a tragedy. If you fight and emigrate—that is a tragedy. The basis is that you hold on and fight. The important thing is that you hold on to the land, and afterward—combat."[16]

16. *Al-Fikr* (Paris), June 1985, 29.

The practice of controlled radicalism, West Bank style, involved formidable difficulties. The impact of fluctuations in PLO-Jordan relations and of power struggles within the PLO was strongly felt in the West Bank. Such developments jeopardized Jordanian-PLO coexistence and threatened the local leadership and the pattern of controlled radicalism. Nowhere was this threat more vividly expressed than in the Rabat summit of 1974 and in the aftermath of the Camp David accords of 1978. Such events increased the support of the Palestinians in the occupied territories for the PLO and enhanced the prestige of leaders affiliated with the radical PLO factions. Yet local leaders continued to see in controlled radicalism an optimal mode of behavior. As long as Jordanian-PLO coexistence prevailed and as long as Israel continued to pin its hopes on political settlements with Arab partners outside the territories, simultaneous reliance on the PLO and Jordan, followed by cooperative relations with Israel, remained the West Bank's preferred mode of action.

It was this stance of controlled radicalism that helped the local leadership retain its standing among the population and rebuff pressures toward extremism from the youth. As a result, the middle class— merchants, officials, and other white-collar workers—were able to pursue their day-to-day activity in the presence of a prolonged occupation.

Israeli Policy and the Local Leadership

In Israel, political stands regarding the territories derived primarily from two political perceptions: the Greater Israel vision associated with the rightist Likud, and the territorial compromise approach espoused by the Labor Alignment.

The Alignment, which was in power until 1977, viewed the West Bank and Gaza in terms of security considerations, whereas the Likud, which succeeded Labor, spoke in terms of historic rights as well. The Alignment, fearful of what demography portended, sought a political settlement that would enable Israel to rid itself of densely populated Arab areas, while the Likud, with an eye on geography—the whole Land of Israel—urged a permanent Israeli presence throughout the West Bank and Gaza. The Alignment advocated selective settlement, chiefly in the Jordan Rift Valley and the Etzion Bloc south of Jerusalem, whereas for the Likud the entire West Bank was a legitimate, indeed vital, target for Jewish settlement.

Under the Likud government, the pace of settlement in the West Bank intensified, the settler population increased, and budgetary allocations for the physical infrastructure in the West Bank were multiplied. Yet, Israeli policy toward the local leadership and the Palestinian population as a whole remained unchanged. Under three defense ministers—Moshe Dayan and Shimon Peres from the Alignment, and Ezer Weizman from the Likud—Israel gave priority to securing calm in the territories through cooperation with the local leadership on day-to-day matters. At the same time, Israel refused to consider these leaders as potential partners for talks on a permanent settlement. Two repercussions followed from the Israeli policy. First, the disinclination to conduct political negotiations with the local leadership encouraged that leadership's continued cultivation of political and economic ties with Jordan and later on with the PLO; and second, Israel's desire to maintain calm relations with the Palestinian population through cooperation with the local leadership meant Israel's acquiescence in the continued influence of Jordan and the PLO in the West Bank and, in consequence, the affinity of the Palestinians in the territories for both alike.

Manifestations of Israel's acceptance of a continuing Jordanian influence in the West Bank were clearly visible as early as 1970. Beginning in that year, Israel permitted Jordan to pump money into the territories to pay the salaries of those who had been employed in the Jordanian civil service until 1967. These included municipal clerks, teachers, doctors, lawyers, and clerics. Israel also allowed Jordan to provide financial aid to local governments and to educational, religious, cultural, and social institutions.[17] The interaction between Jordan and the West Bank was given an additional boost by the Israeli policy of maintaining open bridges across the Jordan River for two-way traffic of persons and goods and in growing cooperation with Jordan in agriculture, education, health, and various economic spheres. A similar, albeit less obvious, tendency characterized Israeli policy toward the PLO's role in the West Bank. From the mid-1970s, the Military Government tacitly agreed to the injection of funds originating with the PLO for local governments and other civilian bodies. The money reached the West Bank via international or inter-Arab organizations.

Israel continued to acquiesce in the local leadership's affiliation with both the PLO and Jordan even after the 1976 West Bank municipal elections. The victory of pro-PLO candidates such as Bassam al-Shakʿa in Nablus, Fahd Qawasima in Hebron, Karim Khalaf in Ramallah, Ibrahim Tawil in al-Bira, Muhammad Milhim in Halhul, Hilmi Hanun

---

17. Moshe Maʿoz, *Palestinian Leadership on the West Bank* (London: Frank Cass, 1984), 77, 171–72.

in Tulkarm, Amin al-Nassir in Qalqilya, Wahid Hamdallah in ʿAnabta, and Bishara Dawud in Beit Jala did not prevent the Military Government from appointing them as mayors. Furthermore, Israel allowed the mayors to visit Amman and other Arab capitals for meetings with Jordanian personalities and senior PLO officials. Israel took no steps to block the continued transfer of funds by Jordan and the PLO to local governments and other institutions. In May 1977, for example, Jordan earmarked half a million dinars for town governments. Earlier that year, Nablus had received a grant of three million dinars made up of contributions collected from Palestinians in Saudi Arabia. In 1980, Hebron received a grant of ten million dinars from al-Madina in Saudi Arabia as part of a "twin cities" pact sponsored by the PLO.

The National Guidance Committee, formed in October 1978, benefitted from the same Israeli policy. The committee's 23 members included the mayors Shakʿa, Khalaf, Qawasima, Milhim, Hanun, Tawil, and Hamdallah, as well as representatives from trade unions, charitable societies, women's organizations, and student associations from the West Bank and Gaza. Also represented were the religious establishment, the business sector, and the press.[18]

The NGC was established with the PLO's encouragement to help in the political struggle against the autonomy plan contained in the Camp David accords. Yet, Israel placed no obstacles in the NGC's way.

Defense Minister Ezer Weizman permitted the NGC to hold public meetings and ordered military governors to tolerate anti-Israeli pronouncements and rallies organized by the NGC. Nor did Weizman prevent committee members from going abroad to hold talks with government officials in the United States and Europe and with political leaders in Jordan, Syria, Iraq, and Saudi Arabia.[19] Israel also acquiesced in the 1978 Baghdad Arab summit decision to provide $150 million annually to the occupied territories, to be allocated by a joint Jordan-PLO committee.

Israel's continued tolerance of the local leadership's dual PLO and Jordan affiliation was not self-evident. Following the municipal elections of 1976, and more intensely after Anwar al-Sadat's visit to Jerusalem in November 1977 and the signing of the Camp David accords, anti-Israeli activities escalated: there were more demonstrations, more school and commercial strikes, more petitions, and a growing readiness

18. Colin Legum, Haim Shaked, and Daniel Dishon, eds. *Middle East Contemporary Survey* (New York: Holmes and Meier, 1978–1980), 3:334; 4:273–74.
19. Maʿoz, 169.

to challenge law and order. A deepening affiliation of the local leadership with the PLO and heightened cooperation between the two was an undeniable fact. Yet, as long as the local leadership did not press its anti-Israeli activity to the point of discarding the pattern of controlled radicalism and as long as the PLO and Jordan continued to operate within that framework, Israel tended to accept the population's simultaneous reliance on both parties.

Israel's stand was an outgrowth of the autonomy talks between Israel, the United States, and Egypt. The Israeli interest was to conduct negotiations on the autonomy plan with a delegation comprised of Jordanian representatives and Palestinians from the territories not identified with the PLO. But Israel was unwilling to pay the price demanded by Jordan and Palestinian leaders to make their participation more feasible. Both Jordan and West Bank Palestinian leaders considered favorably the idea of entering negotiations with Israel on an interim agreement in the spirit of the autonomy plan, provided Israel showed a willingness to stop settlement activity in the territories and commit itself to the character of the future permanent agreement. As far as Jordan was concerned, a final settlement entailed an Israeli withdrawal to the 1967 borders or a mutual exchange of territories. For Palestinian leaders, a permanent settlement meant the creation of an independent Palestinian state at the end of the autonomy period.[20]

In the absence of an affirmative Israeli response to such conditions and taking into account the Egyptian and American positions, which were more responsive to the Jordanian and Palestinian stands, a head-on clash with the local leadership would have inevitably triggered an Israeli showdown with Egypt and the United States. Israel would have been accused of derailing the autonomy negotiations and sabotaging regional peace efforts. A confrontation with the local leadership would thus be a losing proposition for Jerusalem. True, one may argue that the removal of pro-PLO leaders who served as mayors or held key positions in local institutions would have thrown a snag into the link between the West Bank and the PLO. Yet, other considerations should be taken into account: the ensuing aggravation of Israel's relations with Egypt and the United States and the criticism of Israel in the international arena sure to follow would spur the population to show greater solidarity with the ousted local leadership and heighten its support for the PLO. Because

---

20. On the Palestinian stand, see Maʿoz, 176–77; and on the Jordanian stand, see Asher Susser, "ʿEmdat Hussein be-sheʾlat ʿatid ha-Gadah ha-maʿravit" ("Hussein's position on the future of the West Bank"), *Hamizrah Hehadash* 28, no. 3–4 (1979): 242.

there was no real possibility of inducing other local leaders of stature to take over, the almost certain result would be to bring about intensified activity by extremist elements in the PLO. The delicate weave of relations between the Israeli authorities and the local population would be jeopardized.

From Israel's point of view, the continued reliance of the Palestinians in the territories on both the PLO and Jordan, even at the price of the mode of controlled radicalism, seemed the lesser evil. While Israel was hardly pleased by these developments, the probable consequences of a policy entailing the removal of the local pro-PLO leadership seemed worse by far.

It was this cautious approach that guided Alignment policy toward the local leadership up to 1977, and the Likud during the first Menachem Begin government, when Moshe Dayan served as foreign minister and Ezer Weizman as defense minister. Both had recognized the limitations of Israel's power to neutralize the PLO as a politically potent element in the West Bank. Absolute truths and millennial visions were alien to their political thought.

The 1981 appointment of Ariel Sharon as defense minister signaled a turning point in Israeli policy toward Palestinian local leaders. Sharon believed that the political reality that had developed in the occupied territories was detrimental to Israel's national interest of maintaining a permanent presence there. He therefore adopted a policy aimed at severing ties between the PLO and the Palestinians in the West Bank, while creating conditions that would reconcile the Palestinians to the idea that Israel was in the territories to stay. To this end, Sharon availed himself of the services of the Civil Administration in the territories, established as an adjunct to the Military Government at the time he took over at the Defense Ministry, to effect the removal of the pro-PLO urban leadership. In March 1982, the mayors of Nablus, Ramallah, and al-Bira were dismissed and Israeli officers appointed in their place. In the same month, the National Guidance Committee was outlawed on the ground that it was an arm of the PLO. Bir Zeit University was shut down. Strict censorship was imposed on newspapers published in East Jerusalem, and their distribution in the West Bank was prohibited.

The political vacuum created by the removal of the urban leaders was supposed to be filled by the heads of the Village Leagues, who gained the support of the Civil Administration. They were given control of infrastructure budgets—roads, water, electricity, construction of clinics and schools—in their locales. They also became the dispensers of permits needed for building, exporting goods, or visiting relatives in Arab states. Sharon's decision to gamble on the Village Leagues as a substitute leadership was guided by two postulates: one was that the PLO's main strength derived from the urban population, which was the source of the pro-PLO leadership and the prime mover of anti-Israeli activity; the other was that the urban sector accounted for only 30 percent of the West Bank's population, while the remaining 70 percent consisted of a rural population that lacked a developed national consciousness and therefore did not regard the PLO as its representative. It followed that political and material support for the Village Leagues might encourage a new leadership that would supplant the city leaders and weaken the PLO's standing in the West Bank.

The scale of the Israeli investment in the Village Leagues was matched by the disappointment in the dividends. Their leaders, such as Mustafa Dudin, Muhammad Nassir, Yusuf al-Khatib, Tahsin Mansur, and Jamil al-ʿAmla, rejected the notion that the PLO was the exclusive representative of the Palestinian people, and they were ready to hold talks with Israel on a political settlement along the lines of the autonomy plan. But to the Palestinian population, they were traitors and collaborators. In the words of a senior Civil Administration official, the League's attempt to form an all-West Bank anti-PLO movement turned into "a joke."

The failure of the Village Leagues reflects the limitations of Sharon's policy to cultivate a leadership that would stand up to the PLO and its supporters in the territories. In a political climate in which the PLO enjoyed inter-Arab legitimacy and worldwide recognition, it was an illusion to think that a substitute leadership could be formed without the assurance of far-reaching Israeli political *quid pro quos*. Moreover, in Jordan, the PLO found a faithful ally to frustrate the Israeli initiative to form an alternative leadership. Jordan viewed the Israeli initiative as a tangible threat to its existence as a Hashemite kingdom. A Sharon-type Palestinian leadership was perceived in Amman as the first step on the road to implementing a plan that had support on the Israeli Right: to transform Jordan into a substitute homeland for the Palestinians, where they could realize their national desires and live an independent existence. Because Israel dangled no political bait that might induce the Palestinian population in the territories to support a substitute leadership and because it could not dictate with military means a political settlement that ignored the PLO and Jordan, the Palestinians preferred to go on relying simultaneously on Jordan and the PLO.

The 1982 Lebanon War and Sharon's resignation as defense minister, in March 1983, terminated the era of the Village Leagues. Sharon's successors, Moshe Arens of the Likud and Yitzhak Rabin of Labor, understood that a Palestinian local leadership identified with Israel could never gain popular support. Instead, they tried to win the backing of pro-Jordanian urban leaders. Their assumption was that the destruction of the PLO infrastructure in Lebanon would encourage such figures, who were not tainted by association with the PLO, to cooperate with Israel in the conduct of day-to-day affairs. In February 1984, Israel allowed figures from the territories to meet with King Hussein and senior Jordanian government officials. At the same time, they were prohibited to meet with PLO officials.[21] In the same year, the Israeli authorities barred former Gaza mayor Rashad al-Shawwa and retired Jordanian parliamentary speaker Hikmat al-Masri from going abroad to attend a joint meeting between King Hussein and Yasir Arafat.

However, in the political climate prevailing in the West Bank in the post-Lebanon War era, Israel found it difficult to convince pro-Jordanian figures to fill the vacuum left by their pro-PLO predecessors. Jordan's supporters in the territories could not ignore the continued broad support that the PLO enjoyed among the population. They were aware that the PLO's "tribulations and its organizational flaccidity outside [the territories] were far from weakening its standing in the territories.... Arab hostility only awakens in the Palestinians the feeling that they must rely on themselves and reinforces their sense of Palestinian identity. In the light of this tendency, the complaints and qualms that the residents of the territories have about the PLO's mode of operation become insignificant."[22] The pro-Jordanians also paid close attention to the dialogue that took place between Jordan and the PLO following the war in Lebanon, aimed at reaching agreement on a joint drive for a political settlement. Both Jordan and the PLO feared the persistence of the territorial status quo, and both recognized their inability to modify it through separate political initiatives.

Under these circumstances, the prospect that pro-Jordanian figures would respond to Israeli overtures was minimal. To do so would have required them to maneuver in a manner acceptable to both Jordan and the PLO. Israeli acceptance of such a formula would have been tantamount to approval of the PLO's return to playing an active political role in the West Bank. The result was that Israeli army officers continued to

21. Moshe Maʿoz, *ha-Manhigut ha-falastinit ba-Gadah ha-Maʿravit* (Palestinian leadership on the West Bank) (Tel-Aviv: Reshafim, 1985), 218.

22. Mati Steinberg, "Preface," in Menachem Klein, *Du-Siyach veshivro: Yachasei Yarden-Ashaf, 1985–1988* (Antagonistic collaboration: PLO-Jordanian dialogue, 1985–1988) (Jerusalem: Policy Papers 27, Leonard Davis Institute for International Relations, Hebrew University of Jerusalem, 1988), 8.

serve as appointed mayors. Influential local figures willing to do the job could not be found.

On the surface, it seemed to be business as usual. The absence of local mayors did not prevent municipal bodies from functioning normally, and the population continued to abide by the spirit of the occupation's rules and regulations. Many Israeli officials came to believe that, despite the absence of a local leadership, Israel could retain its effective control over the populace.

However, two developments suggested otherwise. Since 1981, the activity of student bodies and youth organizations had been widespread in the West Bank. Their involvement extended to urban neighborhoods, villages, and refugee camps. Besides their activities among young people, these organizations endeavored to aid the adult population in the areas of health, relief, education, and environmental improvement. In the absence of effective leadership, student and youth organizations set the tone in the community, becoming a rising political force.

The growing strength of the young activists was accompanied by a considerable escalation in violence. Three figures show the trend: in 1977, there were 656 disturbances of public order in the West Bank; in 1981, there were 1,556; and by 1984, there were 2,663 incidents.[23] However, the prolonged political dialogue conducted between the PLO and Jordan since October 1982, and the Amman Agreement of February 1985 squelched the volcanic potential latent in the two developments just mentioned. The Amman Agreement spoke about a joint Jordan-PLO entry into peace negotiations within the framework of an international conference with the participation of the five permanent members of the U.N. Security Council and all the parties to the conflict, including the PLO. The agreement also declared that negotiations would be conducted on the basis of the "land for peace" principle and entail recognition of the Palestinian people's right to self-determination, to be implemented in a Jordanian-Palestinian confederation.[24]

The Amman Agreement was consistent with the interests of the Palestinians in the territories, who supported a political solution based on a Jordan-PLO partnership. But sharp disagreements between the PLO and Jordan over Palestinian self-determination and Arafat's refusal to accept Security Council Resolutions 242 and 338 unconditionally, as demanded by King Hussein, led Jordan to suspend the agreement in 1986. The brakes on the young radicals in the territories were thus

---

23. The data are based on material from the Israeli Army Spokesman's Office.
24. Klein, 27.

removed. Jordan's attempts to pressure the PLO to accept its dictates on self-determination by renewing its activities in the West Bank were unsuccessful. The Palestinians in the territories aligned themselves with the PLO. Economic initiatives such as Jordan's five-year plan of 1986 to develop the "occupied Arab lands,"[25] the establishment of an Arab bank in Nablus, and the appointment of local leaders as mayors in Hebron, Ramallah, and al-Bira could not tip the scales in Jordan's favor. In the absence of an effective local leadership, nothing could contain the violent activity of the young generation.

Evidence of the youngsters' volatility was visible as early as December 1986, a year before the start of the Intifada. When two students were killed in a clash at Bir Zeit University, the West Bank and Gaza erupted for ten days, with youths and students leading the demonstrations. This incident was a watershed. Two developments poured oil on the flames: the decision of the PLO's Executive Committee, on the eve of the meeting of the Eighteenth Palestinian National Council in April 1987, to annul the Amman Agreement; and the attempt of Jordan and Syria, during the Arab summit conference held in Amman in November 1987, to undercut the PLO's standing as the sole representative of the Palestinian cause. The West Bank and Gaza experienced more disturbances, more clashes with the army, more petrol bombs, and more stone throwing. The initiative passed into the hands of the youngsters, and no one, not Israel, not Jordan, and not the PLO, could control the unfolding events.

It was Gaza that gave the signal—and set the tone. On May 18, 1987, six members of the Islamic Jihad movement (al-Jihad al-Islami) escaped from the Gaza central prison.[26] On August 8, they assassinated an officer of the military police in Gaza. On October 1 and 6, bloody confrontations took place between members of the group and the Israeli security forces, resulting in the deaths of four Palestinians and one Israeli. On December 8, an Israeli citizen was stabbed to death in the Gaza market. On December 9, rioting broke out in Jabalya refugee camp after four camp residents were killed and seven injured in a road accident near Erez checkpoint at the northern entrance to the Gaza Strip. It was rumored that the road accident had been deliberate and was meant to avenge the death of the Israeli who had been stabbed. On December 10, the flames spread to the other Gaza refugee camps and engulfed the

25. *Al-Dustur* (Amman), Aug. 25, 1986.
26. On the Islamic Jihad's religious vision and its attitude toward Israel, see Ziad Abu ʿAmr, *al-Harakah al-Islamiyah fi al-Daffah al-Gharbiyah wa-Qitaʿ Ghazza* (The Islamic movement in the West Bank and Gaza Strip) (Acre: Dar al-Aswar, 1989), chap. 5.

West Bank as well.[27] Since 1967, Gaza had always known more violence than the West Bank. Gaza, more than the West Bank, is economically pinched, demographically saturated, dense with refugees, and consumed by the fervor of religious faith. These characteristics set the stage for a violent eruption. But this time, the West Bank was ripe to join. The Intifada seized stone and petrol bomb and verbalized its message through poem and underground leaflet.

27. For more details, see Ziad Abu ʿAmr, *The Intifada: Causes and Factors of Continuity* (Jerusalem: Palestinian Academic Society for the Study of International Affairs, 1989), 7–15; Aryeh Shalev, *The Intifada, Causes and Effects* (Boulder, Colo.: Westview, 1991), 27–33; Zeʾev Schiff and Ehud Yaʿari, *Intifada: The Palestinian Uprising—Israel's Third Front* (New York: Simon and Schuster, 1990), chap. 2.

2

PAPER WAR
The Intifada Leaflets

THE LEAFLET PHENOMENON is as old as the Jewish-Arab conflict. During the British Mandate (1920–1948), leaflets were part of Palestinian political life. They served as an instrument to express attitudes and to direct behavior. After 1948, and more intensively after 1967, they continued to appear in the West Bank, the Gaza Strip, and among the Israeli Arabs. Yet, leaflets never played such a key role as during the Intifada. The diversity and frequency of the leaflets, and the scope of obedience and response they elicited, showed their centrality among the population. In the absence of an official and prominent local leadership, leaflets became a substitute leadership during the Intifada.

The leaflets tapped the ideological and organizational sources of two powerful political streams from the pre-Intifada period: the national and the religious. The national camp was identified with four major PLO factions: Fatah, the Democratic Front for the Liberation of Palestine (DFLP), the Popular Front for the Liberation of Palestine (PFLP), and the Palestinian Communist party (PCP). Affiliated with the religious camp were the Muslim Brothers and al-Mujammaᶜ al-Islami (the Islamic Association). The activity of the national camp was more pronounced in the West Bank, while the religious camp demonstrated more presence and greater influence in the Gaza Strip.

It was after the Yom Kippur War of October 1973 that the PLO undertook intensive political activity in the occupied territories. In the years that followed, the organization gained popular support and secured powerful positions in municipal bodies, student groups, trade unions, and charity and welfare organizations. Its institutional inroads were matched by its ideological success. The PLO emerged as a source of political inspiration for the population, both as the embodiment of national aspirations for Palestinian sovereignty and as an ideological guide in the labyrinthine politics of the Palestinian and inter-Arab systems. More often than not, the PLO and the Palestinian issue were perceived as Siamese twins.

The methods of the Muslim Brothers, while less spectacular, were no less effective. Their ultimate objective is the establishment of an Islamic state in all of Palestine through *jihad,* or holy war, against Israel. This however, is considered a long-range goal, for which the foundations must be laid by infusing the people with the spirit of traditional Islam. Consequently, the Muslim Brothers turned their energies to the educational domain and extensive community activity. The mosques became their main arena of indoctrination. In them, the young generation imbibed the Qur'an, and from them the ideological and doctrinal word went forth. The watershed year for the Brothers' activity was 1978. It was then that al-Mujamma ͨ al-Islami, which had been founded five years earlier, obtained recognition by and the cooperation of the Israeli authorities. Its aims were to teach the young generation the tenets of Islam, organize sports activities for youth, provide health services, and assist the needy. Following the success of al-Mujamma ͨ, other associations gained adherents among young women and students. Within this context one might mention the Islamic Young Women's Society (Jam ͨ iyyat al-shabbat al-Muslimat), set up in 1981 with the aim of disseminating Islamic principles, and the Islamic Bloc (al-Kutla al-Islamiyya), which operated in Gaza's religious university.

The decision of the Muslim Brothers and al-Mujamma ͨ al-Islami to focus on quiet, civilian-oriented activity, proved to be a sound one. The two organizations played a prominent role in "mobilizing the masses by means of an impressive organizational structure and by building up a wide network centered around the ... mosques."[1]

The effects of the widespread activity of both camps, the national and the religious, and the deep roots they struck within the local population, became obvious during the Intifada. Both camps were involved, whether directly or indirectly, in writing leaflets and directing events on the ground. There were four major bodies behind the wording of the leaflets: the United National Command (al-Qiyada al-wataniyya al-muwahada; hereafter UNC); the Islamic Resistance Movement (Harakat al-muqawama al-Islamiyya, known as Hamas); the left-wing Palestinian factions; and the Islamic Jihad. Each was identified ideologically or linked

---

1. Reuven Paz, "ha-Amanah ha-Islamit ve-mashm ͨ autah: ͨ iyun rishoni ve-targum" (The Islamic covenant and its meaning: A preliminary perusal and translation) (Tel Aviv: The Moshe Dayan Center for Middle Eastern and African Studies, Tel Aviv University, Sept. 1988), 6 (mimeographed).

organizationally with either the national camp or the religious camp. The two most important groups were the UNC and the Islamic Resistance Movement (Hamas).

The UNC was a coalition of supporters of Fatah, the Democratic Front, the Popular Front and the Communist party. The close interrelationship between the UNC and the PLO was given explicit expression in the lead-in to the UNC's leaflets. Beginning with leaflet no. 3, each such communiqué opened with the same declaration: "No voice can overcome the voice of the uprising, no voice can overcome the voice of the Palestinian people—the people of the PLO." Every leaflet, beginning with the third, stated that it was being issued on behalf of the PLO and the UNC and was undersigned by both bodies.

The left-wing organizations, although affiliating themselves with the UNC, published separate leaflets. By doing so, they could emphasize their sheer presence in the field, as though to say, "We issue leaflets, therefore we exist." In addition, they could demonstrate ideological and organizational independence by stressing their differences with Fatah on key issues, particularly on relations with Jordan and on a political settlement.

Hamas is an umbrella organization for activists of the Muslim Brothers movement in the Gaza Strip and for al-Mujammaʿ al-Islami. The Islamic Jihad, whose orientation is also religious, operated separately from Hamas and put out its own leaflets. Its independent activity was motivated by a profound disagreement with both the Muslim Brothers and al-Mujammaʿ al-Islami on how to advance the creation of an Islamic state in Palestine. The Jihad would launch a holy war on Israel here and now, whereas the Brothers and al-Mujammaʿ advocate educational activity within the community before embarking on a military offensive. The Jihad, its extreme world view notwithstanding, scrupulously maintained organizational ties with Fatah, though it avoided affiliating itself with the UNC. Its cooperation with Fatah appeared to be motivated by logistic considerations—to smooth its activity in the uprising.

The interrelation of the four bodies, both ideologically and organizationally, enabled an intensive level of activity to be maintained and ensured a high level of obedience by the population to the directives contained in the leaflets.

Diversity, Frequency, and Effectiveness

The scope of activity is reflected in the diversity and frequency of the leaflets. The leaflets issued by all the groups were intended for blanket distribution in the West Bank and the Gaza Strip. In practice, UNC and

Hamas leaflets enjoyed the widest circulation. They differed in both style and content. UNC leaflets were longer and more detailed; they were phrased more succinctly, and their authors endeavored to present political arguments couched in clear language. Hamas leaflets, in contrast, drew heavily on religious images and slogans.

With the exception of the UNC, the leaflets of all the groups were homemade; that is, they were drawn up solely by local activists. UNC leaflets were drafted in the territories and then sent outside to the PLO for their final polish.

Besides the countrywide leaflets, there were also leaflets of a more local variety. The initiative for such communiqués generally originated with groups associated with the UNC. Such leaflets were intended to translate the general instructions into specific guidelines geared to local needs. There were also sectoral leaflets issued by professional or voluntary organizations scattered throughout the territories. Here, too, the imprint of the UNC, or sometimes of the left-wing factions, was pronounced.

Leaflets appeared frequently: in the first year of the Intifada (December 1987–December 1988) the UNC issued 31 leaflets and Hamas 33 (Hamas began numbering its leaflets with no. 21, in May 1988). The average in the first year was therefore two or three leaflets a month issued by each body. This was a higher frequency than that, of the left-wing factions and of the Islamic Jihad. Our estimate is that in the first year of the Intifada, all the left-wing factions together issued about 20 countrywide leaflets (besides an unknown number of leaflets issued by local leftist groups). This low figure was probably owing to the fact that these factions also had a hand in UNC leaflets.

Of all the bodies, the Islamic Jihad was the least eager to issue leaflets because it considered the whole Palestinian public to be the leadership of the uprising. However, the Islamic Jihad claimed it was compelled to issue leaflets because other bodies passed themselves off as initiators and leaders of the Intifada. As the first (undated) Islamic Jihad leaflet explained: "Self-interested groups of the heretical left . . . have sought to latch on to our blessed Muslim uprising and claim to be the determiners and deciders regarding our pure and courageous uprising. These elements took advantage of our silence and the fact that we have refrained from issuing leaflets in order to create the impression among the inhabitants that they are the pioneers and leaders of the struggle."

Toward the end of the first year of the Intifada, the Islamic Jihad was wracked by an internal struggle in which it ended split into three separate bodies. The fierce competition between the three factions for the sympathy and support of the population, particularly in Gaza, led to an increase in the range and frequency of leaflets. During the second year of the Intifada, each of the three Islamic Jihad factions issued about 10 leaflets. However, they did not attain the status of the UNC and Hamas leaflets, which continued to enjoy countrywide distribution, compliance, and obedience, even though fewer leaflets were issued: 19 by the UNC and 18 by Hamas.

The leaflets of all the bodies set out to dictate daily routine. However, UNC and Hamas leaflets had the force of governmental decrees. The response and obedience they elicited were correspondingly high. Along with offering encouragement and enumerating the Intifada's achievements, the leaflets provided detailed guidelines on what was permitted and what was prohibited. In comparison with the leaflets of the Left and of the Islamic Jihad, the UNC and Hamas addressed a broad range of issues: work, health, transportation, education, agriculture, commerce; whether a strike was to be full or partial; the hours in which shops could be opened; how to maintain studies despite the closure of schools; who could travel during a strike and who could work. The leaflets called for intracommunal help, contributions, and donations to the needy and to the families of people killed or imprisoned; urged a selective boycott of Israeli products; called on the population not to work in the Israeli agricultural sector and to attack Jewish settlers; and demanded that Palestinians employed by the Israeli Civil Administration resign, particularly policemen, tax collectors, and members of appointed local councils. Hamas leaflets, which were prepared in the Gaza Strip, contained religious instructions regarding prayer, charity, penitence, and the need for good behavior such as obeying traffic rules in the spirit of "Muslim politeness."

The UNC and Hamas leaflets influenced the behavior not only of the local population but of the Israeli authorities as well. They became "working papers" guiding the scale and intensity of activity by the army, the Civil Administration, and other Israeli security bodies.

The "Pamphlet Leadership" of the Intifada

In the absence of a formal leadership, the anonymous writers of the leaflets became the "pamphlet leadership" of the Intifada. If a leadership is measured by its ability to articulate values, define goals, and assure the public's obedience and compliance, the authors of the UNC and Hamas leaflets met those criteria.

The pamphlet leadership of the Intifada differed in two crucial aspects from the previous leadership. First, in the pre-Intifada period, the leadership was identified with dominant political personalities. They held official positions, as mayors, heads of local councils, members of chambers of commerce, leaders of trade unions; or they wielded influence as journalists or lawyers. In contrast, the pamphlet leadership was not comprised of professional politicians, nor were its members a permanent body. Arrests and deportations thinned its ranks. If the pamphlet leadership continued to demonstrate operational effectiveness, this was owing more to the charisma with which its role was perceived and less to its personal composition.

Second, as described in the previous chapter, the pre-Intifada leadership maintained a simultaneous affiliation with Jordan and the PLO. But the pamphlet leadership of the Intifada was saliently Palestinian in orientation. It did not draw its political inspiration from a single source: the national-Palestinian world view espoused by the PLO differs from the world view of the religious camp. Yet, both camps defined themselves as Palestinian movements, and both camps were instrumental in defining the goals and shaping the activities of the Intifada.

The Palestinian State

An analysis of the leaflets shows that the different groups active in the Intifada had two overriding common goals: to undermine the authority of Israeli rule in the occupied territories by means of a civil revolt that would force Israel to withdraw from those areas and to establish a Palestinian state.

Hamas and the UNC were at loggerheads about the character of a Palestinian state and consequently differed over their attitude toward a political settlement with Israel. These differences were inherent in each movement's credo. Hamas, with its religious ideology, aspired to establish an Islamic state in all of Palestine. According to the Hamas charter of August 1988, the soil of Palestine is a Muslim (religious) trust and Hamas is a "distinctive Palestinian movement working to raise the banner of Allah over every grain of soil in Palestine."[2] Hamas saw itself as a link in the chain of *jihad* against Israel. To forgo parts of Palestine was tantamount to forgoing part of Islam.[3]

---

2. Paz, 30.
3. *Jihad*, literally, an effort, is a continuous status of holy war against the unbelievers and is a required duty. *Jihad* must end when the unbelievers have accepted either Islam or a protected status within Islam (for Jews and Christians).

Hamas's adherence to the principle of "not [ceding] one inch" and its emphatic claim to all of Palestine found frequent expression in its leaflets. Leaflet no. 28 (August 18, 1988), entitled "Islamic Palestine from the [Mediterranean] Sea to the [Jordan] River," asserted: "The Muslims have had a full—not a partial—right to Palestine for generations, in the past, present and future. . . . No Palestinian generation has the right to concede the land, steeped in martyrs' blood. . . . You must continue the uprising and stand up against the usurpers wherever they may be, until the complete liberation of every grain of the soil of . . . Palestine, all Palestine, with God's help."

Leaflet no. 22 (June 2, 1988) declared: "For our war is a holy war for the sake of Allah unto victory or death."

In Hamas's eyes, the Muslims' right to all of Palestine leaves no opening for a dialogue or a political settlement with Israel. The following quotations exemplify this approach:

Let any hand be cut off that signs [away] a grain of sand in Palestine in favor of the enemies of God . . . who have seized . . . the blessed land. (March 13, 1988)

"Land for peace" and the "umbrella of an international conference" . . . this is no more than a mirage, deceit. (March 4, 1988)

Every negotiation with the enemy is a regression from the [Palestinian] cause, concession of a principle and recognition of the usurping murderers' false claim to a land in which they were not born. (August 18, 1988)

Arab rulers, who invest efforts for the false peace, . . . and who entreat Israel to agree to a "just" peace. . . . We hope you will fight at least once [in order to prove] that you partake of Arab boldness or Muslim strength. (January 1988)

And, in a rhetorical appeal to Israel: "Get your hands off our people, our cities, our camps, and our villages. Our struggle with you is a contest of faith, existence, and life" (Undated leaflet).

Hamas also adduced political arguments for rejecting any attempt to achieve a political settlement with Israel. Thus, in leaflet no. 28: "Israel understands only the language of force and believes neither in negotiations nor in peace. It will persist in its evasiveness and in building a military entity, in exploiting the opportunity for attack, and in breaking the Arabs' nose." And in the same leaflet: "The Arab world is not so weak as to run after peace, and the Jews are not so strong as to be able to impose their will. . . . How long can Israel withstand all the forces?"

Furthermore, Hamas ascribed to Israel and the Jews demonic traits that justify a refusal to hold a dialogue: Israel is a "cancer which is spreading . . . and is threatening the entire Islamic world" (May 3, 1988). The Jews, according to another leaflet, are "brothers of the apes, assassins of the prophets, bloodsuckers, warmongers. . . . Only Islam can break the Jews and destroy their dreams" (January 1988).

Hamas often draws on historical personalities and events from Islamic tradition in order to underscore the religious character of the conflict with Israel. Names that frequently cropped up in the leaflets are: Ja'far Ibn Abu-Talib, who fought the Byzantines in the Battle of Mu'tah (629); Khalid Ibn al-Walid, who fought the Battle of the Yarmuk (636 C.E.) and was called by Muhammad "the sword of God"; Salah al-Din al-Ayyubi, who vanquished the Crusaders at the Battle of Hittin (1187); and Baybars, who fought the Mongols in the Battle of 'Ayn Jalut (1260). Muslim tradition has it that, during the battle, Ja'far held up the standard with one hand; when that hand was cut off he switched the banner to his other hand; and when that was also cut off, he attached the banner to his chest until he was killed.

The Khaybar affair has also attracted Hamas's attention. Many Hamas leaflets concluded with the call: *"Allah akbar* [Allah is great]—the hour of Khaybar has arrived, *Allah akbar*—death to the conquerors." Khaybar was a wealthy Jewish colony on the Arabian Peninsula. According to a Muslim tradition, the Jews of Khaybar betrayed Muhammad by serving him poisoned meat, which eventually caused his death. The Prophet and his followers had conquered Khaybar in 628 C.E., allowing "the Jews their land in return for binding themselves to turn over half their harvests."[4] For Muslims, Khaybar became a symbol of Jewish treachery. Similarly, the Muslims who reside in the territories are looked on as *mujahidun*—the warriors of the holy war—or as *murabitun*, inhabitants of the Ribat. These were Muslims who settled in the countryside during the period of the Muslim conquests to defend the borders; they were considered to be fulfilling a religious precept. Overall, Hamas advocates a Muslim state throughout Palestine that will ameliorate the ills of the Muslim community. Hamas thus looks with disfavor on Palestinian Christians and is more receptive to Muslims outside of Palestine.

Hamas believes that a political solution to the conflict with Israel would violate the religious precept of a holy war against the Jewish infidels. Its perception of Israel and the Jews as a religious—not a na-

---

4. Carl Brockelmann, *History of the Islamic People* (New York: Capricorn, 1960), 28.

tional—adversary rules out the possibility of a political settlement based on compromise. The alternative, according to Hamas, is "victory or death."

A different picture emerged from the leaflets of the UNC. They perceive reality in secular terms. UNC leaflets, which serve as a mouthpiece for the national camp, have room for both Muslims and Christians. "Religion is God's and the homeland is for all" (al-din li'llah wal-watan li'ljami'),[5] rather than Hamas's "faith is the whole world" (din wadunya). Indeed, UNC leaflets rarely mentioned heroes or events from ancient Muslim history; their allusions were to modern historical figures who became national heroes. Three names in particular were frequently cited: Sheykh ʿIzz al-Din al-Qassam, a pioneer of the armed struggle in Palestine, who was killed by the British in 1935;[6] ʿAbd al-Qadir al-Husseini, who fell in the battle for the Qastel, outside Jerusalem, in 1948; and the writer and poet Ghassan Kanafani, who was killed in a car explosion in Beirut in 1972.

UNC leaflets stressed the ties between Muslims and Christians. Leaflet no. 22 (July 21, 1988), for example, called on the people to "pray for the repose of the martyrs' souls and [to] hold marches and demonstrations in protest at the measures of the occupation authorities against Islamic and Christian holy places." Leaflet no. 30 (December 15, 1988) referred to the forthcoming Christmas celebrations in the following language: "December 24 [is] a day for ringing church bells and calling out *Allah akbar* in the minarets of the mosques, marking the birth of the messenger of peace, the Lord Messiah. We extend felicitations to our Palestinian Christian brothers and urge them to make do with observing the religious rituals."[7]

The UNC perceives the conflict with Israel more in secular-political terms than religious ones. The Palestinian society will be healed, leaflet no. 28 said, through "self-determination and the establishment of an independent state with Arab Jerusalem as its eternal capital," rather than by imposing the kingdom of Islam on the Palestinian world.

---

5. *Al-Hadaf* (Beirut), (PFLP organ), Oct. 12, 1987. Cp. the biblical Psalm, 115 (16): "Heaven is the Lord's, and the earth He gave to man."
6. Fatah views Sheykh ʿIzz al-Din al-Qassam more as a national hero than a religious figure. In his memory, Fatah issued a special publication, *Thawrat al-Sheykh ʿIzz al-Din al-Qassam* (The revolution of Sheykh ʿIzz al-Din al-Qassam (Beirut: June 1977). The Palestinian Left regards Sheykh al-Qassam as a social rebel.
7. The idea is to play down the Christmas festivities and not decorate the streets as in previous years. A similar call, to refrain from holding festivities, went out to Muslims on the Feast of the Sacrifice (ʿId al-Adha).

Like Hamas leaflets, those of the UNC are harsh in their denunciations of Israeli policy and leaders. The detention facilities for Palestinians are "Nazi camps" (leaflet no. 15); Sharon, Peres and Rabin are "fascist dwarfs" (no. 16); Rabin is a "shedder of blood" (no. 11); he is a "terrorist" and Shamir is "arrogant" (no. 25); the settlers are "herds" or a "rabble" (no. 27); and the Israeli military authorities are a "Zionist machine of oppression and fascist executioners" (no. 28). Yet, as the following passage shows, the leaflets also repeatedly recognized the need for a peaceful solution based on the PLO formula of

> an effective international conference under U.N. auspices with the participation of the five permanent members of the Security Council and all parties to the conflict, [including] the PLO, our sole legitimate representative, on an equal footing with the other parties, on the basis of [Security Council] Resolutions 242 and 338, with the right of self-determination for our Palestinian people. This emphasis proves how sincerely devoted our people is in its aspiration to establish a just and comprehensive peace, this against the background of detente in the international arena and the tendency to resolve regional conflicts on a basis of international legitimacy. (leaflet no. 29, November 11, 1988)

The UNC also addressed practical demands to Israel, directly or indirectly, of a kind that indicate that its perception of Israel was pragmatic and not demonic, realistic and not mythological. Leaflet no. 26 (September 27, 1988) contained a typical list of such demands: annulment of the 1945 emergency regulations; removal of the army from Palestinian population centers; release of all uprising detainees and repatriating the deportees; free elections in all the local governments, urban and rural, under U.N. supervision; and cessation of punitive measures, such as economic "siege," demolition of houses, torture, deportations, arrest without trial, and building of settlements.

Some leaflets were addressed to the Israeli public or to specific groups in an effort to explain the rationale behind the Intifada and the need for a peaceful settlement. Leaflet no. 28 (October 30, 1988) offered a striking example of this approach.

> UNC stresses to the Israeli street that our blessed uprising, ... did not aspire to shed the blood of Palestinians or Jews, but was a revolution against the dispossession, oppression, and fascism of the occupation, and [a manifestation of] national determination to establish a just peace in our region, [a peace] which will emerge only with the establishment of our Palestinian state on our national soil. Concurrent with our request that

our National Council adopt realistic resolutions and plans in order to support our people, put an end to the occupation and establish our independent state, we are also taking advantage of this opportunity to underscore the recent appeal made by the PLO and the United National Command to the Israeli street, calling on Arab and Israeli voters to vote for peace forces that support our people's right to self-determination and [the right] to establish an independent state on our national soil.

Examples of calls to specific Israeli groups appeared in leaflets nos. 23 and 25. The former (August 5, 1988) called on Jewish physicians "to intensify their support for our just struggle" and praised those among them "who have disdained the occupation measures about not giving medical treatment to the wounded of the uprising." This leaflet also called on "all Israelis who face harassment because of their support for our people's national rights, to explain to the Israeli street our just rights. [This, because] whoever consents to another's repression cannot himself be free." Leaflet no. 25 (September 6, 1988) was addressed to the Jewish settlers:

> To avoid bottles [Molotov cocktails] and stones, [Prime Minister] Shamir has given the settlers a green light to open fire on the Palestinian inhabitants. We ask them and others: ... Are you aware that the solution to the stone problem and so forth will only come when you remove yourselves from our land and recognize our legitimate national rights, self-determination, and an independent state, and not by talking nonsense, going on the rampage, and exercising oppression?

The conflicting stands of Hamas and the UNC regarding a Palestinian state and the political process often generated friction between the two groups. These disparities were heightened as the UNC increasingly expressed support for a peaceful solution, and PLO diplomatic activity was intensified. As a result, Hamas tended to operate without coordination with the UNC. Thus, in leaflet no. 25 (September 6, 1988), the UNC assailed Hamas's decision to call a two-day general strike on a date different from that set by the UNC. The UNC termed this a blow to unity of ranks and a boost for Israel. The UNC also decried acts of violence against those who did not respond to Hamas's call for a strike.

Hamas was not long in retaliating, and in its leaflet no. 30 (October 5, 1988) absolved itself of all blame.

> The Jews and their supporters are striving to split our ranks and generate disputes by spreading rumors that [the] Hamas is competing

[with other movements] or seeking to replace them. In reaction to these virulent rumors, we call on the people to peruse the covenant of the Islamic Resistance Movement [of August 1988] in order to acquaint themselves with it and learn its goals. The competition will consist of confrontation against the [Israeli] enemy and inflicting grave damage on his camp. We reiterate that we are for unity of ranks, against schism, and for everyone who works faithfully for the liberation of Palestine—all of Palestine. We are against conceding so much as an inch of our land which is steeped in the blood of the Companions of the Prophet and their followers.

Tension between Hamas and the UNC mounted in the wake of the events at the Palestinian National Council (PNC) meeting held in Algiers in mid-November 1988. In this meeting, the PNC declared the establishment of a Palestinian state and endorsed U.N. General Assembly Resolution 181 of November 1947, calling for the partition of Palestine into two states, one Jewish and one Arab. In leaflet no. 29 (November 20, 1988), entitled "The Joy of the Palestinian State," the UNC appealed to

a number of fundamentalist elements to prefer the general national interests, our people's national interest, over their basic assumptions and factional interests . . . and to cease presenting negative stands and manifestations. For, they serve the enemy, whether they wish to or not. They must draw the conclusions from the mass celebrations . . . marking the declaration of the [Palestinian] state, reflecting the deep roots of our legitimate leadership and sole representative, [the PLO]. It is still not too late to fuse all the loyal forces in the melting pot of the uprising and its United National Command.

In reaction, Hamas declared, in leaflet no. 31 (November 27, 1988), that it opposed splitting the ranks but that this might result from "leaflets being planted in the name of the Hamas which the [Israeli] occupier circulated in order to split the ranks and cast aspersions on the [various] currents." And, above all: "preserve the unity of the people. Pay no heed to the enemy's attempts to cause a rift in families, clans, currents of thought, and ideas."

Hamas's response to UNC's charges attest to its complex attitude toward the national camp. On the one hand, Hamas was not eager to aggravate its disagreements with the UNC to the point of a head-on clash. Such a development would have a boomerang effect in the struggle against Israel. On the other hand, Hamas did not undertake to back away from a confrontation in the future if the UNC, together with the

PLO, should assent to a political settlement that jettisoned the principle of liberating the whole of Palestine.

Hamas's covenant sheds light on the movement's ambivalent relations with the national camp. It described Hamas-PLO relations as resembling those in a family: "The Palestine Liberation Organization is one of the closest [bodies] to the Islamic Resistance Movement. It contains fathers, brothers, relatives, and friends. Can the Muslim abandon his family and friends? Our homeland is one, our tragedy is one, and our fate is one." At the same time, the PLO's secularism was not to Hamas's liking: "We cannot exchange the Islamic nature of Palestine in the present and the future for the secular idea. The Islamic nature of Palestine is part of our religion, and whoever relinquishes his religion is on the losing side." When the PLO adopts Islam as a way of life, "the movement's attitude toward the PLO will be as son to father, as brother to brother, and as relative to relative."[8]

The ideological discord between Hamas and the UNC-PLO increased the potential for an irreparable rift between the two camps. Still, along with the conflicting interests in the ideological realm, there was an awareness of common interests in the practical domain, namely, in the day-to-day struggle against the Israeli authorities. As long as Israeli military activity continued on a large scale and as long as a PLO-type Palestinian state had not arisen, it was unlikely that the ideological differences between Hamas and the UNC would lead to a drawing of the battle lines.

The Question of Civil Revolt

A second goal of the Intifada shared by the UNC and Hamas was to undermine Israeli rule in the occupied territories by means of a civil revolt that would force Israel's withdrawal from these areas. On this issue, unlike those noted above, the two groups shared a common approach. This was reflected in their nearly identical directives to the Palestinian public about its role in the uprising.

The population was called on to cooperate in both violent and nonviolent actions. The former included throwing stones and fire bombs, building barriers, burning tires, wielding knives and axes, clashing with the Israeli forces, and attacking collaborators. To ensure that these operations were carried out, the UNC made use of "shock squads" (*al-majmuʿat* or *al-firaq al-dariba*). These units had the task of ensuring that the requisite actions, both violent and nonviolent, were implemented. A

8. Paz, 15-16.

detailed description of their activity appeared in the UNC's leaflet no. 22 (July 21, 1988).

> The United National Command salutes the shock squads for their active role against the [Israeli] occupation forces, their agents, and departments, and against those who deviate from the will of the people. They are called on to strike with an iron fist against whoever has not resigned [from the Civil Administration], and are requested to block roads on general strike days and to allow only doctors' vehicles to pass. They should write national-unity slogans [on walls] . . . and sign only in the name of the United National Command. They should raise flags, organize demonstrations, burn tires, and throw stones and Molotov cocktails.

Leaflet no. 26 (September 27, 1988) called for the "escalation of the daily clashes with the occupation soldiers and the herds of settlers, and sabotage of enemy property." Both this leaflet and the previous one urged action against collaborators.

In the realm of nonviolent activity, the population was called on to take action in three areas: (1) to sever economic ties with Israel and to build up local institutions that would provide substitute public services; (2) to engage in civil disobedience, i.e., disobey laws and regulations; and (3) to carry out activities that promote solidarity.

The directives on severing ties with Israel included: not working in Israel; not working in Jewish settlements in the occupied territories; boycotting Israeli products; withdrawing deposits from Israeli banks; resigning from the Civil Administration; developing a home-based economy, including the growing of vegetables and the raising of domestic animals in one's yard, and, to farmers, "to plant cereals and legumes such as lentils, chickpeas, broad beans, garlic, onions, wheat, and so forth, for storage" (UNC leaflet no. 24, August 22, 1988);[9] expanding local plants and taking on new workers; setting up and expanding popular committees on education, information, guard duty, and agriculture; and establishing and cultivating local bodies for "popular education"—a directive calling on parents, teachers, and students to uphold the routine of studies despite the protracted closure of educational institutions by the Israeli authorities.[10]

---

9. The home-economy aspect rarely appears in Hamas leaflets. The reason is that the population density in the Gaza Strip, which is Hamas's power base, precludes the use of yards for agriculture.

10. The Islamic Jihad was the only body that favored the continued closure of educational institutions. A Jihad leaflet (undated) stated: "A policy of calm in our occupied Muslim Palestine, and the dousing of the fire of the comprehensive uprising, is the aim

TABLE 1

Types of Directives in UNC Leaflets by Periodic Distribution
(absolute numbers)

Type of Directive	Period 1 (Nos. 1–10)	Period 2 (Nos. 11–20)	Period 3 (Nos. 21–30)	Total
Violent	10	32	45	87
Nonviolent:				
Severing Contact	19	21	15	55
Disobedience	18	22	27	67
Acts of Solidarity	23	36	47	106
Total	70	111	134	315
Percentage	22.2	35.2	42.6	

Directives regarding civil disobedience included: nonpayment of taxes and of fines; staging partial commercial strikes; and holding general strikes on specified days. As for activities to enhance solidarity, the population, or at times certain groups, were called on to fulfill the following directives: day-long strikes of solidarity with prisoners; day-long strikes of solidarity with families of victims; memorial days for traumatic events such as the civil war in Jordan that broke out in September 1970; coordination of dealing with prisoners by lawyers, and press conferences to expose conditions in the detention camps; sit-down strikes by students, teachers, and parents in front of foreign missions and closed schools; volunteer work with farmers to help with the olive harvest; assistance to needy families; refraining from raising rent; reducing fees charged by doctors and hospitals; and writing slogans on walls and raising flags.

An analysis of the first 30 leaflets issued by the UNC and Hamas shows a steady and significant rise, over time, in the number of violent and nonviolent directives. Subsequent leaflets maintained the same high proportion of violent and nonviolent directives. Table 1 shows that of 315 directives, both violent and nonviolent, contained in UNC leaflets,

of our crafty enemy. We must say 'no' to this policy a thousand times, and a thousand times 'yes' to the closure of the schools and educational institutions so that our children and youngsters will turn to the sacred stones, to a lengthy and blessed struggle, and so that the sacred hands will turn to the shattering of the injustice and its expressions, and so that Muslim Palestine will be a graveyard for the heretical invaders."

TABLE 2

Types of Directives in Hamas Leaflets by Periodic Distribution
(absolute numbers)

Type of Directive	Period 1 (Nos. 1–10)	Period 2 (Nos. 11–20)	Period 3 (Nos. 21–30)	Total
Violent	11	16	25	52
Nonviolent:				
Severing Contact	10	11	3	24
Disobedience	7	2	19	28
Acts of Solidarity	8	11	16	35
Total	36	40	63	139
Percentage	25.9	28.8	45.3	

70 (22.2 percent of the total) were contained in the first ten leaflets, 111 (35.2 percent) in leaflets nos. 11–20, and 134 (42.6 percent) in leaflets nos. 21–30.

A similar tendency, albeit smaller in scope, is discernible in the first 30 leaflets put out by Hamas.

Table 2 shows that of 139 violent and nonviolent directives in Hamas leaflets, 36 (about 26 percent of the total) appeared in the first ten leaflets, 40 (29 percent) in leaflet nos. 11–20, and 63 (more than 45 percent) in leaflet nos. 21–30.

A comparative analysis discloses that UNC leaflets contained nearly 2.5 times as many directives as Hamas leaflets. Indeed, from the outset of the Intifada, UNC leaflets gave more detailed instructions than Hamas leaflets. This trend continued: as the Intifada progressed, UNC directives became increasingly detailed and specific as compared with those of Hamas. The source of these differences lay in the character and goals of the mother-movements with which each group was affiliated. The PLO, the UNC's referent, had a concrete goal of establishing a state in the West Bank and Gaza within the foreseeable future. Consequently, it encouraged actions based on immediate considerations, which necessitated detailed instructions. In contrast, the Muslim Brothers, the movement behind Hamas, envisaged the establishment of a state in all of Palestine as a long-range goal. The Brothers' religious world view gave

TABLE 3

Types of Directives Contained in UNC Leaflets
by Periodic Distribution
(in percentage)

Type of Directive	Period 1 (Nos. 1–10)	Period 2 (Nos. 11–20)	Period 3 (Nos. 21–30)
Violent	14.3	28.3	33.6
Nonviolent:			
Severing Contact	27.1	18.9	11.2
Disobedience	25.7	19.8	20.2
Acts of Solidarity	<u>32.9</u>	<u>32.4</u>	<u>35.0</u>
Total	100 (70)	100 (111)	100 (134)

rise to goals of an absolutist character. As a result, Hamas's directives were less concrete and more general.

Another reason for the differences was that, as compared with Hamas, the PLO is a mature organization, larger and more complex in structure, and with greater experience in overt political, economic, and social activity among the Palestinians in the territories. These factors not only heightened the PLO's sensitivity to issues that impinged on the day-to-day life of the population but also influenced the expectations placed in the PLO by the public. Yet, the leaflets of both groups showed an identical trend of a steady increase in the number of both violent and nonviolent instructions. The data show further that the increase in the number of directives was accompanied by a significant change, over time, in the proportion between instructions calling for violent or for nonviolent activity.

Table 3 shows a significant rise in the preponderance of instructions calling for violent activity in UNC leaflets during each of the three periods. In the first period, 14.3 percent of the 70 instructions entailed violent action, in the second period the proportion had risen to 28 percent, and by the third period such instructions accounted for a third of the total. Thus, the weight of violent instructions more than doubled between the first and third periods.

Concurrently, a drastic decrease is visible in the number of instructions for severing ties with Israel in the realms of the economy and

TABLE 4

Types of Directives Contained in Hamas Leaflets
by Periodic Distribution
(in percentage)

Type of Directive	Period 1 (Nos. 1–10)	Period 2 (Nos. 11–20)	Period 3 (Nos. 21–30)
Violent	30.5	40.0	39.7
Nonvolent:			
Severing Contact	27.8	27.5	4.8
Disobedience	19.4	5.0	30.2
Acts of Solidarity	22.2	27.5	25.4
Total	100 (36)	100 (40)	100 (63)

services: from 27 percent in the first period to 11 percent in the third. The frequency of the two other types of nonviolent instructions—disobedience to orders and encouragement of acts of solidarity—remained stable.

Where Hamas is concerned, the overall picture regarding violence and the severing of contact with Israel was substantially the same. A comparison of the instructions for violent actions in Hamas and UNC leaflets reveals that the violence level of the former was consistently high from the start of the Intifada. In the UNC, the violence level was initially low but gradually crept upward during 1988. From August 1988 it approached that of Hamas. The difference in the proportion of violent directives should not cloud the fact that both groups evinced an identical trend: a growing number of violent directives, on the one hand, and a sharp decline in calls to break economic ties with Israel, on the other. In UNC leaflets, this trend was discernible already in the second period, while in Hamas it emerged in the third period of 1988.

These trends reflect the contradictory considerations guiding the groups that were behind the uprising. On the one hand, they believed that violence was a necessity: extreme action served as an outlet for the younger generation's ideological fervor and political frustrations. The demographic weight of the younger Palestinians, their level of education and political awareness, together with the organizational frameworks at their disposal, made them leading instigators in the uprising. Moreover, as the violence grew and claimed more casualties on the Palestinian side, the Intifada's political gains increased accordingly. The daily skirmishes between the population and Israeli troops, widely covered in the media, thrust the Palestinian problem and the PLO back into international consciousness. Public figures, politicians, and the press in countries friendly to Israel were sharply critical of Israeli policy, and governments and international organizations condemned the methods employed to suppress the uprising.

The surging violence also deeply affected Israel itself. Many Israelis perceived the occupation as morally indefensible, socially deleterious, economically ruinous, and politically and militarily harmful. Israel's political leadership faced mounting pressure from broad segments of the public to stop trying to quell the uprising by force and to propose political solutions that would put a stop to the bloodshed.

In short, it was the Palestinians' growing awareness of the vital role played by violence in propelling the Intifada and in producing political gains that accounted for the significant increase in the violent directives in UNC leaflets and the consistently high level of violent directives in Hamas leaflets.

On the other hand, the Intifada's real capacity for endurance depended on the Palestinians' economic staying power. In the absence of self-sustaining economic capability, dependence on Israel had become a way of life. Under these circumstances, excessive pressure to sever contact with Israel was ineffective. To obey would mean economic hardship for tens of thousands of workers who earned their living in Israel and a huge loss of revenue for many local merchants and factory owners who maintained commercial ties with Israeli firms. In turn, a severe economic downturn in these sectors could weaken the influence of the UNC and Hamas, stir disobedience, and encourage anarchy. If the Intifada's strength lay in its ability to obtain the cooperation of all social strata and age groups, it is readily understandable how the ideologically heretical suddenly became economically inevitable.

The inability or unwillingness of merchants, factory owners, and workers to break off economic relations with Israel forced both the UNC and Hamas to adapt themselves to the circumstances and bow to the constraints. Hence, the gradual decrease in the number of directives urging an economic break with Israel. Instructions in this spirit continued to appear, but more selectively. This was particularly noticeable as regards work in Israel and the boycotting of Israeli products. Later leaflets noted clearly that the prohibition on working in Israel was confined to days of general strikes or to persons employed in sectors that competed with products of the territories, such as the citrus industry. In the same vein, the leaflets called for a boycott of products for which local substitutes were available, notably milk products, agricultural produce, cigarettes, and soft drinks.[11]

The decline in the number of directives calling for a total economic break with Israel indicates a reassessment by both the UNC and Hamas concerning the limits of strength of the Intifada. This awareness explains why both groups stepped back from declaring a general civil revolt and preferred to hammer home the idea that the uprising was a stage toward a total revolt. This outlook is illustrated in the following examples from UNC leaflets:

> The uprising is a lengthy and protracted revolutionary process that entails hardships. . . . The road to civil disobedience obligates the creation of additional popular committees, neighborhood committees, educational committees, and guard duty, agricultural, information, and solidarity committees. (Leaflet no. 15, April 30, 1988)

> The declaration of the stage of civil disobedience in the uprising depends on the creation of the essential conditions for its fulfillment, the most important of which is to complete the establishment of the apparatus for popular rule in all the towns, villages, and [refugee] camps in the occupied territories. (Leaflet no. 19, June 8, 1988)

> UNC . . . calls on our masses to escalate the uprising as a stage toward comprehensive civil disobedience. (Leaflet no. 21, July 6, 1988)

A similar picture emerges from Hamas leaflets: "Know that victory demands patience and God is on the side of the righteous" (leaflet from January 1988); "Know that the road [of struggle] with the Jews is long and will not end soon" (April 1, 1988); and "Spare no efforts [to fan] the fire of the uprising until God gives the sign to be extricated from the distress. Invoke God's name plentifully, for lo! with hardship goeth ease" (January 1988).

The controlled civil revolt, like the continuous decline in the number of directives calling for the severing of economic ties with Israel, was evidence that the leading bodies of the Intifada had adopted a flexible strategy to further their political goals. The Palestinians were

---

11. A Hamas leaflet, of Apr. 15, 1988, mentioned specifically three soft-drink brands: Crystal, Tempo, and Schweppes.

aware of profit-and-loss considerations. They were avoiding a slide into absurdities in trying to achieve their objectives. They recognized the limits of their strength and were careful not to reach a point of no return in the confrontation with Israel. The Intifada had its share of internal contradictions and conflicting interests; nonetheless, it was able to accommodate such contradictions without succumbing to them.

Modes of Operation and the Ability to Continue

The Intifada's strength has come from its ability to forge a sense of mutual dependence and partnership between the middle class and the radical youth; between the merchants, businessmen, factory owners, doctors, lawyers, engineers, and other members of the white-collar sector, on the one hand, and the "rolling stones" generation that imbibed its doctrine from West Bank universities, Gaza Strip mosques, and youth organizations in both areas, on the other. This younger generation existed before the outbreak of the Intifada. But the conditions conducive to its cooperation with the middle class could not materialize as long as a prominent urban leadership held power and was able to cooperate simultaneously with Israel, Jordan, and the PLO. Thanks to this political cooperation, the local leadership could shield the middle class from radical pressures exerted by the young guard. The enfeeblement of the previous local leadership, a development caused by Israeli policy since the early 1980s, created a vacuum that was filled by the young people. In the absence of an urban local leadership, the middle class was no longer protected. It was pulled, almost willy-nilly, into the radical action of the Intifada.

The cooperation between the youngsters and the merchants and the rest of the middle class accounts for the fury of the outburst but not for its duration. The merchants and the businessmen lost money and complained; so did the Civil Administration employees who had to resign. Their interests were not identical with the interests of the youngsters who were fired by national fervor and a passion for self-sacrifice. The repeated instructions to the merchants to open for business only as set forth in the leaflets and not to raise prices, along with insistent calls to local workers in the Civil Administration to resign, testified to a large measure of unease in those groups. If the solidarity between the middle-class groups and the younger generation persisted, it was owing to the ability of the UNC and Hamas to make effective use of several mechanisms that reduced the danger of a split and enabled the momentum to be maintained. A perusal of the leaflets shows an effective use of three such mechanisms: organizational tools, economic means, and symbolic rewards.

Organizational and Economic Sphere

The leaflets show that the Intifada has been characterized by decentralized activity that emphasized local action. The local activity was carried out by the popular committees that were created in the course of the uprising. There were hundreds of these, in urban neighborhoods, in villages, and in the refugee camps throughout the West Bank and Gaza Strip. As may be gleaned from UNC leaflets, these committees were the equivalent of an executive branch. Their task was to ensure that instructions were implemented in the spirit of the leaflets and to tend to the daily needs of the population, which was under constant Israeli military and economic pressure. Through the committees' various inducements or coercion, if necessary, close supervision could be maintained over those people who ignored the directives.

The leaflets also point to the existence of a broad range of committees organized on a professional or geographical basis. Professional committees include those of merchants, physicians, and lawyers, and committees to care for prisoners. Groups operating on a geographical basis include neighborhood committees, guard and defense committees set up after local policemen resigned, and mutual help committees. The "shock squads" would operate in conjunction with these committees. They would ensure that directives were carried out and, if necessary, would punish those who were unwilling to obey. The operational echelon at the local level also included bodies that existed before the Intifada, whose activity was now integrated with that of the popular committees. Among these were associations of women, workers and students, charity and welfare organizations, and religious societies.

The major objective of the various organizations was to erode the Israeli ruling apparatus in the occupied territories. In large measure, the committees became parallel ruling bodies enjoying popular local encouragement and cooperation. Nor did the leading bodies of the uprising neglect the economic sphere. Financial aid was proffered to those harmed by Israeli actions, such as families of people killed, wounded, or deported, and families whose houses were demolished. Similarly, as mentioned, various steps were taken to reduce general economic hardships. Commercial strikes were usually partial: stores were closed half days, except in general strikes, when they shut down for the whole day; the boycott of Israeli products was selective, and the same holds for working in Israel. Often, the leaflets conveyed to the population that the leadership of the uprising was aware of their plight and was doing all in its power to ensure that the economic burden was shared equally. Examples were the directives calling on property owners not to raise rent and to defer collecting rent from those unable to pay. At the same time, those who did have the means were urged to pay on time. The leaflets called on physicians and hospitals not to increase the costs of medical services, and on lawyers to refrain from raising legal fees.

Symbolic Gratifications

Most striking was the effort to impart to the people a sense that they were participating in a historic event of supreme national importance. The leaflets extolled the activity of the entire populace and lauded its contribution to the Intifada's achievements. Those achievements, as seen from the perspective of the leaflets, have been many and varied.

Economically, the Intifada cost Israel $2 billion during its first year, and far more in the second, according to the calculations of the United National Command.[12] Militarily, it demonstrated that Israel cannot cope with stones and Molotov cocktails. Two-thirds of the Israeli army was said to be engaged in suppressing the riots.[13] Israeli soldiers required psychological treatment as a result. One UNC leaflet quoted the then chief of staff, Lt. Gen. Dan Shomron, as saying that the Intifada could not be crushed by force. In the civilian sphere, the leaflets noted with satisfaction "the dismantlement of the mechanisms and tools" of Israeli rule in the territories and the building of a Palestinian "national government" apparatus.

Politically, the leaflets pointed to the contribution of the Intifada in bringing the Palestinian problem to international consciousness, along with the diplomatic damage and domestic strife it was causing in Israel.

12. The figure of $2 billion, mentioned in the leaflet, is close to the estimates of the former Israeli finance minister, Shimon Peres. According to his calculation, the annual cost of the Intifada for Israel was between $1.5 to $2 billion. See Ha'aretz (Tel Aviv), June 2, 1989. According to the former economy and communications minister, Gad Ya'acobi, the first year of the Intifada cost Israel $0.5 billion. See, Ha'aretz (Tel Aviv), Mar. 12, 1989.

13. The leaflet's assessment that two-thirds of the Israeli army was engaged in suppressing the riots was far from accurate. The Israeli army, regular and reserves, consisted of 498,000 soldiers in 1989. Israeli military experts estimate that, at the height of the Intifada, some 10,000 soldiers were involved in military activity in the territories. See Joseph Alpher, Zeev Eytan, and Dov Tamari, eds. *The Middle East Military Balance, 1989–1990* (Jerusalem: Jaffee Center for Strategic Studies, Tel Aviv University, 1990), 243.

UNC leaflet no. 30 (December 7, 1988) stated: "The unbroken continuity of heroic exploits performed by our generous masses, in defiance of the occupier's strength, tyranny, and wickedness, was a beacon that placed our Palestinian cause at the head of international, Arab, and local interest. The Palestinian issue has become a talking point in every diplomatic and political meeting and discussion in every corner of the world. At the same time, the abhorred occupation has experienced division and political and social schism due to the continuation and escalation of the uprising." Hamas leaflets voiced similar sentiments. From a leaflet dated February 11, 1988: "Our Muslim people . . . heightened the conflict and the split in the enemy's ranks through its blessed uprising."

The leaflets also made much of the sense of pride and self-esteem that the Intifada imbued in the Palestinians in the territories. UNC leaflet no. 23 (August 5, 1988) declared: "You have already proved that the enemy's measures, including deportations, house demolitions, harassment, economic measures, a declaration of war on the popular and national committees, closure of the national institutions, disseminating propaganda through the media and through treacherous agents about the end of the uprising and the fading of its flame—that all these measures will fail in the face of your blazing fire and your readiness for sacrifice."

The picture in Hamas was similar: "The Muslim people is wreaking its revenge and restoring its past glory" (leaflet of February 11, 1988). Hamas, like the UNC, emphasized the population's staying power thanks to which Israel's attempts to impose "collective punishment and political and media stifling . . . are doomed to failure. The thick club has failed, their economic pressures have failed along with the starvation [tactics]" (leaflet of April 7, 1988).

The recourse to varied symbolic organizational and economic modes had proved its worth. The Intifada, which began as a spontaneous outburst, soon took a course of intensive and ongoing activity embracing all segments of the population. Collective steadfastness, a readiness for personal sacrifice, and a sense of national pride in the face of harsh Israeli punitive measures were among the major achievements of the Intifada.

The central bodies behind the day-to-day activity—the United National Command and the PLO, on the one hand, and Hamas, al-Mujammaʿ al-Islami, and the Muslim Brothers, on the other—were able to ensure a considerable degree of obedience to their directives and to obtain broad compliance from the population. In the absence of a local leadership, the popular committees and the "shock squads" narrowed the range of possible deviation by opponents and induced those who showed reluctance to obey the directives. Concurrently, means of persuasion were exerted on those who were indifferent. Carefully calculated directives in the economic sphere, imparting to the population the feeling that the burden was a shared one and that they were full partners in national achievements, heightened the readiness for active participation.

Israel's failure to suppress the Intifada results from its inability to come up with a quick and effective response to the coercion and persuasion mechanisms wielded on the Palestinian population in the West Bank and Gaza by the groups behind the uprising. Israel's difficulties in this sphere have diverse causes: political constraints, domestic differences, legal limitations, and moral considerations that guide the nation's political and military levels. Supposing that these factors will continue to dictate the nature of Israeli activity and that, in turn, this activity will render it difficult for Israel to prevent those behind the Intifada from continuing to gain the obedience and compliance of the population, political dialogue becomes an unavoidable option. If not, the war of the clubs against the stones will not cease, the leaflets will blossom, and the Intifada will continue to be a millstone around Israel's neck.

...

Leaflets of the United National Command (UNC)

• • •

LEAFLET NO. 1

In the name of Allah the merciful and compassionate

Communiqué—communiqué—communiqué

In the wake of our people's glorious uprising, and the need to promote the spirit of struggle and solidarity with our people everywhere, with faithfulness to the blood of the pure martyrs and our imprisoned brothers, and to express our resistance to the occupation and the policy of repression—expressed in deportations and collective arrests, the imposition of curfew and the demolition of houses—and in order to unite our revolution and our heroic masses, and in obedience to the call of the PLO, our sole legitimate representative, to continue with the sacrifice and the valiant uprising, we issue the following call:

All sectors of our heroic people, wherever they may be, are to observe scrupulously the call for a comprehensive general strike from January 11, 1988, until Wednesday evening, January 13, 1988. The strike will embrace all spheres of public and private commerce, as well as the workers and public transportation sectors. The general strike must be strictly observed. The slogan of the strike will be: Down with the occupation, long live free Arab Palestine!

Brother workers,

Your observance of the strike by abstaining from work and by not turning up at the factories constitutes true support for the glorious revolution and for our people, and fealty to the blood of the pure martyrs; [it will] support the demand for the release of our detainees and help ensure that our brothers [who are to be] deported shall remain.

Brother owners of shops and grocery stores, you must scrupulously observe the call for a general strike on the strike days. Your previous strict observance of the call to strike was an extraordinary expression of your magnificent solidarity with and sacrifice for the stand of our heroic people. We will make every effort to protect the interests of our honorable merchants, in view of what they can expect from the occupation authorities.

We warn against following in the footsteps of the "tails" of the occupation authorities.[1] Be assured that we will punish traitorous merchants quickly. Let us go together, in unity, to achieve victory.

Brother owners of bus and taxi companies,

We will not forget your honorable and magnificent stand and help toward the success of the general strike on the day of Palestinian steadfastness. It is our hope that you will support the general strike. We warn owners of the bus companies against not observing the strike, for this will bring in its wake revolutionary punishments.

Brother doctors and pharmacists, you must be vigilant to provide succor for those of our people who are ill. Pharmacists will work normally, doctors will display the special "doctor's symbol" prominently.

A general warning:

We warn against the danger of walking on the roads due to measures that will be taken to intensify the general strike. We warn that glutinous material will be poured on the main and side roads and everywhere, this in addition to the roadblocks and the shock squads,[2] who will be dispersed throughout the occupied homeland.

O our inhabitants, our heroic people, before the strike you must equip yourself with everything you will need during the strike.

General announcement:

The fighters and brother members of the popular committees and the uprising committees who are widely dispersed must proffer whatever help and aid they can to our people and their various sectors, and especially to the needy families among us.

The strike units and the popular uprising squads must adhere strictly to the work plan in their possession. Together, hand in hand, with upraised voice, let us all call:

"Down with the occupation, down with the occupation,"

Long live free Arab Palestine.

The Palestinian Forces

1. *Tails*—the Communists' contemptuous term for collaborators with Israel.
2. In the original: *majmuʿat dariba*—what the Israeli press dubbed "strike units." Also known as *al-firaq al-dariba*.

• • •

LEAFLET NO. 2

No voice will overcome the voice of the uprising

Communiqué—communiqué—communiqué

Communiqué No. 2

Issued by the United National Command
for the Escalation of the Uprising

O masses of our glorious people,

O people of martyrs, descendants of al-Qassam,¹ O brothers and comrades of Abu Sharar, Khalid Nazzal and Kanafani,² O people of the uprising, which has been growing from the roots of our homeland since 1936,³ and with iron force is pitted against the fascist occupation and is burning the ground under the feet of the cowardly soldiers and their commanders. O heroes of the war of the stone and the Molotov cocktail! In order to bolster our people's glorious uprising and their fealty to the pure blood of our people's martyrs; and to enhance the revolutionary chapters recorded by the

---

1. Sheykh ʿIzz al-Din al-Qassam was born in Syria in 1871. He arrived in Palestine in 1921 and became a preacher in Haifa's al-Istiqlal mosque. From 1931, al-Qassam and his followers conducted guerilla attacks against Jewish civilians in Palestine. He became the target of a British manhunt after being involved in the murder of a Jewish officer. Al-Qassam was killed on November 21, 1935, after he and his men were surrounded by a British military unit near the village of Yaʿbed. His funeral turned into a tumultuous mass demonstration. His grave became a place of pilgrimage, and he himself became a model for emulation among the Palestinians.

2. Majid Abu Sharar, Fatah activist, was killed in Rome. Khalid Nazzal, member of the DFLP, was killed in Greece. Ghassan Kanafani, from the PFLP, was killed in Beirut.

3. In 1936, the Arab revolt against the British and the Jews broke out in Palestine.

sons of Jabalya, Balata, ʿAskar, al-Maghazi, al-Bureij, Qalandya, al-Amʿari, Rafah, Khan Yunis, al-Shati, Tulkarm, and all the [refugee] camps, towns, and villages of Palestine, united on the daily battlefield which eradicated the occupation's repression, terror, and policy—collective arrests, poison gas, armored vehicles, the closure of cities and camps; and to deepen our steadfast and absolute unity with the PLO, the sole legitimate representative of our Palestinian people; and to stress yesterday's resolutions of the Central Committee regarding the struggle and unity; and to support the heroic popular uprising—the United National Command calls on all the national action committees and the popular committees to escalate the victorious popular uprising and to improve its methods, by declaring a comprehensive general strike from Monday, January 11, 1988, until Wednesday evening, January 13, 1988, incorporating all forms of revolutionary escalation. And by declaring Friday, January 15, 1988, a day of unity and solidarity to commemorate the martyrs of the uprising by means of requiem prayers and symbolic funerals, vociferous popular demonstrations and chanting loudly and in unison:

With our spirit and our blood we will redeem you, O *shahid* (martyr) . . . With our spirit and our blood we will redeem you, O Palestine.

O youth of Palestine, O throwers of flaming stones, the neofascists will undoubtedly be forced to admit the facts forged by your uprising, which is marking the road to national independence. Let us hoist the flag of Palestine over the walls of holy Jerusalem!

O valiant masses of the working class,

We must make the general comprehensive strike a success by totally stopping work on the strike days. Your pioneering worker role in the general uprising constitutes the answer to the threats and contempt of the authorities and their policy of racial discrimination, and underscores your fealty to the blood of the people's martyrs. Thus will the occupation [authorities] be forced to annul all their deportation decisions, and freedom will resound for our heroic detainees.

O valiant shop-owner fighters,

One of the most important slogans of the uprising calls for stepping up the struggle to abolish all tax measures. It is incumbent upon you to join the uprising alongside all our people's sectors—workers, *fellahin* (farmers), students, women. You must maintain the prominent national role you have played thus far. The people of the uprising will know how to protect the merchants and when to punish severely whoever attempts to emulate those who collaborate with the occupation authorities.

O heroic sons of our people, drivers and owners of bus and taxi companies,

Your honorable national stand was demonstrated on the day of Palestinian steadfastness. We are confident that your steadfastness will persist during the three days of the strike. Whoever deviates from the general consensus is hereby warned that the cubs of the uprising are lurking for him.

The United National Command for the Escalation of the Uprising emphasizes the continuation of the struggle in all its forms, under the banners of the PLO, until the attainment of our people's exalted goals: the return [to the homeland], self-determination, and the establishment of our independent Palestinian state under the leadership of the PLO. [We] call on all the masses of our heroic people to struggle for the realization of the paramount urgent slogans of the uprising:

An end to the iron-fist policy, immediate abrogation of the outmoded Emergency Laws,[4] including all the deportation decisions.

An end to the desecration of the holy places, evacuation of the terrorist [Ariel] Sharon from the Old City of Jerusalem.

Removal of the army from the cities, camps, and villages. An end to their provocations. A ban on opening fire against the defenseless sons of our people.

Dissolution of municipal committees, village councils, and [refugee] camp committees that were appointed by the occupation authorities. The holding of democratic elections in all the municipal and village councils in the West Bank and Gaza Strip.

The immediate release of all detainees of the uprising, the closure of the prisons of Farʿah, Ansar 2, and Ansar 3 (al-Dahariya).

Abolition of V.A.T., which is levied arbitrarily on our people's merchants.

An end to the expropriation of our lands and to the building of settlements and provocations by the herds of licentious settlers.

A prohibition on raids against or the closure of educational institutions, trade unions, and popular institutions, and a ban on intervention in their affairs by the occupation authorities.

O masses of our people, heroes of the uprising, and forgers of the tremendous Palestinian glory,

Let all roads be blocked in the face of the occupation forces.

Let the cowardly occupation soldiers be prevented from entering the camps and major population centers by the erection of Palestinian

---

4. The term "Emergency Laws" refers to the Defense (Emergency) Regulations of 1945, promulgated by the British Mandate government in Palestine.

barriers and the burning of tires. Let Palestinian stones rain down on the heads of the occupation soldiers and the collaborators.

Let Palestinian flags be hoisted on the turrets of mosques, churches, roofs of houses, electricity poles, and in every place.

Let the siege on our people's camps be lifted through rebellion against the present curfew orders and those yet to come.

O people of martyrs, O most illustrious of revolutionaries, lion cubs, youth and students, workers, *fellahin,* women, the elderly, clergy, and imams of the mosques, O our whole people!

We will burn the ground under the feet of the occupiers. Let the whole world know that the eruption of the volcanic uprising which was generated by the Palestinian people will not be extinguished until the achievement of independence in a Palestinian state with Jerusalem as its capital.

Let our people's glorious uprising be intensified! Down with the occupation!

Glory to our heroic people! Eternal life for the martyrs!

The United National Command for the Escalation
of the Uprising in the Occupied Territories
January 10, 1988

LEAFLET NO. 3

Communiqué—communiqué—communiqué

*No voice will overcome the voice of the uprising
No voice will overcome the voice of the Palestinian people
—the people of the PLO*

Communiqué No. 3

Issued by the Palestine Liberation Organization/
The United National Command of the Uprising

O masses of the magnificent Palestinian people, O masses of the stone and the Molotov cocktail, O soldiers of justice who are taking part in the uprising of our heroic people! May your arms of steel be strengthened, O heroes, may your hands be strengthened, O workers and *fellahin,* students, merchants, and women . . . May your valiant arms be strengthened, O lion cubs of Palestine, O generation of the future, O builders of the independent Palestinian state! May your arms be strengthened, O young commanders, the new generals of our people! Blessed be this glorious people, which has registered the most magnificent spectacles of struggle, this people that heeded the call to duty, the call of the PLO and of the United National Command of the Uprising, which shook the ground from under the feet of the occupation during the past week.

Salutations of pride and honor to the masses of this struggling people, salutations of respect and admiration for the precious victims, the sacrifice in every sector of our generous people, salutations of challenge, steadfastness and pride, salutations of the resistance that the children of the stone and the Molotov cocktail are inscribing in the history of our people and the contemporary revolution.

Salutations to you, descendants of al-Qassam, salutations to the spearhead that repulses the enemy's soldiers in the byways of the camps, villages, and towns throughout our occupied homeland.

Salutations of the wound that triumphs over the knife of Shamir, Sharon, and Peres and stands proudly against their war machine, their armored vehicles, their airplanes, and their suffocating and poisonous bombs.

A thousand thousand salutations, endless honor and glory, exaltation and eternal life to you our people's martyrs, heroes of the uprising, who saturate the soil of the beloved homeland with rivers of your spilt blood, hoist the banners of freedom and independence, and with your pure shed blood pave the way to victory and the independent state under the leadership of the great and powerful PLO.

For the millionth time we reiterate: may your hands be strengthened, heroes, in Sheykh Radwan, Kafr Nueʿima, Rafah, Bittin, Jabalya, Qalqilya, in the camps, the villages, the neighborhoods, and the byways. We reaffirm our esteem and our pride in the masses, who in an uplifted and united voice called out:

> With spirit and blood we will redeem you O *shahid* . . .
> With spirit and blood we will redeem you O Palestine.

To the masses of our glorious people,

On the way to the escalation and continuation of the uprising, on the way to the removal of the occupation and the realization of the slogans of the uprising, we urge the national action committees and the popular committees to ensure the escalation and advancement of the victorious popular uprising by declaring a general and comprehensive strike from the morning of Tuesday, January 19, 1988, until the eve of Friday, January 22, 1988.

Let our people remain in their houses on Wednesday and Thursday, let the prayers, the symbolic funerals, and the vociferous popular demonstrations resume on Friday to commemorate the martyrs of the uprising. Let the bells sound in the churches in all the villages and towns throughout the occupied homeland.

O heroic merchants,

You who have recorded a glorious and honorable struggle with steadfastness, you who experience the arbitrariness of the occupation and its daily repression. You who valiantly defy the closure orders, the brandished rods, the war machines, and the armed soldiers, you who maintain a commercial strike despite all the measures of the occupation, we salute you and your central role in our people's uprising and in the victories that are achieved every day.

We urge you to observe the general strike that has been called even if the army increases its presence and in spite of the measures it will take. We further urge you to continue establishing and expanding special committees for merchants in every street and city, village, and camp, in order to formulate a united stand and form a united plan that will endorse a collective abstention from paying V.A.T. With all the masses of the people and its national movement behind you, the threats and measures of the occupation, whatever they may be, will not succeed in dissuading you from implementing this slogan, which is one of the paramount slogans of our people's heroic uprising.

O masses of our people from all sectors and strata,

From this day we will begin to boycott Israeli merchandise and products that our industry also manufactures. We note especially the boycott on Israeli chocolates, milk, and cigarettes.

O masses of the Palestinian working class,

Indeed the bronzed arms of steel have succeeded, by virtue of their broad and active participation in the general strike, in bringing to a stop the production line and the wheels of industry in thousands of Israeli plants, projects, and workshops. The pioneering role of the workers in the uprising was prominent and honorable. Persist in your labor strikes in Israeli plants, our valiant workers. Do not be intimidated by the frightened threats being voiced by the Zionists, authorities, rulers, and owners. All we have to lose in our uprising are the chains, the suppression, and the exploitation that we groan under. Let the wheels of Israeli industry grind to a halt through damaging the Israeli economy and deepening the economic crisis in Israel. This is one of our weapons on the road to attaining our rights of return, self-determination, and establishment of the independent national state.

O masses of heroic pupils,

You who disturbed the rest of the occupiers for years, let us teach the occupation a lesson it will never forget, we will teach the occupation that its policy of closing down educational institutions, universities, institutes, and schools will bring it nothing but trouble. Just recently the occupation authorities closed down all the educational institutions. Let us transform the masses of students in the villages, the camps, and the cities, mobilizing them for the school of revolution, the schools of the struggle in the streets, so that they can help shake and burn the ground under the feet of the occupiers. Let us therefore organize the ranks and mobilize all the student forces from the schools of the struggle in order to escalate and advance our people's heroic uprising.

Our heroic taxi and bus drivers and owners of taxi companies,

Having seen your actions in previous strikes, the United National Command calls on you to desist from activity completely in all places on the strike days, with the exception of Friday. We urge you to cooperate with the national and popular committees and to punish the few drivers who do not accede to the obligatory call.

To the sector of doctors and health services,

We call on you to remain vigilant and to join immediately the medical committees and bodies that are organizing medical-aid activities in the camps and besieged locales that have been adversely affected. We also call on all doctors, pharmacists, male nurses, and lab technicians to take part in these aid actions in the camps and in the occupied areas where the medical situation is poor and disease is rampant due to siege, the starving of the population, and the use of noxious and suffocating gas.

To the owners of the warehouses and the drugs industry and the pharmacies,

We call on you to contribute medicines and equipment to the medical committees and the medical bodies to enable our wounded to receive free treatment.

To the owners of the national capital and all persons of means,

We call on you to take a substantial part in contributing merchandise and goods as well as funds, in order to supply food to the camps and the besieged areas that have been adversely affected. Contributions should be made to the national and popular committees and to the local supply committees [*lijan al-tamwin*].

To the academics and practitioners of the various professions,

The uprising needs the effort of each and every one of you. You must join the national and popular committees and the functional committees, take an active part in the uprising, in the supply and aid operations, or do literary writing, compose poems, songs, and slogans, take part in information campaigns, organize marches and sit-down strikes against the occupation policy.

The PLO and the Uprising Command take pride in the large forces of the masses that have been given expression in our people's heroic uprising. We urge you to continue escalating the uprising in accordance with the missions and slogans already determined. We also call for the closing of all the streets—main and side streets—in the villages, camps, and towns to prevent the movement of soldiers on these streets. Likewise the closing of the roads leading to settlements in order to block the access of the settlers.

Let Palestinian flags be raised over every house and building, over the churches and the turrets of the mosques.

We say yes to our people's right of return, self-determination, and building an independent national state.

Victory to the uprising of our people, down with the occupation!
Glory and eternal life to our people's virtuous martyrs!

The Palestine Liberation Organization
The United National Command of the Uprising
in the Occupied Territories
January 18, 1988

. . .

LEAFLET NO. 6

Communiqué—communiqué—communiqué

*No voice will overcome the voice of the Palestinian people—
the people of the PLO*

Communiqué No. 6

Issued by the Palestine Liberation Organization/
The United National Command of the Uprising

Let us unite our efforts for the continuation
and escalation of the uprising

O masses of our valiant people ... O multitudes rising up in the camps, villages, and towns of Palestine ... O you whose will and determination have triumphed over the policy of perpetuating the Zionist occupation and have made your thunderous voice heard throughout the world, O relentless fomentors of the uprising, O you who have seized the initiative from the rulers of Tel Aviv and thrust them into a position of political siege and international condemnation ... You who by your struggle daily and hourly are paving the road to victory, the ousting of the occupation, and the establishment of an independent Palestinian state under the leadership of the Palestine Liberation Organization.

O masses of the uprising ... At this time especially, when American imperialism and its agents in the region are conspiring in an attempt to rescue the Zionist enemy from its certain defeat, and in a desperate effort to overturn your magnificent national achievements. American imperialism and its agents are revealing plans and solutions whose sole aim is to coerce us into submission, such as the Mubarak plan that would eliminate [the Palestinian issue] and the desperate attempts by the American State Department to spruce up and resurrect a few mummified local figures. All this has the goal of presenting an "alternative leadership" in place of our sole legitimate leadership, the Palestine Liberation Organization.

Here stands the salt of the earth that is rising up and calling for unity of representation by the PLO and for the Palestinian people's right of return and self-determination and [its right] to establish an independent state, and calling for dissociation from the yellow leaves[1] that go up [in pilgrimage] to sit with a representative of the dirty trinity.[2]

O masses of our glorious people,

The United National Command, mindful of the martyrs' blood and the tortures endured by the thousands of wounded and incarcerated, and heedful of the commitment to act in line with the PLO program, emphasizes its rejection of the Mubarak plan and the dubious efforts of the Jordanian regime and its supporters, which seek to gain acceptance for the capitulation plan of the functional division or any other plan that ignores our people's inalienable rights. In addition, [the United Command] asserts that it rejects the objectives of the envoy of American imperialism Philip Habib, and of the forthcoming visit by [Richard] Murphy. The multitudes of insurgents will lurk in wait for anyone who tries to impose himself on them and stress that all such will be doomed to disappointment and abject failure.

O our people... Let us unite all the efforts of the popular forces, activities, organizations, and goals into a struggle of a unified will of devotion to and escalation of the uprising, in order to better its methods, and let us create diverse forms of suitable organization, such as committees and teams, in every locale, in every village and town, and in every camp... in order to reach every neighborhood and street, to pave the way toward general civil disobedience, as the action of an intensifying struggle.

The United National Command of the Uprising, desiring to pave the way for every mission, calls on the masses of our people to...

First: continue and escalate the general strike involving Zionist projects and refrain from working in settlements.

---

1. The term "yellow leaves" refers to those who collaborate with opponents of the Intifada. The same epithet is used for the pro-Jordanian newspapers published in the West Bank and East Jerusalem and for leaflets and other publications suspected of being forgeries.

2. The "dirty trinity," i.e., the United States, Zionism, and the Arab conservative regimes.

Second: calls on all municipal and village councils and committees in the camps that were appointed by the Zionist occupation authorities to resign immediately.

Third: to complete the formation of the merchants' committee with the aim of [launching] a campaign for an immediate cessation of tax payments and forcing the authorities to retract their rapacious policy.

Fourth: we call on property owners to follow in the footsteps of those who have abstained from collecting their due rent from shop owners because of the circumstances produced by the strike, in solidarity with the fortifiers of the magnificent uprising, our brother merchants.

Fifth: we urge all relatives and families of detainees to cease categorically to pay the heavy fines imposed by the Zionist courts against the imprisoned heroes of the uprising.

Sixth: encouraging the national economy, local national industry and promoting household economy, instruction and reduced consumption, this to support the uprising and with a view toward finding alternatives to Israeli merchandise which is to be boycotted.

Seventh: a revolutionary reaction against the policy of beatings and breaking [of bones] by escalating the war of the Molotov cocktail and the stone.

O masses of our valiant people,

The basis of the resistance must be expanded. Let mass demonstrations, marches, and sit-down strikes be staged, let prayers be held in the churches and mosques, let a comprehensive strike be held on Sunday and Monday, February 7–8, 1988, marking two months since the eruption of the glorious uprising and commemorating the burial of the first martyrs, and stressing the persistence and escalation of the uprising.

Let us hoist national flags in the skies of Palestine, to emphasize today and every day our steadfast determination to go on struggling until we have attained all our legitimate national rights, above all the rights of return, self-determination, and the establishment of an independent Palestinian state under the leadership of the Palestine Liberation Organization.

Glory to our people and eternal life to our pure martyrs on the road to liberation

We will surely triumph.

The United National Command of the Uprising
in the Occupied Territories
February 5, 1988

• • •

LEAFLET NO. 10

In the name of Allah the compassionate and merciful

Communiqué—communiqué—communiqué

No voice will overcome the voice of the uprising

Communiqué No. 10

Issued by the Palestine Liberation Organization/
The United National Command of the Uprising

Our vow is to continue the popular armed revolution until [the establishment of] the independent Palestinian state. To our brother Arabs [in the Arab states] we say: We have had enough of speeches and applause . . . Here is the stone . . .

O proud struggling masses of our people! O giants of the twentieth century! O makers of glory, honor, and pride. The uprising has entered its fourth month strongly and powerfully, one wave after another, momentum following momentum, bidding farewell to one group of martyrs after another on its road to liberating the Palestinian homeland and pushing out the enemy. Its acts of heroism are destroying the myth of the unbeaten army, daily it is defeating the occupation on all planes and all levels—political, military, economic, propaganda, and cultural, defeating Kissinger, Shultz, and Shamir, who are one body and a single spearhead [incarnating the image of] the neofascist and the neo-Nazi in their oppression of peoples and in trying to exorcise their [national] will.

Our sweeping and violent uprising—the stones, the fire bombs, the various forms of popular struggle, and above all the legitimate armed struggle against the occupiers—is shaping the picture of the homeland with the help of Palestinian free will. It is this will that foiled Shultz's plot, whose main objective was to gain time and [unleash] a bloodbath against our people, our revolution, and our ingrained just rights. As a result of the fiery truth of our uprising and the flame that rises from it, we are pushing out the occupation and thus Shultz went home defeated.

The Palestinian flood has drowned and rejected anyone who even tried to defy or ignore the PLO, our sole legitimate representative ... From your uprising, O masses of the exalted uprising, it became known both near and far that the United States is our principal enemy, not a mediator. Things have reached a pass where it is Shamir who is visiting Arab capitals in the guise of the American Shultz. You, the sons of our valiant people, have proved to the whole world that we and our Command will let no one speak in our name. [Likewise] we will not give any support whatsoever to the attempts by a number of Arab capitals to compromise our uprising and our revolution. These attempts are expressed in the form of hints uttered at the splendid receptions tendered during Shultz's shuttle mission and in his criminal thesis that rejects the right of peoples to [national] rights.

O our people, we will not ask for our rights or plead for them from anyone, we will take them forcibly, in a prolonged and unrelenting struggle.

We, together with you and through your strength, O our heroic masses, hereby reaffirm our resolute insistence that there is no solution but the Palestinian solution! We welcome [the initiative] to convene an international conference to be vested with full powers, while emphasizing that the PLO's right [to participate] is equal to that of the other parties to the conflict and the five permanent members of the Security Council.

The United National Command of the Uprising in the Occupied Territories, as the PLO's organizational arm, esteems and lauds the stand of Algeria, the sister [state], the state of martyrs, in the face of the Arab silence. [The Command] further stresses unequivocally the latest communiqué of the PLO's Executive Committee, published in Tunis on March 5, 1988. This communiqué gave faithful, revolutionary, and lucid expression to the aspirations of the Palestinian people inside the occupied homeland and throughout the diaspora. In its statement, the Executive Committee called for the convening of an urgent Arab summit, a conference of the uprising and its martyrs, in order to assist our people, the cause of our Palestinian people, and our Arab nation, in all possible political and material ways. The United National Command of the Uprising esteems and lauds the stand of all the forces of peace and freedom, and the stand of all the democratic forces, the Jewish forces of progress ... who, in different ways, have supported our prolonged struggle to attain our rights, above all the right to return to the homeland, the right of self determination, and the establishment of an independent Palestinian state under the leadership of the PLO—our sole legitimate representative. In addition, [the United National Command] calls for unity among our people and for support throughout the occupied homeland, in Nazareth, Galilee, the Triangle, the Negev, the Gaza Strip, and the West Bank, and throughout the [Palestinian] diaspora. This is clear and overwhelming proof of our common destiny and future and the unity of the struggle on all planes. [This unity] is a source of pride for our Palestinian people. In its great revolutionary steadfastness in which cohesion, support, and the united struggle attained a hallowed level, [our people] aroused amazement, appreciation, and feelings of respect throughout the world for its great revolutionary staying power and its hallowed cohesion, support, and united struggle.

O our tremendous struggling masses! By virtue of your forward-moving steadfastness, your united stand and in the spirit of the plan for the violent and comprehensive uprising, which expresses our aspirations, the United National Command of the Uprising entrusts to your faithful hands the following decisions:

1. Unity of our masses is the certain guarantee to preserve the impressive achievements of the uprising. Therefore, we call for further cohesion, unity, support, and manifestations of consideration for others. At the same time, we urge you to strike with an iron fist against anyone who attempts to undo your achievements by spreading tendentious rumors and twisted reports. With this in mind, we ask that additional united popular committees be formed as well as shock squads—the fighting arm of the comprehensive uprising.

2. We appeal to all our masses in the various areas to agree on a uniform time for opening shops, gas stations, and display booths, as was decided previously—three hours a day in accordance with the conditions in each area.

3. The call that was directed to civil administration employees to resign was meant for policemen and tax department staff only. The masses of the uprising and the shock squads reiterate the call to all policemen and tax department staff to resign immediately. The shock squads and the will of our people will not bend in the face of the Zionist occupiers. At the same time, our people and the United Command affirm that they do not abandon their responsibility regarding the right of those of our people who heed the call for national duty.

4. We renew our call to our heroic masses not to pay taxes. It is the responsibility of the accountants and our steadfast merchants not to submit or fill out any tax forms. The popular committees and the merchants' committees have the task of monitoring this issue. The shock squads will punish whoever tries to disregard the calls of homeland and duty.

5. We call on our brave merchants and noble masses to boycott Israeli and foreign products, especially those for which local substitutes exist, such as cigarettes, detergents, locks, milk products, and others. We underscore the importance of dealings between merchants and local factories and the importance of the undertaking by industries to serve our people and not to exploit them. We urge that prices be lowered and that no attempt be made to erode workers' wages or working hours and that no dismissals be effected. The relevant bodies will monitor this issue. We also urge the vegetable dealers on all levels to boycott Israeli agricultural produce and to buy local agricultural produce, thus ensuring the steadfastness of our farmers.

We call on all sectors to reduce prices. This is incumbent upon merchants, factories, doctors, pharmacies, pharmaceutical factories and lawyers, for this is a period of solidarity with all sectors of our people.

6. We urge our masses to reduce the Zionist pressure on the besieged areas through struggle and through material and moral support. Let us as one person offer support and donations in cases of siege.

7. Intensifying the mass pressure against the occupation army and the settlers and against collaborators and personnel of the Jordanian regime. We are proud of our people for punishing them and pressing them to desist from their ways by publishing this resolution in mosques, churches, and before the popular committees.

8. Each region will draw up a plan for beginning to break into educational institutions, according to local circumstances, with the presence there to be limited to three hours, from the morning until 11:00 A.M., as in other sectors of our struggling people.

9. Besides this, we reaffirm the resolutions in leaflet no. 9 and the earlier leaflets.

O masses of the heroic uprising, in this great month of March and on the road of the uprising, we declare the following:

1. The days of the uprising are milestones of heroism and union for our people against the occupation, the settlers, and the collaborators.

2. March 14 is declared a day of Palestinian solidarity with the detainees and wounded of the uprising, by means of sit-ins, visits to their parents, and giving moral and monetary support.

3. Tuesday and Wednesday, March 15–16, are declared days of a comprehensive strike under the slogan There is no alternative to an independent Palestinian state under the leadership of the PLO, our sole legitimate representative. Let these be days of rage and heroic marches.

4. March 21, the eternal remembrance day for [the battle of] Karameh, is declared a day of Palestinian dignity (*karameh*), a day of violent clashes with the occupation [forces].

O masses of the valiant PLO, great glory and esteem to the [Palestinian] woman for her devotion and generosity to her people, as well as to the mothers, fathers, girls, and children—the flowers and the lion cubs, and all the selfless generations. Utmost esteem to the shock squads and to all free people in the world, to the reporters who are uncovering one truth after another about the fascist Zionist practices.

Glory and greatness to our pure martyrs and the martyrs of the actions in the villages.

Public announcement: The Voice of the Revolution, the Voice of the PLO—broadcasts and programs from Baghdad between 6:30 P.M. and 9:30 P.M.—covers the news of the uprising and the revolution, and contains many surprises. May Kissinger and his henchmen go to hell . . .

We will surely triumph.

The Palestine Liberation Organization
The United National Command of the Uprising
in the Occupied Territories
March 11, 1988

LEAFLET NO. 11

Communiqué—communiqué—communiqué

No voice will overcome the voice of the uprising
No voice will overcome the voice of the Palestinian people—
the people of the PLO

Communiqué No. 11

Issued by the Palestine Liberation Organization/
The United National Command of the Uprising

Land Day Proclamation

Let us mark Land Day as an occasion
to escalate the Palestinian national struggle

O masses of our struggling people! Your ongoing response and your precious sacrifice for your homeland is daily paving the way toward the independent state. Daily the masses of the stone and the Molotov cocktail evince their national will. The occupation stands with hands bound in the face of the heroes who are making history toward the liberation of their people and is bewildered in the face of the flaming uprising that burns the occupiers and their henchmen. Now Rabin, the shedder of blood, imposes economic punishments and starvation on our masses and imposes curfew on our masses in the Gaza Strip, trying, in vain, to generate a split between our masses in the West Bank and our valiant people in the heroic Gaza Strip. This policy attests to and underscores the occupation's abject failure and political distress as a result of the uprising. The masses of the uprising will continue to defy—today, tomorrow, and every day—all the tactics of the occupation: siege, starvation, and the enforcement of ignorance. The many major changes that have been caused in the international arena by the uprising today call for a united Arab effort and support for our masses as they face the Zionist forces.

The United National Command reaffirms the call of the fighting President Chedli Ben Jedid[1] for an emergency Arab summit meeting to express support for the uprising, and requests all Arab monarchs and presidents to respond to this call and to convene an Arab summit as soon as possible in order to formulate resolutions of support for our people's struggle for their inalienable national rights—the right of return, self-determination, and the establishment of our independent state under the leadership of our sole legitimate representative, the Palestine Liberation Organization. [The summit must also] react forcefully to the decision by the American Congress to close the office of the PLO's U.N. mission, a decision that demonstrates the shameful one-sided bias of American imperialism on the side of the Zionist entity.

The United Command also appeals to President Hafiz al-Asad[2] to grasp the necessity of improving relations between fighting Syria and the PLO. There is no longer any justification for the break between those who are engaged in the same struggle against the enemies of our Arab nation.

O our masses!

The United National Command continues to be with you in the struggle and together with you follows on a daily basis the achievements of the uprising—the increasing sectors of the population that are taking part in the uprising and your full response to the appeals of the calls issued by the united leadership, such as the mass resignations of policemen prompted by the Palestinian national decision. [The leadership] is certain that our people will be capable of organizing their own affairs by themselves—because, O our people, the struggle raises the level of responsibility borne by each of us. Each of us is responsible for the security and well-being of our people. Each of us must exercise caution at home, on the street, and while driving. It is the responsibility of each and every one of us to fight the attempts of the occupation authorities to heighten the anarchy among our people.

At this time the United National Command stresses the following points:

1. We congratulate the merchants, professionals, craftsmen, and all who boycott the payment of taxes. [We welcome] your national decision to

---

1. President of Algeria.
2. President of Syria since November 1970.

defy the orders of the occupiers and to persist in your refusal to pay taxes levied by the Zionist authorities. We underline the need to organize the people in these sectors within the framework of the special committees in order to intensify the implementation of the national decision.

2. The United Command praises the role of the courageous workers who have been in the forefront of the struggle, and especially their broad general participation in bringing work to a halt in Israeli projects, and their absolute refusal to work in the settlements. We ask all our productive sectors to employ as many of them as possible.

3. The United Command appreciates the high and sweeping level of response [to the call for their resignation] evinced by policemen, workers in the tax and customs department, and some Civil Administration officials in the West Bank and Gaza Strip.

4. Popular committees must continue to be established everywhere, in every town, village, and [refugee] camp, in every quarter and neighborhood, to act as the arm of the United National Command across the whole length and breadth of the homeland.

5. Efforts must be made to boycott Zionist products. To strengthen the boycott, the United Command calls for supervision of consumption, preparation for a long-term struggle, cultivation of auxiliary sectors (raising chickens and rabbits, and [planting] garden vegetables), and of production (sewing and knitting).

6. Intensifying the manifestations of solidarity with the families of the heroic martyrs, wounded, and detainees.

7. Organizing the professional sectors (academics, doctors, engineers, pharmacists, etc.) for protest activities such as marches, sanctions, and press conferences to denounce and combat the occupation policy.

8. Repulsing the useless attempts of the occupation authorities to undermine the merchants' strike plans in the various areas. We emphasize that these attempts will fail as surely as did the tactics to cause a split between our struggling people and its United National Command.

The United National Command—the struggle arm and political arm of the PLO—reaffirms the determination to continue the struggle until the defeat of the occupation, and calls on our people as follows:

1. To continue the demonstrations against the occupation army and escalate them: to pelt the army and the herds of cowardly settlers with a hail of stones, Molotov cocktails, and iron bars.

2. Thursday, March 24, 1988, is declared a day of Palestinian defiance (a teaching day) against the policy of enforced ignorance and of turning some of our schools into detention centers and bases for the Zionist invasion army. Teaching staff, [administrative] workers, students, and

their families will enter the educational institutions and hold marches and sit-ins. In this way they will violate the decision of the occupation authorities. In government schools and in UNRWA schools in the Gaza Strip which are unaffected by the closure order, studies will take place from 8:00–11:00 A.M.

3. Friday and Sunday, March 25 and 27, will be days of prayer in the mosques and churches to commemorate the martyrs of Land Day and the martyrs of the uprising. Symbolic funerals will be held, Palestinian flags will be raised, and wreaths will be placed on martyrs' graves.

4. Saturday, March 26, 1988, is declared a day of struggle against the [Israeli-]appointed municipal, village, and [refugee] camp councils. Marches will be held to oust the appointed councils. The masses of the uprising will settle accounts with them trenchantly. The masses will settle accounts with everyone who deviates from the decision of the *al-Ijma*ʿ[3] and refuses to resign immediately.

5. Monday, March 28, 1988, is declared a general-strike day, on which workers will abstain from reporting for work at Israeli plants and commerce and public transportation will be halted.

6. Tuesday, March 29, 1988, is declared a "day of penitence." This day will offer an opportunity for all those who have deviated from the will of the people to return, hand over their weapons, and cleanse their conscience.

7. Wednesday, March 30, 1988, Land Day, is declared a general-strike day to be marked by mass demonstrations against the occupation forces and the settlers.

8. March 31 and April 1 are declared days of return to the land and sowing [the land].

Long live our people's valiant uprising
Long live the Palestinian Land Day
Glory and victory to our people
Glory and eternal life to our sacred martyrs.

The Palestine Liberation Organization
The United National Command of the Uprising
in the Occupied Territories
March 19, 1988

---

3. *Ijma*ʿ means unanimous consent. It is one of the four sources of religious law in Islam (*ussul al-fiqh*). *Al-Ijma*ʿ—consent by speech, action, and silence—is a precept of faith that took root in Islam based on the principle, laid down by Muhammad, that the commonalty cannot be wrong.

LEAFLET NO. 12

Communiqué—communiqué—communiqué

*No voice will overcome the voice of the uprising
No voice will overcome the voice of the Palestinian people—
The people of the PLO*

Communiqué No. 12

Issued by the Palestine Liberation Organization/
The United National Command of the Uprising

Qastel Proclamation

We will die upright and we will not surrender! They shall not pass! The uprising will triumph!

O masses of our great people, the people of the stone and the Molotov cocktail, the people of the exalted uprising, the people of heroism and sacrifice! In letters of blood and light you are inscribing the history of your Arab nation, you are kindling light with the oil of your blood to illuminate the Arabs' long dark night. O heroes of the victorious uprising, the uprising continues dipped in pure and immaculate blood, day after day, watering the soil of our precious homeland, registering cardinal achievements and being strengthened step by step through little triumphs that accumulate, one on top of the another, layer after layer, to foment the great and magnificent victories that will build the independent Palestinian state.

Despite the cruelty of the Zionist enemy, the arms of steel are able to withstand all the military orders and the Zionist arrogance that threaten to suppress the uprising wrought by our children, women, youth, and old people whose sacred stones and surging fury are being [unleashed] against the occupation and its collaborators.

O our fighting people, people of al-Qassam and ʿAbd al-Qadir al-Husseini,[1] O people of the struggle and sacrifice, our triumphant uprising and popular revolution is entering its fifth month. The Palestinian masses are confronting more than two-thirds of the Israeli occupation army and all the herds of the Zionist settlers who were sent into the streets of our camps, villages, and towns against our defenseless people. This revolution will not be uprooted or liquidated—not by the breaking of bones, not by killing and fascist terrorism, not by mass arrests and not by economic restrictions. Because hundreds of thousands of Palestinians throughout our beloved homeland declare today that there is no turning back and that the revolution of the stone will not end until the establishment of our independent state. Thus did two million Palestinians display their allegiance to the one and united people on Land Day. Now they are arising in united ranks behind the banner which will never be lowered, the flag of the PLO, the banner of the United National Command, the banner of liberation and the independent homeland. It is to hoist this banner over the hills of Jerusalem that the Palestinians are rising up in every town, village, camp, and street.

O Palestinian people, O people of the PLO, heroic people of the United National Command . . . After failing to extinguish the fire of the uprising with repression and terror, the occupation has now resorted to the dissemination of lies and forged statements, [supposedly] signed by the United National Command, in an attempt to generate suspicions among our people, individuals, and groups and to sow communal factionalism and discord. Thus [the occupiers] spread lies about having arrested the authors of the leaflets of the United National Command, with the aim of weakening our incandescent uprising. The United Command is certain that our people can withstand all the false rumors of the occupation. The United National Command affirms that all the strata, groups, and sectors of the people are involved in the uprising. The United National Command constitutes the band of martyrs whom the

---

1. The linking of the two names, ʿIzz al-Din al-Qassam and ʿAbd al-Qadir al-Husseini, is meant to denote the historical connection that existed between "Ikhwan al-Qassam" and the "al-Jihad al-Muqaddas," which was headed by ʿAbd al-Qadir al-Husseini. Following al-Qassam's death, in November 1935, Ikhwan al-Qassam united with al-Husseini's movement. The mention of the names of al-Qassam and al-Husseini in the same breath should be read as a call to religious Muslims to cooperate with the United National Command.

uprising has led and will lead day after day in order to drench the soil of the homeland. It is the children and youths of the stones and the Molotov cocktails. It is the thousands of women who have miscarried due to the noxious gas bombs and those whose husbands and sons are incarcerated in the Nazi prisons. It is the thousands of farmers and laborers who have stopped working in Israeli settlements in order to defend their villages, camps, and towns day and night against the brutality and terror of the settlers and the occupation soldiers.

O masses of our generous people . . . O mothers of the martyrs, detainees, and wounded, O all mothers of Palestine. The rulers of the Zionist entity think that mass arrests and night raids will break our spirit and weaken our faith, but they do not know that our people is accustomed to self-sacrifice for the sake of the homeland. No matter how harsh the repression and its fascist measures become, no matter how many children and men of the uprising are detained, they will not be able to put an end to the surging revolution, the revolution of the sacred stone. For our people today advance like a single giant, smashing all the theories of the Zionist entity, heightening their distress and dilemma, and intensifying the confusion of their soldiers. Therefore, increase your self-sacrifice, for it is the dawn of the freedom that is carving out a way through the darkness of the prisons and the oppression as a harbinger of the independent national state.

As we stand at the threshold of the fifth month of our illustrious uprising, marking these days the fortieth anniversary of the battle of heroism and sacrifice (the Battle for the Qastel) in which the hero commander ʿAbd al-Qadir al-Husseini fell, the United National Command notes the following:

—We deplore the attempts to cancel the convening of the Arab summit in mid-April. It should meet as soon as possible in order to support the struggle of the people of the uprising on the soil of Palestine. The Arab monarchs and presidents should be aware that it is not money we seek. We are ready to go hungry and naked rather than submit. We will die martyrs rather than forsake our rights until the glorious victory. We expect the summit to adhere in practice to its previous resolutions and affirm our people's inalienable right to establish an independent state under the banner of the struggle and our sole legitimate representative, the PLO, and to undertake that the international conference will possess full powers and that the PLO will participate. We call on the Arab summit to close the doors of the Arab states to the Shultz plot whose goal is to liquidate the uprising, to reject it vigorously by closing Arab airports to his shuttles and to all other U.S. emissaries. Thus, Shultz and all the Arab regimes that follow his lead will know that he can turn only to the PLO, for it is an interested party and the sole legitimate representative.

—The United National Command and the masses of the uprising denounce the latest measures of the suppression authorities, such as isolating the West Bank and Gaza, coercing the Gaza Strip by imposing a three-day curfew, and declaring certain areas closed to civilian traffic and to journalists—in their abortive attempt to prevent the people from celebrating Land Day. Our reply is that all these moves are doomed to abject failure and that the will of the revolution of the stone and the insurrection will overcome their fascist and Nazi methods.

—We deplore the occupation authorities' decision to outlaw the Shabiba Movement and to close trade unions and [other] institutions. These measures conflict with human rights and with all international conventions and laws. The United National Command asserts that such measures will only heighten our determination to continue the uprising.

—The United National Command and the masses of the uprising welcome the unified collective stand taken by merchants in the Ramallah region who vowed at a public meeting attended by 300 of them not to pay taxes and who upheld their oath. We regard this as an example for all merchants throughout the West Bank and the Gaza Strip.

—The United National Command greets the members of the municipal and village councils who acceded to the call of the United National Command and the masses of the uprising to resign. The [UNC] herein declares that it places beyond the protection of the law the person and property of the council heads and members who have not complied. The masses of the uprising will trample everyone who acts against the national consensus and everyone who refuses to comply with the call of the uprising.

—The United National Command esteems the resignation of the tax and customs personnel in the Gaza Strip and urges the staff of these departments in the West Bank to do the same. It congratulates the policemen who acceded and demands that the others resign at once. The United National Command also urges all the national and popular committees to complete the establishment of committees for maintaining and protecting the public order, this to block attempts by the enemy authorities to sow sabotage and confusion. The United National Command appeals to all industrial institutions, in cooperation with the national and popular committees, to employ the policemen and tax and customs personnel [who have resigned]. The United National Command calls on agronomists, owners of plant nurseries, and experts capable of rendering all assistance, direction, and guidance to the masses of *fellahin* and striking workers so that they can meet their needs and withstand the occupiers' measures of economic coercion. Tilling and sowing of the soil must continue so that we can satisfy our requirements and provide help to the closed areas—for to go on strike does not mean to cease cultivating the land.

The United National Command is continuing on the long and exhausting road to vanquish the occupation and establish our independent state. It calls on the masses of the uprising to carry out the following militant actions:

1. Monday, April 4, 1988, is declared a general-strike day to express the rejection of the Shultz plot by the masses of the uprising. We reiterate the PLO's stand that every meeting with him or with any other American envoy is to be boycotted.

2. Monday, Tuesday, and Wednesday, the 4th, 5th, and 6th of the month, are declared days of struggle by the masses and their uprising committees and shock squads in their various national frameworks against the Shultz visit. These will also be days of solidarity with the detainees and the wounded, including sit-ins and mass demonstrations with the participation of women.

3. Tuesday, April 5, has been designated a day of national work on which all the national institutions and enterprises will operate at full productivity for the benefit of the families of the martyred, the wounded, and the incarcerated, and for the sake of the closed areas and the unemployed, both those who left their jobs and those who resigned from their [Civil Administration] posts. The popular committees in every town and every camp will distribute the produce of this day to the needy. You may rely on them to carry out this deed.

4. On the occasion of World Health Day, April 7, the United National Command salutes all doctors, pharmacists, and nurses who have done their duty in the uprising and have visited the wounded in the camps, villages, and towns, and calls on all these personnel to step up their dispensing of medical aid.

5. Thursday, April 7, is declared Qastel Battle Day, on which ʿAbd al-Qadir al-Husseini fell.[2] On this day, fierce clashes are to be initiated

---

2. Following pitched battles, the Qastel was captured by Jewish forces on April 9, 1948. Among those killed in the fighting was ʿAbd al-Qadir al-Husseini, commander of the Arab irregulars in the Jerusalem area and the nephew of the Mufti, Haj Amin al-Husseini. ʿAbd al-Qadir was venerated as a national hero and was buried on the Temple Mount in Jerusalem. Faysal al-Husseini is his son.

against the occupation authorities and the settlers, clamorous demonstrations staged in the streets, and all the camps, villages, and towns will become the uprising's bastions of confrontation.

6. Saturday, April 9, is declared a memorial day for the first victims of the uprising, and of commemoration for the martyrs of the Deir Yassin massacre,[3] and the onset of the fifth month of the uprising. On this day, processions will be held to the graves of the martyrs, and sit-ins will take place in municipalities and institutions. Demonstrations are to be staged everywhere, and the day is to be declared a day of rage against the occupation authorities [expressed in] a march against their acts of suppression and the burning of the ground beneath the feet of the occupiers.

7. April 8 and 10 are days of prayer for the repose of the martyrs' souls. Demonstrations and processions will continue, as well as sit-ins in the mosques and churches.

8. Monday, April 11, is designated a general-strike day and a day of general volunteering by our masses to work the land for the development of the Palestinian village and household economics.

O people of the uprising, continue . . . forward . . . forward . . . O lion cubs of the stones, advance . . . advance . . . For they shall not pass . . . The uprising shall triumph . . . triumph . . .

The Palestine Liberation Organization
The United National Command of the Uprising
in the Occupied Territories
April 2, 1988

---

3. Deir Yassin, on the western outskirts of Jerusalem, was attacked on April 9, 1948, by the Irgun, the Lekhi, and a Palmach unit. Some 200 residents, including women and children, were killed in the assault. Arab politicians and commentators cite the Deir Yassin attack as an example of Israeli maltreatment of Arab civilians.

LEAFLET NO. 14

Communiqué—communiqué—communiqué

No voice will overcome the voice of the uprising
No voice will overcome the voice of the Palestinian people—
the people of the PLO

Communiqué No. 14

Proclamation of the martyred commander, teacher, and symbol,
our brother Khalil al-Wazir, Abu Jihad[1]

O masses of our fighting people everywhere, O brothers and comrades of the hero martyr Abu Jihad, O masses of the heroic uprising, the Zionist entity's hand of neo-nazism and neo-fascism has reached out to add yet another crime to the chain of despicable crimes it perpetrates daily against our heroic Palestinian people and against its leadership and symbol of its struggle, the PLO, the sole legitimate representative of our people wherever they are—in a desperate attempt to foil the magnificent uprising. Thus has the racist fascist entity become mired to its neck in the sea of immaculate blood which was shed on the soil of the resistance and the legitimate struggle to achieve the national right of our valiant people.

Even if your pure body has fallen, O dedicated son of Palestine, symbol of resistance, struggle, and devotion, you will continue to inspire the sacred revolutionary activity; even if the bullets of poisonous

---

1. A senior PLO leader. Born in Gaza in 1935, he was among the founders of the Fatah organization and served as the head of the PLO's military arm. In this capacity he was responsible for the PLO's military and civil activities within the territories.

enmity were thrust into your pure body, you will continue to be the teacher and inspirer for generations of our rejuvenated people who are fighting until victory. You will remain alive, towering above the hills of Palestine, in the hearts and minds of the children, the old people, the women, and the young men and women of our glorious people. We swear to you, martyr-symbol, teacher of generations, that we will continue on the road of the pledge and the vow to fight until our people's goals and aspirations are attained in full. Your blood and the blood of our martyrs shall never be shed in vain. We shall lay down our lives or we shall raise the banner to which you devoted your life over holy Jerusalem, capital of our independent Palestinian state. The pledge is a pledge and the vow a vow, unto victory or unto death on the road of freedom and independence.

O masses of our struggling people, the fascist Zionist entity thinks that by applying its oppressive measures and its policy of murder, killing, collective punishment, various forms of economic siege on our towns, camps, and villages, deportation decisions, house demolitions, lengthy curfews, sealing off areas, smashing limbs and bones, using poison gas bombs, night raids, destruction of inhabitants' property by the fascist forces, in disregard of all international conventions and treaties and the principles of human rights . . . [sentence not completed]

The policy of the Zionist enemy attests only to the degree of his confusion and bewilderment and to the force of the blows that the heroic uprising is meting out to its invading forces and its economy, which is based on sucking the blood of our masses.

O our devoted masses, let us have more cohesion and unity, let us direct more painful blows to the enfeebled body of the fascist entity and its forces, with stones, Molotov cocktails, metal projectiles, bow and arrow, marbles, fireballs—whatever you have. Burn the earth beneath the invaders' feet. Let us take revenge with all the means at our disposal against the murderers of our people, and be true to the blood of the martyr, the paragon Abu Jihad, and all our virtuous martyrs.

O our dear ones, O our forbearing, steadfast people, you are continuing on the road of the struggle with full pride and glory, with your magnificent means, escalating your tremendous and heroic uprising. You are laying the firm foundation to attain [the stage of] full-scale civil disobedience.

Our splendid Command, whose intensive political activity is resulting in the most superb achievements, is gaining increasing support for our people's victorious revolution, and securing constructive assistance and cooperation with sympathetic forces—particularly the PLO and the friendly Soviet Union—with a view to the convening of an international conference possessing full powers and Palestinian representation by an independent delegation which will give expression to our people's legitimate rights: return, self-determination, and the establishment of an independent Palestinian state, rights which have been recognized by most states. These accomplishments are the fine fruit of our magnificent uprising. Continue to escalate the struggle against the occupation and its mechanisms and against its collaborators, especially the appointed municipal committees. Expand and establish new popular committees, shock squads, neighborhood committees, guard committees; intensify the implementation of the uprising program contained in the previous leaflets. Step up the boycott of Zionist products that have local substitutes and utilize everything that can be beneficial. Merchants must abide by the boycott and not purchase Zionist goods. Step up the boycott of the bloodsuckers, the customs and tax system. Intensify the resignation of those who are still hesitating to resign from the police and the tax department. We urge you urgently to join your colleagues and not to evade the issue under cover of taking vacations, for the eyes of the people are penetrating and the hand of the people will reach all who deviate from the march of the victorious uprising.

O masses of our splendid uprising, in harmony with the struggle plan, we make the following appeal:

1. We emphasize the importance of scrupulously refusing to pay taxes to those who are sucking the blood of our people.

2. We esteem highly the role of the inhabitants and of the agricultural and popular committees and the neighborhood committees, in responding to the call of the land by carrying out home planting and working the land by means of agricultural cooperatives, until every bit of the soil of our beloved homeland is included.

3. We urge our masses and people to continue economizing, to reduce outlays during the month of Ramadan, the month of sacrifice, mutual help and giving.

4. We call on our workers to intensify the boycott of work on the Zionist settlements, to the point of a total boycott.

5. [We urge] that the spheres of work of all the medical committees be expanded. A helping hand must be extended to our people everywhere, and additional courses in first aid, preventive medicine, and health consciousness organized. We call on the brother doctors to lower their prices for visits of the uprising masses.

6. Adherence to the decision of the PLO's Executive Committee to assist resignees from the police and tax departments and our courageous

workers who refuse to work in the Zionist settlements. The popular committees and the other committees will give a helping hand to them all.

7. We greet the heroic masses of the Golan [Heights] and extol our [common] struggle. We salute the Palestinian and Arab masses in the Zionist entity and in the Arab states for the help they have given the uprising. Let us all rise up against the occupation and the dispossession! We call on Arab governments to release the Palestinian and Arab prisoners in their jails as a service to our people's uprising.

8. We call on the [department] directors working in the Civil Administration offices in the Gaza Strip to resign immediately.

9. We emphasize the need for the International Committee of the Red Cross and UNRWA to assume responsibility for supplying food and medicines to the besieged and curfewed towns, villages, and camps.

O masses of our tremendous uprising, in adherence to the struggle plan of the United National Command, the PLO's fighting arm, we call on you [to observe] the following:

1. Fridays and Sundays are declared days of prayer for the eternal bliss of the soul of our martyr, the symbol [Abu Jihad], and for all the martyrs of Palestine. Symbolic processions and funerals should be staged in which black banners and Palestinian flags will be raised.

2. Monday, April 23, 1988, marks one week since the fall of the Commander Abu Jihad. This is declared a special day in which all struggle activists will take part.

3. April 28, 1988, is declared Deportees Day. A general strike will be held as well as events to express solidarity with our deported fighters and to denounce the policy of arbitrary deportation.

4. The other days will be days of rage and escalation, in condemnation of the policy of murder and killing, the policy of house demolitions, the imposition of lengthy curfews, the murder of children with poison gas, and arbitrary mass arrests. All activists will take part in a special mode of struggle. We call on the popular forums and the operational committees of all kinds to carry out all the struggle actions and to employ all means and ways to execute the decision of the United National Command, [that is,] to turn the days from April 22, 1988, to April 29, 1988, into days of Palestinian rage on which painful blows will be delivered to the Zionist entity, its forces, and its herds of settlers. These will be days of escalation against the murderers of our pure martyrs.

O our masses, O brother martyr Abu Jihad, our symbol, and all the pure martyrs, step up your giving, step up your sacrifice, step up national unity and cohesion, step up the utilization of means and resources, step up the throwing of sacred stones and Molotov cocktails, strike with a mailed fist at the enfeebled body of the fascist entity. Let us shake the earth beneath the feet of the invaders, for the cascade of Palestinian blood is not dry. We swear to our martyr hero Abu Jihad and to all our pure martyrs that the day will come when our Kalachnikov will sing in every corner of Palestine, in every village, camp, and town, its bullets putting an end to Zionist fascism so that our people will obtain their legitimate national rights through the leader of its struggle, the PLO. The pledge is a pledge, the vow a vow: victory or death for the sake of a free, independent Palestine.

We will surely triumph.

The Palestine Liberation Organization
The United National Command of the Uprising
in the Occupied Territories
April 20, 1988

LEAFLET NO. 15

In the name of Allah the merciful and compassionate

Communiqué—communiqué—communiqué

*No voice will overcome the voice of the uprising
No voice will overcome the voice of the Palestinian people—
the people of the PLO*

Communiqué No. 15

Issued by the Palestine Liberation Organization/
The United National Command of the Uprising
in the Occupied Land

The Workers Proclamation

O masses of our glorious people, heroes of the uprising, and makers of its splendor, you who with your stones and incendiary bombs shook the ground beneath the feet of the occupiers. By your resistance and steadfastness you adhered to the goals and slogans of the uprising. By virtue of thousands of victims, martyrs, wounded, incarcerated, and harmed by all the forms of fascist oppression and through its achievements to date, the uprising has paved a sure road to the stage of full-scale civil disobedience. In addition, the uprising has also put a forceful end to the manifestations of hesitation and trepidation in the face of the oppression and terror of the occupiers, and has left us with no choice but to escalate the struggle and deliver painful blows to the fascist entity on the way to realizing the goals of your victorious uprising for freedom and independence.

Despite all the manifestations of oppression—the isolating of towns, the besieging of camps and villages, starvation, murder, arrest, deportation, the crime of assassinating the Commander Abu Jihad, and the psychological warfare being waged by the agencies of the Zionist occupiers with the aim of foiling the uprising, our people have not retreated and will not retreat. With its creative powers, it is inventing new forms of confrontation in reaction to the occupiers' escalation tactics, this while readying itself for a lengthy struggle until the expulsion of the occupiers and the establishment of an independent state.

Notwithstanding all the occupiers' calls for surrender, our people see in the daily achievements a firm basis for the uprising's continuation and development. The uprising has created a new way of daily life, economically and socially. Your way of life derives from the fact that the uprising is a lengthy and protracted revolutionary process that entails hardships, victims, and a reduced income. But it has produced achievements that have deepened national unity among all segments of our people and its national forces. This unity is visible in the way the people have rallied around the popular committees, the shock squads, and the guard committees; the widespread return to the land; the establishment of cooperatives; and the unexampled social harmony. The uprising's dazzling achievments are revealed not only in the thwarting of America's reactionary plots and the Zionists' dreams of seizing control of the occupied lands but also in the spreading atmosphere of international support for our just goals. More than ever before, and particularly in the light of the joint Soviet-Palestinian accord, conditions have emerged for the successful convening of an international conference with full powers based on our people's legitimate national rights and compelling the Zionist entity and its ally, American imperialism, to obey the will of the world community whose support for our people's goals increases from day to day. The uprising's unmistakable impact was shown clearly in Resolution 605 of the United Nations Security Council, which underscored the need to realize the legitimate national rights of the Palestinian people, and in the Palestinian, Algerian, Libyan, and Soviet efforts. Manifestly, Syrian-Palestinian relations are also moving in the right direction, with their zenith coming in the meeting between a Palestinian delegation led by Brother Abu ʿAmmar,[1] chairman of the PLO's Executive Committee, and Syrian President Hafiz al-Asad. We call on Syria to establish a fighting alliance

---

1. Yasir Arafat.

with the PLO on the basis of respect for the independence of Palestinian national decision. We urge the national Arab states to establish a new militant foundation of steadfastness which will have as its top priority the convening of an Arab summit conference to assist the uprising, as well as the formulation of an Arab political stand against the machinations of U.S. imperialism, above all the Shultz plan. The influence of the uprising is also evident among our people who are standing steadfast in the Lebanese arena, enabling them to expand their struggle and alleviate their suffering. Likewise, this development opens a broad path for Palestinian factions unaffiliated with the PLO to return to and join the PLO's institutions according to the program of the 18th meeting of the Palestinian National Council.[2] At the same time, the uprising has engendered a qualitative change in the world balance of forces in favor of our people's national rights of return, self-determination, and the establishment of an independent Palestinian national state under the leadership of the PLO.

The United National Command reaffirms its adherence to the just national goals of our people and thus refutes the allegations of the Zionist enemy which are misleading world public opinion regarding the aims of our just struggle, intensifies [the enemy's] stifling isolation, and heightens our people's optimism about the attainment of a just solution for its national problem.

O masses of our glorious people. The fifteenth leaflet is being issued on the eve of May Day, World Workers' Day, and on this day marking the struggle of the workers of the world, our Palestinian people takes pride in the revolutionary role of our workers and their unions and of the Palestinian wage earners, along with the other sectors of our people, and lauds their great sacrifices in defense of our national cause. The United Command takes pride in the struggle of our heroic workers despite the suffering entailed in the continuation of the uprising, and calls on international bodies and international labor organizations to express solidarity with the Palestinian workers' movement against decisions to deport, arrest, and persecute union activists and against decisions to shut down labor unions, break into their offices, and ban their activity.

On May Day, the United National Command greets our heroic workers with esteem for their militant role. It urges them to boycott completely work in Zionist settlements and to show steadfastness in working

---

2. The 18th session of the Palestinian National Council convened at Algiers in April 1987.

in the occupied territories. A shift must be effected to working the land, and every opportunity must be exploited to find substitutes for work inside the Green Line. On this occasion, we also call on our heroic workers to intensify their self-sacrifice as an expression of the united Palestinian will. In addition, we call for the establishment of united workers' committees and for unifying the ranks of the workers' and union movement.

The United National Command salutes with esteem the merchants' steadfast and honorable stand. We welcome the action of the courageous merchants in Jerusalem who rejected the authorities' dictates. We urge all merchants not to accede to the authorities' calls to open their shops in contradiction of the national stand. We emphasize the importance of adhering fully to [the decision on] the nonpayment of taxes by all sectors and stress the importance of maintaining prices [at a low level].

The boycotting of work in the Zionist settlements and the boycott of Zionist products will undoubtedly intensify the collapse of the Zionist entity's economic and social foundations.

The United National Command salutes the masses of our people in the Gaza Strip and its besieged camps for their steadfastness, and calls on our people in al-Shati, Deir al-Balah, and other camps to foil the authorities' plot to confiscate residents' I.D. cards as a means of striking at the uprising.

The United Command appeals to international institutions and to the United Nations Relief and Works Agency (UNRWA) to expedite [the delivery of] full supplies to all the inhabitants of the camps in the Gaza Strip, in order to reinforce their heroic steadfastness in the face of the Zionists' fascist actions.

The United National Command calls on our masses to deliver the severest blows to employees of the police and of the appointed municipal and village councils who are deviating from the will of our people, particularly al-Wazir, al-Tawil, Khalil Musa, Jamil Sabri, Khalaf, and others, and emphasizes that the measures taken against them until now were only a warning.

Having committed itself to [uphold] the recommendations of our courageous merchants' committees and of our people, the United National Command calls for shops to be opened for three hours in all areas, from 9:00 A.M. until 12:00 noon. This includes gas stations, with one Arab gas station to remain open on a shift basis [outside these hours]. Industrial zones will adhere to the hours set for them, from 8:00 A.M. until 1:00 P.M.

O masses of our fighting people,

On the way to actuating civil disobedience and with commitment to the struggle plan of the United National Command, the combative arm of the PLO, we urge you to carry out the following:

1. May 1st will become a national day of confrontation with the racist occupation forces, a day of popular marches and demonstrations in the villages, towns, and camps; Palestinian flags are to be hoisted and slogans sounded condemning the occupation. Institutions, factories, and companies are urged to consider this day an official paid holiday for their workers.

2. May 4—A general strike, a day of national construction; all the activists and the various committees will work the land and rebuild houses demolished by the racist occupation.

3. May 5—The authorities' decision to close down the academic institutions will be violated. We stress the importance of strictly maintaining studies in academic institutions from 9:00 A.M. to 12:00 noon.

4. May 7—A day of solidarity with our valiant merchants on which all will open shops with the backing of our people and the shock squads.

5. May 9–10—General-strike days on which activity in all spheres and transportation will stop in honor of the first group of martyrs of the uprising and to mark the onset of the uprising's sixth month. In this strike, the rule of the people will be expressed by attacking the occupation forces and their collaborators. All operations and forces should be utilized to escalate the uprising against the fascist occupier.

6. May 11–12 will be days of intensive activities and days of Palestinian rage. Fridays and Sundays will be days of prayer for the repose of the martyrs' souls. The United National Command calls on all popular and national committees to name streets and institutions after martyrs of the uprising in order to perpetuate their memory for the generations to come. Vociferous demonstrations will set out from the mosques and churches against the usurper occupier and the herds of settlers.

The road to civil disobedience obligates the creation of additional popular committees, neighborhood committees, educational committees, and guard duty, agricultural, information, and solidarity committees.

Intensify self-sacrifice, ranging from bettering the methods of the daily struggle and heightening the use of popular means and the use of the sacred stones, to the Molotov cocktail that burns all our enemies.

Our people, young boys and girls of Palestine! Augment the shock squads, intensify your sacrifices for Palestine. Every blow to the enemy's body brings us closer to the great victory. The blood of our righteous martyrs shall not be shed in vain. With you and through you, we will continue toward the attainment of our objectives, freedom and independence.

We emphasize that the PLO is the only party to be approached for conducting a dialogue regarding our legitimate national rights.

Greetings to our steadfast masses and to all the national, Arab and international efforts supporting our victorious uprising.

Together we march on the road of the glorious uprising.

We will surely triumph.

The Palestine Liberation Organization
The United National Command of the Uprising
in the Occupied Territories
April 30, 1988

LEAFLET NO. 16

Communiqué—communiqué—communiqué

*No voice will overcome the voice of the uprising
No voice will overcome the voice of the Palestinian people—
the people of the PLO*

Communiqué No. 16

Issued by the Palestine Liberation Organization/
The United National Command of the Uprising

Palestine Proclamation [1]

O masses of our people,
 Forty years have passed since the expulsion of our people from its homeland and the attempt to liquidate its existence and its national existence, but our valiant people is stronger than the expulsion and the efforts to suppress its identity. Its national revolution has succeeded, through the continuous processions of martyrs and victims, in thwarting those attempts and in gaining international recognition for its legitimate national rights [and] for its exclusive representation by the PLO. In the forefront of these rights is the right of return, self-determination, and the establishment of an independent national state under the leadership of the PLO.
 The achievements of the Palestinian revolution, the glory of the magnificent uprising which is entering its sixth month, are continuing tirelessly and relentlessly. When our people declared the uprising, it

understood the scale of the sacrifices that would be required for liberation and independence.

Our people, who declared the uprising, is aware of the dimensions of the sacrifice that will be demanded of it on the road to national liberation. The people consciously pay the price for its aspirations in the form of victims, wounded, detainees, and deportees. [It] grasps the nature of the enemy with whom it is locked in struggle, his barbarism and the actions of his fascist forces, such as the use of poison gas, bullets, house demolitions, and a criminal war of starvation. Despite this, our people has chosen the road of struggle and sacrifice as the only road through which to achieve its national rights.

Just as our people grasps the essence of the enemy, so it is also aware of the character of the war it is waging. Our war is a lengthy one. It is a war of attrition in which each passing day raises the economic and political price paid by the occupier, intensifies his international isolation, exposes the ugly truth about the occupation, and shatters the illusion of coexistence that the enemy has tried to foster. Moreover, it reinforces our legitimate national rights.

The glorious December uprising was launched to demonstrate the solid strength of the fighting array and to raise the [people's] struggle and its national cause to a new level of which the axis is the continuation of the struggle and the resistance and escalation of the confrontation toward civil disobedience.

The United National Command of the Uprising, as it pursues the struggle with you and through you, under the banners of our sole legitimate representative, the PLO, reaffirms our people's readiness for great sacrifices and devotion, to move toward civil disobedience, meaning primarily the liberation of our masses from the occupation and all that this entails: sacrifices and belt-tightening, storing basic foodstuffs, storing medicines, suffering for the sake of the homeland, and relentless and tireless forbearance and determination. The United Command stresses the determination of the uprising masses to remove all the obstacles on the road to civil disobedience, involving especially the resignation of all [the personnel in] the mechanisms of the occupation such as the tax apparatus, the police, and the appointed municipalities.

O our glorious masses,

The United National Command welcomes the removal of the obstacles on the road to normalization of Palestinian-Syrian relations and on the road to perfection of Palestinian national unity through a constructive democratic dialogue. Marginal disputes must not be encouraged. We must turn to democratic dialogue as the only means for settling internal disputes. [The United Command] condemns those who deviate from the unity of our people and are splitting its ranks, while welcoming the national role played by Libya and Algeria in strengthening the PLO's unity and forging an alliance of Arab national forces to counter the imperialist plots of liquidation, above all the Shultz scheme. Likewise it praises the efforts being made to renew the Palestinian-Syrian-Lebanese "steadfastness trinity," which causes the organs of the Zionist enemy to tremble. At the same time, it deplores the Zionists' criminal invasion of southern Lebanon. This is merely a desperate attempt to weaken the uprising, to divert attention from the heroism of our masses in the face of the occupation, and to raise the Zionists' deteriorating morale. The United National Command furthermore stresses that the Zionist invasion of Lebanon, like the media blackout the occupier is imposing on the events of the uprising which is at fever pitch everywhere, cannot stem the erupting volcano of our people. To which end [the United Command] emphasizes the following points:

1. We praise the heroic role of the masses and the considerable escalation of the uprising in the Gaza Strip [refugee] camps. In particular we single out al-Shati, Jabalya, and Khan Yunis [camps], which outdid themselves in violating curfews. We call on the masses of the uprising in valiant Gaza to continue the heroic escalation, whose peak will be the foiling of the new Nazi plan to replace the [inhabitants'] I.D. cards. This plan must be boycotted completely, and fines and taxes must not be paid.

2. The immediate resignation must be effected of department directors in the Civil Administration in Gaza, especially Kheyri Abu Ramadan in the health department and Muhammad al-Jiddi in the education department. Let there be no mistake: the masses of the uprising and the shock squads will punish those who deviate from the will of the people and the decisions of its Command when they see fit.

3. Establishment of the popular committees and their dispersal in all areas must be completed. There must be no delay in executing this struggle mission. The other functional popular committees have the task of organizing the inhabitants' lives and ensuring proper services—food supplies, medicine, education, and security. For the popular committees are the government of the people and the uprising, a substitute for the collapsing occupation mechanisms, and a political tool for introducing civil disobedience and making it succeed.

4. Beat vigorously policemen, collaborators, and members of appointed municipal councils who, by not resigning from the service of the enemy, deviate from the national consensus.

5. Persist in refusing to pay taxes. The shock squads of the uprising will resist the attempts of the occupation authorities to seize control of a number of residents in order to force them to pay taxes. The same applies to whoever deviates from the national consensus. Likewise, no taxes or fees are to be paid to the appointed municipal councils that are betraying the people and the revolution.

6. Be steadfast in boycotting Zionist goods that have a local substitute or can be done without. The shock squads will oppose attempts to market these goods everywhere, and trucks bringing them in are to be attacked.

7. Intensify the boycott of work in the Zionist settlements and refrain completely from providing services to the herds of settlers.

8. We salute the role of the lawyers in defending detainees but at the same time urge them to reduce their fees, denounce the actions of the occupier in the prisons, and expose the inhuman conditions endured by inmates in the prisons of the fascist occupation.

9. We call on all teachers, men and women, to cooperate extensively in the popular education effort. They must escalate their struggle in protest at the measures of the occupier who has stopped paying their salaries and continues to shut down educational institutions.

10. All areas must adhere scrupulously to the general commercial strike and the opening of shops from 9:00 A.M. until 12:00 noon. A halt must be made to the phenomenon of stalls and carts being set up [to sell merchandise] outside the stipulated time frame.

Our people, as it marks the painful memory of the expulsion by standing up for its national rights, manifesting a high readiness for sacrifice, and for changing its way of life and fitting it to the new conditions of the struggle, welcomes together with the Muslim world the blessed ʿId al-Fitr[1] and declares the following struggle program:

1. Holding requiem prayers for the repose of the souls of the uprising martyrs following the services of "orphan" Friday[2] on May 13. After the prayers, symbolic funerals, marches and demonstrations will be staged to commemorate the martyrs.

2. May 15, which denotes the *nakba*,[3] will be a day of national mourning and a general strike; public and private transportation will cease, and all will remain in their houses.

3. To commemorate our people's martyrs and to protest the Arab and Islamic silence in the face of the crimes perpetrated by the occupa-

---

1. Marking the end of the fasting that accompanies the month of Ramadan.
2. The last Friday of Ramadan.
3. Disaster, referring to the defeat of 1948.

tion authorities against our people and its holy places, the United National Command has decided to cancel all festivities relating to ʿId al-Fitr and to make do with religious ceremonies:

The first day of the holiday is declared a day in commemoration of the martyrs. Processions will be staged after the holiday services, wreaths will be laid on the martyrs' graves, Palestinian flags will be raised, and mass demonstrations held.

The second and third days will be days of solidarity amongst our masses—visits to the wounded of the uprising and the families of martyrs, detainees, and deportees. Committees of mutual guarantees for prisoners will be established and assistance rendered to the uprising's casualties.

4. Saturday, May 21, is declared a general-strike day to consolidate the rule of the popular committees in all areas, organize their activities, and complete their formation.

5. The period between May 12–22 is to be regarded as a time of struggle activities and national actions so that the banner of the uprising will continue to fly on the path to liberation and independence.

Long live the uprising of our victorious people.

We will surely triumph.

The Palestine Liberation Organization
The United National Command of the Uprising
May 13, 1988

• • •

LEAFLET NO. 18

Communiqué—communiqué—communiqué

No voice will overcome the voice of the uprising

Communiqué No. 18

Issued by the Palestine Liberation Organization/
The United National Command of the Uprising

The Palestinian Child Proclamation

O masses of our heroic people,

You who have shattered the illusions of the occupation which lasted for more than twenty years, you who have refuted the lies about our people's coexistence with the occupation, you who have smashed all the attempts to find wretched alternatives to the PLO, the sole legitimate representative of our people, and have rejected substitutes for the right of return, self-determination, and an independent national state. You are continuing to pave the way—by your suffering, your immense sacrifices, and the vast stream of blood—to the attainment of freedom and independence for our fighting people. The exalted uprising is eradicating the mechanisms and industries that were established to serve the interests of the fascist occupation, and with the aim of binding to it the interests of our masses. On their ruins, you are building the apparatus of the people's self-government through the popular committees with their various tasks. Your uprising is restoring our national cause to its natural dimensions while presenting it as the cause of a people that is fighting for its legitimate national rights. [Our cause] has become an important item on the agenda of the Moscow summit and the major issue at the Uprising Summit in Algiers.

O our valiant people,

These days we are in the midst of the 21st commemoration of the Arab regimes' defeat and the occupation of what remained of our precious homeland.

Even as the Moscow summit and the Arab summit are being held in the shadow of George Shultz's attempts to renew the plot to foil the uprising, our masses are daily escalating their exalted uprising—for there is no return and there is no retreat until the occupation is ousted and an independent Palestinian state is established, a PLO [state].

O masses of the martyr and symbol Abu Jihad and our virtuous martyrs, our people have embarked on the road of the indefatigable struggle to achieve their rights. More than twenty years of suppression, persecution, harassment, and attempts to obscure our identity and our people's national cause have forged the generation of the uprising, the generation of freedom and independence, builders of an independent national state on our sacred national soil, a generation that is exacting from the occupiers the full price for desecrating our land and our holy places, and that is transforming the occupation into an inferno that sears the occupiers, the soldiers, and the murdering settlers. The United National Command of the Uprising urges our masses to heighten the escalation. To deal painful blows to the neo-Nazis, to expand the mechanisms of the uprising, the functional committees, and the strike units, on the road to implementing general civil disobedience. Implementation of the slogans and demands of the just uprising is an important start toward securing our people's legitimate national rights of return, self-determination, and establishing an independent state. We demand the application of the four Geneva Conventions: sending observers to ensure the necessary protection for our people; removal of the army from the towns, villages, and camps and the lifting of the siege; release of the detainees; the return of the deportees to their homeland; annulment of the occupation laws regarding taxation and other matters; the holding of democratic elections to the municipal and village councils; the lifting of the restrictions on our national economy to enable the development of industrial, agricultural, and service sectors. The PLO, the United National Command, and together with it the masses of our people who are waging their arduous struggle from a stance of deep national unity, demand that the heads of the Arab summit meeting assume responsibility before all nations and before history by supporting this Palestinian struggle, not by abstract condemnations and other speechifying but through:

1. Taking a clear and united political stand before the entire world, which will stress their support for the PLO as our people's sole legitimate representative, and finding various modes of support in order to assist our people to pursue its struggle.

2. Rejecting all the liquidation solutions, above all the Shultz initiative; adherence to the [idea of] convening an international conference with full powers, with PLO participation in an independent delegation on an equal footing with the other parties.

3. Releasing all political prisoners in Arab jails, granting democratic freedoms to the Arab masses so that they can express their solidarity and identity with our people's exalted uprising, and permitting *fida'is*[1] activity from across the Arab borders into occupied Palestine.

UNC[2]/PLO, moving toward the implementation of full civil disobedience, emphasizes the following:

—The immediate resignation of the workers in the traffic, licensing, planning, housing, I.D. and population registry departments.

—Now that the occupation authorities have been forced to open the schools, it is essential to maintain the curriculum scrupulously in order to make up the material that the students missed, especially those students who are sitting for the high-school final exams. Since it is certain that the schools will continue to be fortified bastions of the uprising, popular education should play a supplementary role in enhancing our students' ability.

—An absolute ban on contacts with the occupation mechanisms that enslave the inhabitants and restrict their movement, this by boycotting confirmations of tax payments and severing relations with those who drop off[3] and with the collusionist municipal committees. It bears stressing that the popular committees in all areas are called upon to play an informative role among the inhabitants and encourage them to abide by the national position.

—Boycotting the various types of taxes and boycotting Zionist products and merchandise, both industrial and agricultural, and a total boycott of work in the Zionist settlements.

---

1. *Fida'is*, in Arabic, means self-sacrificers. The term has a religious meaning. It refers to those who murder enemies of the true faith, a task designated by their master as well-pleasing to God, and the execution of which will assure them of the joys of Paradise.

2. UNC is the English equivalent of the Arab initials for the "United National Command" (al-Qiyada al-wataniyya al-muwahada, or QWM), which also means people or nation in Arabic. The use of the acronym was adopted as a counterweight to Hamas, the acronym of the Islamic Resistance Movement (Harakat al-muqawama al-Islamiyya).

3. Referring to collaborators with Israel. The term used in Arabic is *mutasaqitin*.

—Our people in the Gaza Strip will boycott the receipt of the new I.D. cards. The popular committees will have to play an informative role toward this end in order to reinforce the boycott and adhere to the decisions of the PLO/UNC.

—Augmenting the establishment and organization of the popular committees and the neighborhood, health, guard, security, agricultural, popular education, and information committees, of the shock squads—the combat arm of the United National Command—and of the committees for the economy, household economics, and training for consumerism and consumption.

—To step up the blows against those who deviate from the people's will [by not resigning from] the appointed committees in the villages and municipalities, the customs department, and the police. The use of popular-struggle means should be intensified—from stones to Molotov cocktails—against all our enemies.

O masses of our fighting people . . .

PLO/UNC calls on all sections of our people to turn the following days into days of tremendous popular rage that will accompany the coming memorial days and political events, by engaging in struggle activities as follows:

1. May 28–29—Days of mass marches and demonstrations with the participation of all national forums and personalities, in order to make our voice, the voice of the uprising, clearly heard by the personages at the Moscow summit.

2. May 30—A general strike and a pronounced escalation of the struggle on the occasion of the Gorbachev-Reagan summit. Intensified writing of nationalist slogans and the hoisting of flags in all villages, towns, and camps.

3. June 1st—World Children's Day. Marches of children are to be held, and Palestinian slogans and flags raised. The various committees, and in particular the committees of solidarity with the sector of the casualties among our people, will bring gifts to the children of martyrs, wounded, detainees, and deportees.

4. June 3–5 will be days of a general strike to mark the Shultz visit, the invasion of Lebanon, and the 21st anniversary of the Zionist occupation. On these days, our masses and the shock squads will hold demonstrations of defiance against the enemy and his collaborators. Make the ground burn beneath the feet of the fascist occupier and his collaborators.

5. June 7—This day will be declared as the day of Arab solidarity with the uprising of our glorious people. Mass demonstrations should

be held and the Arab masses should be urged to stage demonstrations of support for our exalted uprising.

The Palestine Liberation Organization
The United National Command
May 28, 1988

… … …

LEAFLET NO. 19

In the name of Allah the merciful and compassionate

Communiqué—communiqué—communiqué

*No voice will rise above the voice of the uprising
No voice will rise above the voice of the Palestinian people—
the people of the PLO*

Communiqué No. 19

Issued by the Palestine Liberation Organization/
The United National Command of the Uprising

The Detainees of the Uprising Proclamation

O masses of our glorious people! O you who are fulfilling your unity by advancing and escalating the popular uprising [and by] upholding our people's legitimate national rights—of return, self-determination, and the establishment of an independent state—and by rallying unflinchingly around your sole legitimate representative, the PLO. [O you] who firmly oppose all the plots, schemes, and alternatives—from Camp David and functional division to the Shultz plan—which seek to usurp your national rights and eradicate your cause.

O masses of our heroic people! Now, after the movement [that was achieved] at the Reagan-Gorbachev summit, it emerges that they have still not reached agreement on the Middle East issue and the Palestinian question, due to the intransigent American stand which is hostile to our people's aspirations and its legitimate national rights. We welcome the Soviet stand which supports our cause and stress our categorical rejection of the Shultz initiative and his travels in the region. [This initiative is] the latest link in his desperate efforts to foil your exalted uprising, and yet another attempt to bring American pressure to bear on a number of Arab parties so that they will influence the political resolutions of the Arab summit, the Uprising Summit which will take place in Algiers. Likewise, Arab reactionary elements are trying to disseminate the Shultz plan and the distinctive solutions which conform with American imperialist aims and machinations in the region.

The meetings that were held between the Zionist war minister Rabin and a number of figures from the occupied land constitute an attempt to invent a feeble alternative to represent our people, and their purpose is to sidestep our sole legitimate representative, the PLO.

The same can be said about the dubious activity of the collusionist newspaper *al-Nahar* in the form of the establishment of a special research center and the poison that drips from its pages, as well as the dubious activity of its directors, who are trying to mislead our people and sow confusion and division in their ranks, in order to divert them from the proper national course. The United National Command of the Uprising, in condemning all meetings with any American or Zionist politician, asserts that no talks with our people will be complete other than through our sole legitimate representative, the PLO.

O masses of our struggling people, O you who refute, by your unified will, your immense devotion, your sacrifices, and your renewed hymn to the uprising, all the claims that the uprising is fading and that your spirit has ebbed. Despite all the brutal methods and the fascist oppression which the occupation authorities are wielding against the victorious masses of the uprising, the uprising is registering, day after day, new achievements on the road to our freedom and independence. You who are intensifying the break [with the occupation] and escalating the boycott of all the apparatus of the occupation. The resignations from the departments of the Civil Administration, nonpayment of taxes to those who suck our people's blood, stepping up the boycott of [Zionist] products and boycotting Zionist national industries, desisting from work in the settlements, engaging in intensive agriculture on our lands and breeding domestic animals, giving instruction in consumerism, practicing the principle of family mutual assistance and strengthening social solidarity, storing essential foodstuffs, reinforcing the mechanism of popular rule, escalating the struggle against the fascist occupation forces and the collaborators, and the overall commitment of all the sectors of our people to the struggle plan and decisions of the PLO, the United National Command—all these measures are advancing the uprising to a new stage in the struggle, the stage of general civil disobedience. The declaration of the stage of civil disobedience in the uprising depends on the creation of the essential conditions for its fulfillment, the most important of which is to complete the establishment of the apparatus for popular rule in all the towns, villages, and camps in the occupied territories.

O masses of the heroic uprising!

The United National Command of the Uprising hails the [steadfast] stand of our valiant detainees in the new Nazi camps in the Negev, al-Dahariya, ʿAtlit, Ansar, Megiddo and al-Farʿah, and all the other detention centers.

1. The United National Command demands the immediate resignation of the appointed village and municipal committees, policemen, [and] tax, customs, traffic and housing, and population registry personnel—as well as a boycotting of work in Zionist settlements, nonpayment of taxes, a boycott of Israeli goods, and the disavowal of any commitment or responsibility [toward the authorities].

2. The Command salutes the workers in government departments and agencies who have responded to the call of the uprising and have resigned, especially those who left and have refused to return. The Command promises to stand by them.

3. The Command applauds the role of the population in the Gaza Strip, its heroic stand in the face of the oppressive measures, and its defiance of [the scheme] to replace I.D. cards.

4. The Command salutes our valiant merchants for maintaining the commercial strike by opening their shops [only] until 12:00 noon.

The Command cautions our people against the psychological and communications war being conducted by the authorities and their agents via the media and leaflets and against the false announcements and the new tactics being employed by Zionist intelligence to carry out surveillance and make arrests, such as [using] cars with West Bank and Gaza Strip license plates, and dressing in traditional Palestinian garb. The United Command salutes the heroic students for their role in the uprising, and stresses that the resumption of studies is one of the achievements of the uprising. The opening of the educational institutions reflects the occupation authorities' distress and spurs our children the students, teachers, and academic institutions to adhere rigorously to studies and make up for lost days [by holding classes] during the official holidays. The importance is emphasized of observing in full the general-strike days, of working until 12:00 noon on regular days, and of intensifying popular studies in order to compensate students [for lost school days] and to raise their level. We also call on our pupils to continue to take part in the uprising and to organize sit-down strikes, processions, and demonstrations in solidarity with their brother detainees.

The United Command calls on our heroic workers to establish united worker committees and join existing professional frameworks in order to maintain their rights and enhance their national struggle. We stress that not a single worker is to be fired or have his working hours increased, or have part of his salary deducted due to general-strike days.

The United Command underscores the need to remove the booths of the peddlers, who are deviating from the directives concerning the opening of businesses, and it warns all those who are distributing Israeli products under Arab names. The strike units are urged to act on this.

O masses of our heroic uprising,

The PLO/United National Command send you faithful greetings upon the uprising's entering its seventh month. It applauds your resolute decision to pursue the uprising on the road to the realization of our people's right of return, self-determination, and an independent state. It hails our people's stand in places where curfew is imposed, our loyal fighters in the detention centers, the wounded, and the families of the martyrs and the deportees. The United Command calls upon you to carry out the following program:

1. June 9, 1988, a general strike marking the onset of the seventh month of the uprising and the fall of the first group of martyrs.

2. June 11, 1988, a day of solidarity with the detainees. On this day sit-ins, marches, and demonstrations should be organized, to be supervised by the committees for solidarity with the detainees, at Red Cross centers.

3. June 13, 1988, a day for bolstering rule by the people. On this day the public will work to establish and strengthen popular and specialized committees in all areas.

4. June 15, 1988, a general strike in solidarity with incarcerated students and for intensifying popular education.

5. June 16, 1988, a day for storing food, medicines, fuel, and other essential commodities.

6. June 18, 1988, a day of mass escalation on which mass rallies will be held under the slogan of uniting around the PLO and demonstrating adherence to our people's right of return and self-determination in a national state. [On this day] punishment will be meted out to those who break ranks and to the occupation authorities.

7. June 19, 1988, a day on which our masses will completely boycott Civil Administration offices in order to intensify mass resignations and [enhance] the laws of the people's rule.

8. June 20, 1988, Martyred Palestinian Youth Day. Youth marches and visits to the families of martyred youths are to be organized.

9. June 22, 1988, a general strike—a day of return to the land on which the land is to be reclaimed and sown, while destroying and burning enemy industrial and agricultural property and facilities.

10. On Fridays and Sundays, prayers will be said for the repose of our martyrs' souls, and mass marches and demonstrations will be held.

O our people! Resistance to the forces of the alien occupation and the herds of settlers must be increased through the use of all modes of popular resistance, from the sacred stone to the Molotov cocktail. We advance and struggle in the light of the martyrs' last testament.

We will surely triumph.

The Palestine Liberation Organization
The United National Command
of the Uprising in the Occupied Territories
June 8, 1988

LEAFLET NO. 21

In the name of Allah the merciful and compassionate

Communiqué—communiqué—communiqué

*No voice will overcome the voice of the uprising
No voice will overcome the voice of the Palestinian people—
the people of the PLO*

Communiqué No. 21

Issued by the Palestine Liberation Organization/
The United National Command of the Uprising

The blessed al-Aqsa [Mosque] Proclamation

O our heroic people ... Our people's tremendous uprising is entering its eighth month with [growing] strength and a heightening of the struggle, achieving victory after victory on the road to liberation and independence. You are valiantly withstanding the acts of dispossession and the crimes being committed against you by the new Nazi authorities. Day after day, you are demonstrating your determination to continue the uprising and the struggle until the realization of our people's national and inalienable rights of return, self-determination, and establishment of an independent Palestinian state under the leadership of the PLO, our sole legitimate representative.

The uprising has accorded our people and its representative the PLO a major political victory in the form of the Uprising Summit in Algiers, which affirmed the establishment of an independent state and the PLO's exclusive representation. Our masses demand that the summit leaders implement [in practice] the resolutions. On the international plane, the uprising has generated a substantive change in world opinion, both public and official, in favor of our national cause. The uprising has generated unprecedented support for our people's right of return, self-determination, and establishment of our independent state. The uprising has buried forever all the liquidation schemes and demeaning alternatives [to the PLO] that are designed to eradicate our legitimate rights, while stressing that there can be no substitute for freedom and national independence.

The UNC [United National Command] of the Uprising asserts that our people is struggling to survive and to restore its usurped national rights. Our people is the victim of acts of dispossession by the occupation authorities, including house demolitions, torching of crops, destruction of property, siege of villages and refugee camps, deportation, arbitrary arrest, and the murder of infants, women, and the elderly with bullets and toxic gases. Our masses urge the international community and the U.N. to intervene urgently for the withdrawal of the Israeli army from population centers in the West Bank and Gaza Strip, to provide international protection for our defenseless masses and to close the fascist detention centers, especially the notorious prison in the Negev desert. Our masses stress that there will never be stability in the [Middle East] region or the world, without the attainment of a just and comprehensive solution to the Palestinian problem through the convening of an international conference with full powers, with the participation of the PLO, on an equal footing with the other parties, as our sole legitimate representative, and the participation of the permanent members of the Security Council.

UNC takes pride in the firm national unity that marks the uprising masses and calls on our people wherever they are to close ranks and consolidate their efforts. It condemns the barbaric shelling of the Shatila camp—the symbol—by the gang of the renegade Abu Musa,[1] who is thus stabbing the PLO in the back.

The United Command imputes to Syria the responsibility for not preventing the destruction of the Shatila camp, as the only side capable of doing so. The United Command demands that Syria act immediately to put an end to the acts of massacre and the liquidation of the militant Palestinian entity in Lebanon.

1. Abu Musa left the Fatah of Arafat following the Lebanon War and set up an independent organization under Syrian auspices.

O masses of the uprising, UNC, as it salutes our revolutionary masses everywhere and praises the heroic role of the Jerusalem masses who are resisting the desecration of our Islamic and Christian shrines, calls on our masses to escalate and develop the uprising as a stage toward comprehensive civil disobedience, and stresses the following:

—To intensify the boycott of Zionist products and prevent their reaching local markets. The local press is called on not to advertise Israeli products. Strike units will be lurking for anyone who advertises or distributes Israeli products.

—Not to pay bail or fines to the occupation authorities' coffers.

—To withdraw savings accounts from Israeli banks.

—It is essential that our national enterprises should double their output while undertaking to pay overtime and improve work conditions. Factory owners are called on not to deduct wages on general-strike days. Trade unions should conclude work agreements with local employers to help serve the national interest in view of the successful experience in this regard.

—A grave warning against attempts of the occupation authorities and their agents to erode our people's unity by inciting communal conflicts, as occurred in Nablus, Bethlehem, and Gaza. Whoever takes part in these criminal schemes will encounter firm opposition.

—A grave warning against agents, who conceal themselves under the guise of religion and nationalist names and are trying to twist the image of the uprising and stab the PLO and its United Command in the back. It is essential to verify the identity of collectors of donations and to strike with an iron fist at all forms of crime, theft, and fraud, as occurred in the Gaza Strip and the northern area of the West Bank. Likewise, the poisonous programs transmitted by the Zionist media must be shunned.

—Praise to those who resigned from the Civil Administration apparatus. Step up the blows against those who have not resigned from the departments which they were called on to leave.

—To expand the establishment of popular committees and committees for health, popular education, storage, household economy, and guarding. We emphasize the obligation to turn to the popular committees and not the ruling authorities in the event of any disputes that may arise.

—To form special guard committees for crops and property in Jericho, the Jordan Rift Valley, and the northern areas in order to protect them against harassment by settlers and occupation agents.

—To strengthen the national economy, household economics and agricultural cooperation, and intensify the various forms of mutual aid.

—A warning to headmasters who violate UNC instructions regarding teaching and impose sanctions on pupils. It is essential that teachers mobilize for popular education on strike days and while schools are closed. [The schools] should become a base for forging national consciousness and a combative spirit. We call on students to complete the formation of their united committees so that the academic process can be organized.

—UNC hails the city of Nazareth and the 13th [annual] voluntary work camp,[2] its organizers, and participants, and salutes our masses inside [Israel] for supporting our uprising. UNC is confident that the masses will continue to back the uprising. UNC greets the progressive and democratic forces and the Jewish peace forces that support our people's national rights. We ask them to step up their manifestations of support for these rights.

UNC condemns the massacre perpetrated by the occupation forces and settlers in the al-Aqsa mosque compound on July 3. It praises the heroic resistance of the al-Maqdes [Jerusalem] masses in the defense of our shrines.

We urge our masses to show greater vigilance and not permit the licentious settlers and the Zionist politicians to desecrate our shrines. We request the help of the Organization of Islamic States, the Arab states, the Vatican, the U.N., and all our friends throughout the world to intervene urgently in order to put a stop to desecration of our Muslim and Christian holy places.

UNC greets our students, who hold the pen in one hand and the stone in the other; those who with their arms are building our national economy; our merchants, who are implementing our decisions; our peasants; and our forces, who are striking at the enemy's forces and settlers; and calls for the implementation of the following struggle program:

July 7—A day of solidarity with the besieged villages, towns, and refugee camps. National activities will be carried out to help them break the siege imposed on them.

July 8—al-Aqsa Day. A day of pronounced escalation on which all will take part in mass activities to protect al-Aqsa. The strike units will deal blows to the enemy forces and the herds of settlers.

July 9–10—A general strike to mark the eighth month of the uprising and the fall of the first band of martyrs. These two days shall be days of

---

2. A voluntary project held annually at the initiative of the Israeli Communist party, with the participation of youngsters from Israel and abroad.

national mourning in memory of our people's martyrs in the Shatila and Burj al-Barajneh camps. Black flags will be flown.

July 12—A day of cooperative work and turning to the land. A day of strengthening agricultural cooperatives and the agricultural economy.

July 14—The eighth anniversary of the heroic strike in Nafha Prison. A day of solidarity with the [inmates of the] prison in the Negev desert. Our institutions and mass organizations will carry out solidarity activities. The people are urged to forgo one meal on this day.

July 16—A day of activities to protest the closure of the schools and their invasion, and the detention of students.

July 18—A day of a general strike in solidarity with the detainees in the Negev prison.

The days from July 6–20 shall be days of confrontation and activities against the occupation forces and its organs. The initiative will be in the hands of the popular committees and the shock squads in preparation for the people's rule.

Make extensive use of the means of popular struggle . . . Step up heroic confrontations against the occupation.

Strengthen solidarity and national unity on the road to freedom and national independence.

The Palestine Liberation Organization
The United National Command
in the Occupied Arab Territories
July 6, 1988

LEAFLET NO. 23

In the name of Allah the merciful and compassionate

Communiqué—communiqué—communiqué

No voice will overcome the voice of the uprising
No voice will overcome the voice of the Palestinian people—
the people of the PLO

Communiqué No. 23

Issued by the Palestine Liberation Organization/
The United National Command of the Uprising

The Deportees Proclamation

O masses of our struggling Palestinian people, O masses of the victorious uprising, your uprising is these days entering its ninth month and recording ever more achievements on the road of the lengthy and difficult struggle toward freedom and independence, toward realizing the just national hopes and aspirations of our people for return, self-determination, and the establishment of an independent state with Jerusalem as its capital.

The latest Jordanian moves of severing the legal and administrative link with the West Bank constitutes one of the major achievements of the great popular uprising, a practical step toward implementing the resolutions of the Algiers summit. [The latter] strengthen the PLO's standing as our people's sole representative, as the only party with the authority to negotiate in all the spheres of responsibility relevant to our people in the homeland and the diaspora. Jordan and the other Arab states are called on to assist our people everywhere, especially in the occupied land, to enable them to continue their struggle and their uprising.

This achievement is added to your earlier achievements. Economically, you have caused the enemy damage of more than $2 billion, and you have forcibly extracted three Security Council resolutions which refer, for the first time, to "the occupied Palestinian territories." You have exposed before the whole world the occupation's racist and fascist aspect, and you have consolidated our people's legitimate national rights in the Uprising Summit that met at Algiers, following the attempt to obscure them at the Amman summit. You have traversed an impressive path toward dismantling the apparatus of the Military Government and its branches and toward building the cells of the people's future national government, represented by the popular and national committees. You have laid the foundations for a new way of life based on cooperation and self-reliance. Let us all take pride in these achievements, and [let us] be ready to preserve, advance, and develop them.

The visit to the Middle East region of the American envoy [Richard] Murphy is a follow-up to the Shultz plan and an attempt to give that plan a blood transfusion after the uprising had eliminated it completely. Therefore, the United National Command of the Uprising demands the continued boycott of the American envoy and any other envoy of the American administration, as long as it continues to deny our people's national rights and our sole legitimate representative, the PLO. We call on our people to greet Murphy with large-scale demonstrations and violent clashes with the occupation forces.

UNC, and with it the masses of the uprising, welcomes Iran's acceptance of Security Council Resolution No. 598 regarding the Gulf War [between Iran and Iraq, 1980–1988], and views this as a positive step toward putting an end to a war that is destroying the material and human potential of both countries [and a step toward] the expulsion of the American navy from the Gulf. The cessation of this war may do a considerable service for our people's uprising and national struggle.

In the name of the masses of the occupied land, UNC greets the leaders of our people and of its revolution, who are convening in Baghdad for a meeting of the Palestinian Central Council. [UNC] appreciates their efforts toward the adoption of resolutions that support our people's uprising and that strengthen national unity within the framework of the PLO, on the basis of the collective leadership and the resolutions of the 18th session of the Palestinian National Council, with the emphasis on the convening of an active international conference with the participation of the PLO as sole legitimate representative on an equal footing with the other sides, as the means to realize our people's national rights of return, self-determination, and the establishment of an independent Palestinian state on our national soil.

O our valiant people, the Zionist enemy is deluding himself that by deporting many of you from your homeland he can contain the ongoing uprising. In the last eight months you have already proved that the enemy's measures, including deportations, house demolitions, harassment, economic measures, a declaration of war on the popular and national committees, closure of the national institutions, disseminating propaganda through the media and through treacherous agents about the end of the uprising and the fading of its flame—that all these measures will fail in the face of your blazing fire and your readiness for sacrifice and involvement. UNC urges that you confront the enemy and his apparatus with the emphasis on the following: persecution of occupation agents and those who have not resigned [from the Civil Administration], of distributors of enemy merchandise, of disseminators of deliberate rumors; and placing the emphasis on the boycott of work in the Jewish settlements, and nonpayment of taxes, fines, and monetary levies.

Intensify solidarity activities with the men and women detainees in the enemy's prisons and detention centers, and especially with the detainees in Ansar 3. The women's committees and forums are charged with special responsibility to organize sit-in strikes and other appropriate activities.

UNC of the Uprising sends greetings to the peoples struggling for freedom and independence in Namibia, South Africa, and Chile and urges people of true conscience to work for the release of prisoners of freedom and conscience, foremost among them the fighter Nelson Mandela.

Greetings to the Jerusalem masses who defend the capital of their independent Palestinian state. They are called on to maintain a constant presence in the area of the holy al-Haram [the Temple Mount] in order to prevent the authorities from carrying out excavations and to be ready to confront any possible danger to the holy places of Islam and Christianity.

Heighten and expand the manifestations of revolt and disobedience to the orders of the occupation authorities regarding the erasure of nationalist slogans, summonses, lowering of Palestinian flags and removal of barriers and roadblocks, and collective resistance to the campaign of arrests, tax collection, and house demolitions—such as occurred in the heroic village of Beit Furiq.

Utmost caution must be exercised in the face of the occupation authorities' methods of operation which are intended to generate a rift in our merchants' united stand by offering inducements to some of them, such as tax exemptions in return for their renewal of vehicle licenses, the goal being to bring about further collaboration with the enemy's institutions.

We commend the stand of the European Common Market member-states in not ratifying the economic agreement with Israel. We ask Palestinian farmers not to export their produce via the Israeli Agrexco firm. We warn against a number of local authorities and persons who are suspected of maintaining ties with Agrexco. We demand that they establish national import-export institutions. In addition, the United National Command asks the popular committees to market local agricultural produce and to set up marketing and support committees. This, in order to support the Palestinian farmer and foil the enemy's attempts to prevent certain areas from marketing their produce.

UNC stresses that the closure of the universities, colleges, and schools, and the early termination of the academic year, show clearly that the occupation is acting to render our people ignorant. Hence, we have no choice but to rely on ourselves, to acquire education by ourselves, and to educate our children by organizing and developing popular education. We ask our universities and lecturers to find ways to renew university education, especially for students in their senior year. We urge the Council for Higher Education to assume responsibility and to demand the reopening of the universities and colleges.

UNC praises the [response of] those Jewish physicians who have disdained the occupation measures about not giving medical treatment to the wounded of the uprising, the journalists who are subjected to repression for speaking out against the occupation, and all those who face harassment because of their support for our people's national rights and calls on them to intensify their support for our just struggle and to explain to the Israeli street our just rights. Whoever consents to another's suppression cannot himself be free.

UNC calls on the national and progressive forces [inside Israel] to discard their differences, cease their tirades of mutual vilification, and unify their ranks and potential in the service of our people's victorious uprising and efforts to realize its legitimate national rights.

UNC is proud of the marches staged by the shock squads, their members wrapped in the national colors, in the old quarter [Qasba] of Jabal al-Nar [Nablus]. It esteems highly the role of the masses in the Gaza [refugee] camps who are withstanding the enemy's policy of repression, and in Nablus, Jenin, Qabatya, Hussan, Qalqilya, Beit Sahur, ʿIdna, Bethlehem, Beit Jala, Tulkarm, ʿAzun, and the [refugee] camps of al-Jalazun, al-Amʿari, al-Duheisha, Jabalya, al-Shati, al-Bureij, and all the population centers of our people. It urges that the level of popular organization be raised and that the roles of the popular and special committees and the strike forces be strengthened, and it calls on all positions to intensify the uprising and execute the following actions:

1. Aug. 8, 1988, a day of solidarity with the Palestinian detainees, especially those in Ansar 3. Solidarity activities should be organized, with women's groups doing their part in this regard.

2. Aug. 9, 1988, shall be a general-strike day to mark the start of the ninth month of the uprising.

3. Aug. 10 shall be a day of information activity in the occupied lands to explain the demands of the uprising and its achievements at the popular and international levels. Journalists should play a prominent role in this regard.

4. Aug. 13, a day on which the national and popular committees will assess their roles in order to raise the level of their implementation and organization, and draw up plans to advance the uprising.

5. Aug. 17, Jerusalem Day, a general-strike day in honor of the capital of our future Palestinian state, and to protest the suppression and arrest campaigns to which its innocent sons are subject.

6. Aug. 21, the 20th anniversary of the burning of al-Aqsa mosque by the Zionists. This shall be a day of demonstrations and clashes with the occupiers in denunciation of this shameful act and the attempts to defile and destroy the holy places by means of excavations and other modes. This day shall be al-Aqsa Mosque Day.

7. Aug. 22 shall be a general-strike day in protest at the tax authorities' measures against the courageous merchants and in solidarity with their struggle.

Heightened escalation and clashes with the occupation's soldiers, organs, and agents. Greater unity and revolutionary vigilance.

We will surely triumph.

Announcement: No one, no matter who, is permitted to speak, make a declaration, or issue a leaflet in the name of UNC without its knowledge or its directive. Utmost caution [is required] regarding statements to the press and leaflets attributed to the United National Command.

The Palestine Liberation Organization
The United National Command of the Uprising
August 5, 1988

• • •

LEAFLET NO. 24

Communiqué—communiqué—communiqué

No voice will overcome the voice of the uprising

Communiqué No. 24

Issued by the United National Command of the Uprising

The Uprising Martyrs Behind Bars Proclamation

Let us swear that the uprising will continue until national independence despite all the provocations

O masses of the magnificent uprising, the insurrection has now entered its 36th week without respite, with full momentum and response, and it declares before the whole world that there is no going back from our people's achievements on the road to establishing an independent state on our national soil under the leadership of the PLO.

O our people, in an attempt to suppress and restrain the uprising, to extinguish its brilliant flame, and because of the prominent role being fulfilled by the popular committees in building the people's independent rule and dismantling the apparatus of the occupation regime, the terrorist Rabin and his fascist government have now outlawed the popular committees and threatened their members with arrest and deportation. The popular committees are one of our people's creations in the shadow of the uprising, and a natural result of its struggle. If Rabin thinks that by means of mass deportations and lengthy detentions he will succeed in murdering the uprising, he is going to be disappointed.

Just as our people foiled his decision to outlaw the Shabiba committees and close the institutions, associations and unions, our people's response will be clear and decisive, namely, the establishment of more such committees in all the villages, cities, camps, and neighborhoods. Our whole people constitutes popular committees. They are its lungs, and it will not forsake them. Rabin's mass deportation of many of our people's cadres for participating and leading the mass committees is merely the implementation of the "transfer" policy that the fascist political parties proposed in his name. Does Rabin think that such a policy will quench the flame of the uprising? In place of every deported fighter, dozens of cadres will spring up; and just as the deportation tactics failed in the past, they will fail once more. Our people's response will be to escalate the uprising and intensify and develop its fire. Our people and its fighters, who were seared by the deportation decisions, understand that their stay outside the homeland will not be a long one and that the day of their return to their homeland and their independent Palestinian state, of which there are emerging signs, is not far off. The whole world understands better than at any time in the past the importance of a solution to regional conflicts, and as the racists were thrown out of Namibia, the occupiers be thrown out of our land so that we can build our independent state and its capital Jerusalem.

O our battling people, O people of the proud Gaza Strip, the imposition of curfew on the Gaza Strip and the bar on the entry of journalists and the media, are nothing but a doomed attempt to extinguish the fire of the uprising on the front line. The reaction of our people in the Gaza Strip was unequivocal. Thousands of Gazans went out to repulse the occupier's vehicles in denunciation of the loathsome crime of the burning of three workers. The world heard and learned about what is happening in the sealed Gaza Strip, despite the occupiers' efforts. Your reaction is an example of disobedience to the occupiers' orders which deserves to be emulated, and a prelude to the general national revolt.

O our people in Ansar 3 and in all the Zionist prisons, glory to you, you who are throwing back [the enemy] with your hardened bodies, unarmed, with nothing but faith in your people and in its just cause. Glory to the victims of the uprising who are behind bars, the martyrs of Ansar 3 and the two martyrs of torture in the isolation cells of the Russian Compound and in al-Dahariya. The enemy's resort to the murder of fighters reflects the hysteria that has seized him due to the uprising's intensification. Our people in the occupied homeland (the big prison) and in the diaspora is convinced that you will persist in your struggle against the conspiracies of liquidation and humiliation being conducted against you. Your struggle is part of your people's struggle to attain its legitimate national rights and national independence.

O free people of the world, UNC appeals—in the name of our people who are under curfew and in the jails, in the name of the bereaved families, in the name of the children, the women and the elderly who have suffered and are suffering under the occupation's repressive measures—to world public opinion and to all human-rights organizations to stand by our battling people and exert pressure on the Israeli authorities to halt its policy of wholesale deportation-transfer—to close Ansar prison in the desert and to release the more than 3,000 Palestinian fighters being held in that camp, which resembles the Nazi detention camp Auschwitz.

Therefore, the United National Command asks the international community to do its duty and provide international protection for our unarmed masses, and it appeals to the Israeli street and warns it against the consequences of the policy of despotism and oppression of Shamir, Rabin, and Peres toward our Palestinian people. If it continues, this policy will cause you damage.

O masses of our battling people, UNC asserts that Jordan's moves in abrogating its legal and administrative ties [to the West Bank] are an important political achievement, one of the achievements of the uprising which has restored a Palestinian right that had been usurped for 40 years of custodianship and annexation. We stress that there is no such thing as a so-called political vacuum, as our people in the occupied lands have always regarded the PLO as unassailably its sole legitimate representative, its political leader, and the leader of its struggle. UNC greets our National Council, which is holding an extraordinary session. It is certain that the council will draw up a clear and comprehensive political program which can mobilize the broadest international support for our people's national rights and will take practical steps to assist and advance the uprising. We stress that it is the PLO and its central leadership institutions that constitute the political expression of our people's aspirations, and that the just solution for our Palestinian problem will be effected through international authority that will derive from an international conference possessing full powers in which the PLO will participate on an equal footing with the other parties to the conflict.

O our people's masses across the Green Line, UNC again urges you to avoid marginal disputes, to cease engaging in media attacks, and to close ranks in order to withstand the policy of repression and eradication of your Palestinian Arab identity which the Israeli authorities are conducting against you, and to thwart the official insane attacks against your leadership.

O our heroic masses, UNC greets our masses who are fighting in Tulkarm, Qabatya, ʿAzun, Tell, Burka, Nablus, Kafr Malik, al-Jalazun, al-Amʿari, Balata, Qalandya, al-Duheisha, Bethlehem, Beit Jala, Beit Sahur, Bani Naʿim, al-Dahariya, al-ʿArub, al-Fawar, and all the camps and centers of our people in the heroic Gaza Strip. We bow our head in respect and blessing to the victims of the uprising behind bars and call on our people to affirm the following principles in their daily struggle:

Popular education: UNC calls on all teachers, high school pupils and students, and especially elementary school pupils, to mobilize for the success of the popular education operation on September 1st, in order to foil the authorities' policy of closing the schools and inculcating ignorance in our children. Popular education is a national responsibility, and all must commit themselves to it.

Rumors and "planted" leaflets: UNC calls on our people to heed only the central and regional leaflets and to beware of planted leaflets. We caution against enemy attempts to set the national and religious forces at each other's throats, as occurred recently in the Gaza Strip, when the enemy tried to burn a car belonging to a member of al-Mujammaʿ al-Islami. We also caution against manifestations of slander against loyal citizens and the manufacture of marginal problems in the name of the national cause, as occurred in the Gaza Strip and Tulkarm. We ask our people to safeguard our people's property and to beware of thieves sent by the enemy, in an abortive attempt to convince our people of the need for a police presence.

National agricultural produce: We stress the duty to boycott Israeli agricultural produce and to purchase only national produce. We emphasize that shopowners and fruit and vegetable vendors must be strict about this.

National agriculture: UNC calls on all our masses to continue working and readying the land in preparation for the coming winter and to plant cereals and legumes such as lentils, chickpeas, broad beans, garlic, onions, wheat, and so forth, for storage.

Payment for medical treatment: We call on our private hospitals and our doctors to be considerate of the difficult conditions of our people and to reduce considerably fees for medical treatment.

Positive initiatives: UNC commends the many positive initiatives taken by the popular and national committees in the territories, such as declaring a car strike in the Gaza Strip, distributing questionnaires to merchants to enable them to take an inventory of Israeli goods in order to bolster the boycott principle, distributing medicines free of charge, and distributing cards for medical treatment at reduced prices to families of casualties in Hebron. These initiatives conform with the uprising's escalation program.

O our insurgent masses, UNC is proud of the spirit of intensifying confrontation shown by our masses and the unrelenting attacks that the shock squads perpetrate against the enemy forces, agencies, and settlers and calls on the uprising masses to step up their confrontation against the occupation and carry out the following militant operations:

August 23—The day of the deportees, on which our masses will rise up to denounce the deportation policy (the day of the Molotov cocktail).

August 24–25—Two days of general strike to honor the memory of the uprising martys behind bars.

August 26—Commemorating the al-Buraq revolt of 1929.[1] We ask our masses to mark this day by various struggle events.

August 27—On this day, the strike units will deliver blows to those who were told to resign but did not do so.

August 30—General strike in solidarity with the deportees.

August 31—General strike to protest the burning of three of our Palestinian laborers in Tel Aviv by the fascists.

September 1—On this day, the detainees will declare a hunger strike to protest their detention conditions. On this day, the masses will fast and hold sit-ins in offices of international organizations.

In the first week of September, the popular committees will devote themselves to developing and establishing additional committees.

Friday and Sunday will be devoted to prayers for the repose of the souls of the uprising martyrs. Intensify the unity, cohesiveness, and escalation of the exalted uprising of our people until national independence.

We will surely triumph.

The Palestine Liberation Organization
The United National Command of the Uprising
August 22, 1988

---

1. The al-Buraq revolt refers to the clashes between Arabs and Jews, in the spring of 1929, over the prayer arrangements at the Western Wall in Jerusalem. These clashes led to the riots of August 1929 in Palestine and to the establishment of a British commission of inquiry.

LEAFLET NO. 25

In the name of Allah the merciful and compassionate

Communiqué—communiqué—communiqué

*No voice will overcome the voice of the uprising
No voice will overcome the voice of the Palestinian people—
the people of the PLO*

Communiqué No. 25

Issued by the Palestine Liberation Organization/
The United National Command of the Uprising

The Martyrs of the Massacres Proclamation

O our glorious masses,

Your uprising is now concluding the ninth month of its long life and is inaugurating its tenth month, more courageous and more determined to continue escalating, despite the forms and means of the fascist suppression and the collective punishments, the policy of starvation, the economic strangulation, the demolition of houses, extensive arrest campaigns, deportation from the homeland, the bulldozing of neighborhoods, the murder of fighters, the destruction of property and prolonged curfews. Your great popular uprising is continuing its daily struggle on a large and massive scale on the road to the eradication and dismantling of the apparatus and tools of the occupation regime, while building the people's national authority in the form of the popular committees and the United National Command of the Uprising.

On the brink of its tenth month, your magnificent uprising has succeeded in registering new achievements to be added to the totality of the struggle's political achievements during the past months. Panic-stricken, the American administration has rescinded its previous decision to close down the office of the PLO delegation to the U.N. The U.N. itself, according to Secretary-General de Cuellar, following his meeting with PLO chairman Brother Abu ʿAmmar, is emphasizing Palestine and the soil of Palestine. The U.N. Security Council has again unanimously condemned the policy of deporting Palestinians from their homeland. Most of these achievements are contained in the resolutions on the uprising adopted by the conference of nongovernmental organizations held in Geneva, especially those resolutions stressing the need to provide international protection for our masses—one of the uprising's key slogans and demands. We also heard the recent declarations by [Lt. Gen. Dan] Shomron, chief of staff of the Zionist despotism and oppression, again stressing the inability to quell the uprising militarily, and these came on top of statements by the Zionist Avraham Tamir, director of the enemy's Foreign Ministry, who stressed that the PLO is the body that represents the Palestinians, whether the Israelis like it or not.

To all this must be added the hysterical fear in the face of the Molotov cocktail and the stone that has seized the settlers and brought about the evacuation of some settlements, showing how useless are the pledges of the terrorist Rabin and the arrogant Shamir to accord them greater security and expand the [settlers'] authority to open fire on our people. Heightening all this is the growing crisis on the enemy's economic front. This crisis is reflected openly in the rising numbers published daily by the economic and planning experts in the Zionist ministries.

O our heroic masses,

The evil attempts by the occupation authorities to implement the transfer policy by means of what they call temporary deportation, under which fighters are expelled from the soil of their homeland for different periods provided they sign an undertaking not to take part in the struggle and to ensure quiet in their regions, so that they will be able to return to the homeland—this is considered to be in clear contravention and a shameful violation of the Geneva Convention concerning occupied lands. In form and substance it is no different from the deportation policy condemned by the Security Council and the entire world. UNC urges our masses to struggle against this policy.

O masses of our valiant people,

In these days, you remember with bitterness the massacres of Black September and Sabra and Shatila, which cut down thousands of our people in the diaspora and sought to finish off what was begun at Deir Yassin, Qibya, Duweima, and Kafr Qassim,[1] with the aim of obliterating our people's distinctive national identity. Now we assert loudly to your butchers: shame on you, you have reaped only the contempt of history and the curse of humanity. We are stronger and more mature than ever before in the past, for we have always emerged from your massacres and your slaughterhouses with head upright, standing erect despite our wounds and continuing on the road on which our forefathers embarked, headed by the warrior Sheykh al-Qassam and ʿAbd al-Qadir al-Husseini.

O our struggling masses,

UNC and with it the masses of the occupied land commend the wise decisions taken by the PLO regarding the payment of the salaries which have been stopped by Jordan, and the sincere decision made by Colonel Muʿammar al-Qadafi on this subject. [UNC] appeals to the leaders of the Algiers summit to uphold their financial, political, and information commitments to the uprising, the PLO, and the Palestinian cause. It also greets the emergency session of the Palestinian National Council [PNC] and stresses the importance of passing clearly defined and significant political resolutions based on the permanent national principles and mobilization of all resources to preserve and extend the achievements of the uprising and the revolution on the road to securing our people's national rights of return, self-determination, and the establishment of an independent state on our national soil under the leadership of the PLO.

Our masses and their shock squads,

UNC is proud of the march of the 20,000 who walked through the streets of noble Gaza in defiance of the curfew and of the masses in Jabal al-Nar [Nablus] who did likewise, and of the shock squads in Yatta that carried out the verdict of the people against those who sold their soul to the occupation and betrayed their people and homeland. It calls on our masses to show understanding for the following steps and to act accordingly in your daily struggle:

Hamas:

In the past few days the national arena saw attempts by Hamas, which is a branch of the Muslim Brothers, to impose its control on the na-

---

1. Qibya refers to a military operation that took place in October 1953 as an Israeli reprisal against acts of murder and sabotage perpetrated in Israeli territory. In the Qibya raid, a large number of local inhabitants were killed, including women and children. Duweima was a village ruined by the Israeli army during the 1948 War. The inhabitants either escaped or were killed. Kafr Qassim, an Arab village in Israel. On the eve of the Suez War in October 1956, forty-seven villagers were killed by the army while returning home from work during a curfew imposed when they were out.

tional street and to declare a general strike for Sunday, August 21. Our masses, with their strong instincts, saw this as a move conflicting with the national platform as approved by our United National Command and which united the will of the entire people against the enemy. UNC emphasizes that every blow to the unity of ranks is tantamount to doing the enemy a significant service and harms the uprising. We extended our hand in the past, and we continue to do so, to every force that wants to take part in national activity, and we do not exclude Hamas from our efforts to unite the fighting ranks. The attempts to impose a stand on our masses by force and the reaction to these efforts in the form of strife and clashes serve the enemy's interests and his plans to derail the uprising. Within this context, we denounce the attacks of burning, destruction, and ruin against a number of shops and against property owned by persons who did not heed Hamas's call to strike. At the same time, we urge the affirmation of the united stand not to violate the consensus and to strive to take part in the general national stand through lines of coordination with the sides in the United National Command and its active forces.

We praise the efforts being made by the imams in the mosques, who do not cease to call for uniting the ranks within the framework of the national consensus to preserve the uprising and its continuation.

The U.N. and the international community:

UNC urges the U.N. and the international Security Council, and all international institutions, to intervene immediately to put a stop to the violations of international custom, treaties, and laws by the [Israeli] authorities and to provide international protection for our people in the face of all the forms of despotism and oppression and the insane attacks that aim at uprooting [our people's] existence. UNC demands international supervision by the U.N. over the occupied lands until the implementation of Israeli withdrawal, and the convening of an international conference possessing full powers with the PLO's participation in an independent and equal delegation.

Closure of institutions and the universities:

Following the closure by the [Israeli] authorities of the institutions, colleges, universities, and [trade] unions, they have [also] begun shutting down a large number of societies and associations, including charitable societies. [This in the wake of Jordan's] juridical, legal, and administrative disengagement from the Palestinian [West] Bank. UNC believes that this closure process reflects the sensitivities of the occupation authorities toward every existing Palestinian institution, which they regard as part of the government of the Palestinian people and state. We urge all our institutions, associations, and unions to thwart the closure decisions by continuing to fulfill their missions despite the closure.

Education:

In view of the authorities' continuing shutdown of the educational institutions, as part of their policy to inculcate ignorance in our people, UNC calls for a struggle for the opening of these institutions. At this stage, students should not leave the homeland in order to study [abroad]. [UNC] appeals to UNESCO, to Arab circles, and to international organizations to raise this crucial issue at the highest levels, including the international Security Council. To deprive a people of education is a barbaric measure which violates a basic human right, granted by international custom and treaties, notably the Declaration of Human Rights and the Fourth Geneva Convention. In this context we stress the importance of reinforcing and intensifying popular education and thus offering a more practical and effective response against the Zionists' policy of inculcating ignorance.

Popular committees:

UNC emphasizes the importance of continuing to establish the independent people's authority on the road to independence and freedom. It calls on our masses to join [the popular committees] in the most comprehensive manner, as only this will frustrate the authorities' decision to outlaw them and the insane offensive against them, whose main purpose is to make our masses fear the committees in order to isolate them and leave them vulnerable to attack.

Persecution of collaborators:

UNC praises the [activity of the] shock squads, the core of the popular committees [against collaborators] in Yatta, Hebron, ʿAar, Jenin refugee camp, Qabatya, Bidya, al-Jalazun, Jabalya, Deir al-Balah, and elsewhere, and for executing the verdict of the uprising and the people against some of them. It calls on the shock squads to continue purging the internal front of the filth of those who sold their soul and honor to the occupation and betrayed their people and their homeland.

Attacks by the fascist mounted police:

Our masses in Jerusalem, the capital of our future Palestinian state, are urged to oppose with force attacks of the fascist mounted police against peasants displaying their agricultural wares at Bab al-ʿAmud [Damascus Gate] and Bab al-Zahr [Herod's Gate] in order to alleviate their bitter lives by providing their children with a slice of bread. They are beaten by the vicious horsemen who then destroy their produce and do not hesitate to use it as feed for their horses in full view of the owners.

Money changers:

UNC demands that the money changers cease causing havoc in the economic situation and cease disseminating rumors and contributing to the creation of an atmosphere of anxiety among the public, as occurred in the past few days. The result was that many ordinary people gambled their savings, the fruit of years of labor, by exchanging the dinars they had saved for dollars. Whoever helps foment this anxiety is abetting, whether deliberately or not, the process in which our people's savings are being squeezed dry by the Israeli and American banks.

Merchants' committees:

UNC urges the heroic merchants to establish merchants' committees, to develop and activate those already in existence, and to intensify the boycott of tax payments, to resist collectively the barbarism of the tax officials, and to reinforce the economic boycott against the enemy. This was detailed in the leaflet of the merchants' committee in the occupied Palestinian lands. Likewise, we call on our heroic merchants in the Gaza Strip not to obey the orders issued by the army and the authorities to hang a sign on their shop door containing details about the merchant, his address, etc.

Vendors' stalls:

UNC urges insists that the arrangements concerning vendors be adhered to scrupulously. They must heed strictly the times for the opening and closing of shops, as the continuous appearance of stalls in a number of places throughout the day adversely affects the partial commercial strike. [UNC] calls on the shock squads to organize this matter.

Rental rates:

We demand that property owners reduce their rental rates by at least 25 percent, and that leasers begin implementing this and paying their debts immediately and without delay.

O masses of the uprising and its shock squads,

UNC pities the Israelis for the confusion being shown by their leaders due to the intensification of our people's uprising. This state of affairs became clear from the demand by the fascist Sharon to deport the families of stone throwers, and Arens's demand to prevent [access] to Palestinian streets. To avoid bottles and stones, Shamir has given the settlers a green light to open fire on the Palestinian inhabitants. We ask them and others: why do you shut your eyes to the truth and try to hide the sun with a sieve? Are you aware that the solution to the stone problem and so forth will only come when you remove yourselves from our land and recognize our legitimate national rights, self-determination, and an independent state, and not by talking nonsense, going on the rampage, and exercising oppression?

UNC greets the Palestinian arms that have imbued the stone with the characteristics of revolutionary struggle, and calls on these arms to rain down more stones and more Molotov cocktails on the enemy forces and the settlers relentlessly and in every place, and calls on our masses to carry out the following actions:

1. September 8—A general strike marking the conclusion of the ninth month of the uprising and the start of the tenth month.

2. September 10—A day of solidarity with the institutions, trade unions, and charitable societies shut down by the authorities, by means of a sit-down strike outside these institutions.

3. September 13—Protest rallies outside the European consulates in Jerusalem on the occasion of the meeting of Brother Abu ʿAmmar with [members of] the European Parliament. Petitions will be sent to European states urging that supervision and defense be applied in the occupied lands.

4. September 15—Operations to purge the internal front of collaborators and hounding of those who have not resigned in order to expedite their resignation.

5. September 17—A general strike in memory of the martyrs of Black September, Sabra and Shatila, and all the massacres perpetrated against our people.

6. September 18—A day of clashes with the military forces to protest what has befallen our people.

7. September 22—Commemoration of the establishment of the All-Palestine Government [*Hukumat ʿummum Filastin*] in 1948.[2] On this day the people's authority should be strengthened and additional popular committees established on the road to the proclamation of independence.

8. A general strike in solidarity with the detainees and to protest the existence of the Ansar 3 detention camp.

Together on the path of struggle and escalation until the realization of our national aspirations, freedom, and independence.

We will surely triumph.

The Palestine Liberation Organization
The United National Command of the Uprising
September 6, 1988

---

2. The "All-Palestine Government" was established in September 1948 in Gaza with Egyptian encouragement and the support of the Arab League. It was supposed to seize the reins of government in Palestine following the anticipated victory of the Arab states in the war against Israel. The "government" ceased its activities in the wake of the Arabs' defeat, although a formal announcement to this effect was not made by the Arab League until 1952.

LEAFLET NO. 26

Communiqué—communiqué—communiqué

*No voice will overcome the voice of the uprising
No voice will overcome the voice of the Palestinian people—
the people of the PLO*

Communiqué No. 26

Issued by the Palestine Liberation Organization/
The United National Command of the Uprising

Palestine Proclamation [2]

O our struggling masses,

Your uprising, now in its tenth month, has registered new achievements, such as the meeting of nonaligned states which affirmed your just demands and called for a total Israeli withdrawal from the occupied territories and the stationing of temporary international supervision of those territories in preparation for our people's realization of its right to self-determination. Likewise the European Parliament, following its meeting with a Palestinian delegation headed by Abu ʿAmmar, who delivered an historic address to [the European Parliament], stressed the urgent need to find a just solution for the Palestinian problem through negotiations with the PLO and recognized that body as the sole legitimate representative of our people. The Zionist enemy also admitted again, via Shamir himself, that it is impossible to end the uprising by force.

O our valiant people, the continuation of your popular uprising is the only guarantee that the American administration will be vanquished, and it will make [the U.S.] abandon its arrogance and the untenable conditions it is trying to force on our sole representative, the PLO. Just as the uprising has buried forever [both] the plot for a functional division and the Jordanian option and has forced King Hussein to acknowledge the failure of his plan on the soil of occupied Palestine, so every alternative option will fail except for the Palestinian option. At the same time, Israel will be forced to recognize our permanent national rights. Let American imperialism, which supports our enemy with all its strength, know that it must present concessions to our people, and not vice versa. It must recognize the PLO as the sole legitimate representative of our Palestinian people, and [that people's] right to self-determination and the establishment of an independent state on its national soil with Jerusalem as its capital. Let Israel know that its despotism and its offshoots will not lessen our stones [which are thrown] at it and will not extinguish the spark of hope in the eyes of our infants. Israel is no stronger than America, and our people no less [strong] than the people of Vietnam.

O masses of the uprising,

We are a free and struggling people. The glorious uprising has taught us that through it, [and] through our struggle, our sacrifices, and the political, economic, and material losses we are inflicting on the enemy, the occupation's profit sheet can be transformed into a debit sheet entailing a high and costly price, thus bringing about a true change in the local and international balance of forces which will aid us in registering additional achievements on the road to freedom and independence. Your uprising is like a thunderous voice of protest against official Arab impotence. You have declared resonantly: No to the occupation! Yes! a thousand times yes, to freedom and independence! From the depths of this thunderous voice, UNC has repeatedly articulated your political demands, both general and direct, in the leaflets. The United Command, together with our masses, appeals to the 43rd session of the U.N. General Assembly to affirm our people's national rights, to take all measures necessary to implement them, and to force Israel to undertake the following:

1. Israeli withdrawal from the Palestinian and Arab lands occupied since 1967, including Arab Jerusalem.

2. Annulling all annexation measures and removing the settlements that have been established on the occupied lands.

3. Placing the occupied Palestinian lands under U.N. supervision in order to assure our masses' well-being for a few months, thus secur-

ing the activity of the Palestinian people in realizing its right of self-determination.

4. Convening an international conference with full powers under U.N. auspices, on the basis of its resolutions pertaining to the Palestinian question, which is the heart of the Middle East conflict—in preparation for the total Israeli withdrawal, and placing the occupied territories under U.N. supervision. The international conference shall commit Israel to undertake the following:

    a. Immediate implementation of Security Council Resolutions 605, 607, 608.[1]

    b. Annulment of the 1945 Emergency (Defense) Regulations, as well as all the decrees and military orders [issued under] local and international law.

    c. Removing the army from Palestinian population centers.

    d. Releasing all uprising detainees and repatriating the deportees.

    e. Holding free elections in all the municipalities and local councils—urban and rural—under U.N. supervision.

    f. Implementing the Fourth Geneva Convention of 1949, and all the other international treaties that regulate the occupier's relationship toward the occupied lands.

    g. Ceasing the punitive measures against our people such as: economic siege, demolition of houses, torture, deportations, administrative detentions, and building of settlements.

O our fighting masses,

The road to the attainment of all these legitimate demands and to forcing the arrogant enemy to recognize us inevitably entails the continuation of the struggle at all levels, the escalation and development of the uprising, while preserving continuity and initiative. To this end we call for adherence to the following lines of action:

—Aggressiveness against the occupier. Assaults on the occupier must be continued by the entire public. To strengthen further the shock squads, guard committees, and popular committees. We must enhance secretiveness, covertness, and internal and external unity of ranks. We must take to the streets as liberated Nablus did when masses of masked youths staged an organized march, heralding the appearance of the future Palestinian people's army. They deserve all our esteem, along with the uprising masses in the besieged areas, the heroes in Qalqilya, Tulkarm, ʿAnabta, Kafr Malik, and the Gaza Strip, whose merchants refused to obey the

---

1. All three resolutions call for Israel to respect the human rights charter and not to expel Palestinians from the territories.

authorities' demand to write their names and addresses on the doors of their shops.

—The uprising initiative. The struggle is now being directed against the appointed municipal councils, the severance of all contact with the Civil Administration, its branches and its Arab officials, and action against the treacherous collaborators. Let the heroic activity against them continue as it did in Gaza, Nablus, Jenin, Yatta, Sinjil, and so forth. Let collaborators be boycotted and all contact and communication with them be broken off.

—Education of the masses. The object of educating the masses is not only to supplement the curriculum but also to eradicate adult illiteracy and to inculcate the national culture. This means education in every house and neighborhood without fear of the enemy. We must demand that all educational institutions do their duty and set criteria for evaluating and promoting the pupils in the popular education system. Our slogan is "Education for insurrection (*muqawama*)."

—The workers. We appeal to all our workers not to work on days of general strikes and not to submit to the pressures of Zionist factories to sleep over inside the Green Line on the eve of strikes, ostensibly out of concern for their lives in case of revenge, as happened to three of our workers from Gaza.

—Merchants and owners of factories and workshops. The United National Command reaffirms the need to refrain from paying taxes. It is up to the merchants' committees to follow up this matter and to continue boycotting Israeli goods and merchandise for which local substitutes are available, by publishing lists [of such goods]. There must be no price gouging, and [lower] prices must be set for our national products. We also urge employers to pay wages on a regular basis and to heed the directives regarding [the hours for] opening and closing shops and businesses. In particular, wages must be paid scrupulously for general-strike days.

—Agriculture and cooperatives. UNC calls on the public to turn out in its masses in order to help with the [olive] harvest, to encourage a regime of mutual assistance, [and to engage in] cooperative work in order to extract and reap the full profit from every Palestinian olive. [UNC] also calls on farmers and dealers in olive oil to sell their products at reasonable prices, since it is our oil and we shall consume it if it is not exported.

—Unity of the internal front. UNC affirms the great importance of strengthening the internal front which stood like a [solid] rock on which all the forms of suppression and terror were shattered. We call on the public to fight every phenomenon of communal controversy which the enemy and his agents are trying to stir up. [UNC] asserts that the attempts of the authorities to inflate [out of all proportion] a few differences in order to play up the existence of a force [which is a rival to UNC] will not succeed in transforming that force into an element able to compete with the United National Command.

—The hunted. UNC greets all the hunted [i.e., by the authorities] among our people who fought and rebelled against detention orders, and calls on the public to assist them and lend them a hand.

O masses of our self-sacrificing people,

[UNC] sends messages of encouragement to our heroic masses in besieged Qalqilya. By means of stones, firebombs, and nails, [Qalqilya] struck fear into the hearts of the settler herds and jolted the very being of the generals of the Zionist oppression and escalated its struggle against the means of suppression. [We also send messages of encouragement] to the inhabitants of Khan Yunis, who forcibly resisted the minister of oppression Rabin and his entourage. [UNC] also calls on the popular committees, special committees, and shock squads to prepare a provisional struggle program in accordance with local conditions in order to execute the following struggle operations:

1. Escalating the daily clashes with the occupation soldiers and the herds of settlers and sabotaging enemy property.

2. Purging our internal front of all collaborators.

3. Expanding voluntary assistance for farmers, especially during the [olive] harvest.

4. Expressing solidarity with all our besieged locales [and support for] their maintenance, by supplying food and medicines and taking care of their [agricultural] crops.

5. Solidarity with all the casualties of the uprising—prisoners, wounded, families of martyrs, deportees, owners of demolished houses, those dismissed from their place of work—by means of visits, sit-in strikes, and providing maximum assistance.

6. Let Monday, October 3, 1988, be a general-strike day to protest the authorities' continuing closure of the schools and other educational institutions.

7. Let Monday, October 9, 1988, be a general-strike day to mark the start of the eleventh month of the uprising.

To intensify cohesiveness, struggle, and confrontation on the road to the attainment of our people's permanent national rights.

We will surely triumph.

UNC / The Palestine Liberation Organization
September 27, 1988

LEAFLET NO. 27

In the name of Allah the merciful and compassionate

Communiqué—communiqué—communiqué

*No voice will overcome the voice of the uprising
No voice will overcome the voice of the Palestinian people—
the voice of the PLO*

Communiqué No. 27

Issued by the Palestine Liberation Organization/
The United National Command of the Uprising

The National Council Proclamation

O masses of the heroic uprising,
 O you who are forcing siege and international isolation on your Zionist enemy,
 Your heroic uprising has now entered its eleventh month with firm steps toward the attainment of your rights of return, self-determination, and establishment of an independent national state under the leadership of the PLO, our sole legitimate representative, despite the Zionist enemy's desperate attempts to quench the flame of your uprising.
 The latest attempt has been [the] policy [of] comprehensive surprise raids on Saturdays and on general-strike days, with all that this entails, including murders, arrests, harassment of old people, women, and children, and the imposition of prolonged curfews on villages, towns, and refugee camps. This reflects the serious distress in which

the occupation finds itself and the amount of damage it has sustained in all areas. O bearers of the torch of the independent Palestinian state, your uprising is continuing in the battle arena, and at the same time our historic leadership, in the form of the PLO, is sparing no effort to translate our daily victories into international triumphs for our cause—thus intensifying the isolation of our enemy and, as a byproduct, of American imperialism. As the Palestinian struggle continues, our leadership is planning to convene the 19th emergency session of the Palestinian National Council [PNC], whose resolutions will constitute a new weapon in the hands of our masses, and will provide the clearest answer to the demands of our people, the people of the PLO, the people of the uprising—for freedom and independence.

We are confident that our National Council will endorse the appropriate steps to fill the vacuum created by the Jordanian decisions, and will approve plans and modes of action capable of translating [operatively] the slogan of our uprising for freedom and independence, in order to gain greater international support for our permanent rights.

UNC—the United National Command of the Uprising—which is the struggle arm of the PLO in the occupied territories, is absolutely certain that decisions like these, and the plans that will be approved by the [PNC], even if the hostile forces and their allies will try to block their adoption, will undoubtedly put an end to the attempts to exclude the PLO from representing our people at an international conference possessing powers as an independent delegation on an equal footing with the other parties.

The PLO leadership is clearly capable of bursting into the international arena, as was manifested in Brother Abu ʿAmmar's appearance at the European Parliament last month, and on this occasion the masses of the uprising are called on to hold comprehensive mass demonstrations throughout the occupied territories while the [PNC] is in session and to send messages and cables of support [to the PNC].

On the occasion of the anniversary of the founding of the U.N., which falls this month, UNC calls on the U.N. to assume full responsibility for applying its resolutions, which include our people's right of return, self-determination, and establishment of an independent state under the leadership of the PLO. It takes this opportunity to congratulate the secretary-general of the U.N. and all the peoples throughout the world who support our rights, and reaffirms the need to accede to the following legitimate rights:

1. Withdrawal of the occupation forces from centers of Palestinian population.
2. Annulment of all [British] Mandate and occupation orders and regulations that are in effect.
3. Cessation of the settlement and annexation policy and removal of the existing settlements.
4. Release of the uprising detainees and closure of the military detention camps.
5. Assuring international protection for our unarmed Palestinian masses for a period not exceeding a few months, in preparation for the establishment of our people's independent state with its capital, Jerusalem.

O masses of the uprising! UNC, which is full of esteem for your stand that stunned the enemy's generals, in the face of the apparatus of Zionist oppression and the expansionist policy, the siege, and the plastic bullets, bows its head in honor of the stand of our masses in courageous Hebron who are fighting bravely, with determination and heroism, against the occupation forces and the herds of settlers, confirming that [Rabbi Moshe] Levinger and his rabble will not pollute the Tomb of Abraham (al-Khalil al-Rahman). Likewise [UNC] esteems the stand of the masses in steadfast Gaza who transformed a funeral into a violent demonstration against the occupation and its agents and their defiance of curfew orders. A thousand greetings to all our masses in the occupied territories.

O builders of the future Palestinian state,

The enemy is indiscriminately intensifying his methods to suppress the uprising, and this obligates us, more than ever before, to show greater unity and closeness of ranks under the flag of the PLO, and to adhere to the resolutions and plans of its leadership. On this occasion UNC extends its hand in sincerity to all the honorable people who are struggling for greater coordination and unity of effort in order to thwart the enemy's plot which plays on splitting the national ranks.

In order to promote struggle plans that will ensure a firm stand in the face of the enemy's unbridled assault, UNC calls on you to adhere to and implement the following actions:

1. Education:

The decision of the occupation authorities to prolong the closure of the schools, universities, and colleges, and to deprive tens of thousands of our sons of their right to education, a right which is guaranteed them under local and international law, is merely an expression [of the fear that has gripped] the occupation leaders in the face of the education weapon.

Therefore, UNC calls on all international human rights institutions, particularly UNESCO, to intervene immediately to put an end to the policy of inculcating ignorance being conducted by the occupation authorities. It calls on the Council for Higher Education and the administrations of the universities [and] colleges, teachers' unions, parents, and student councils to shoulder their responsibility and coordinate an extensive information campaign which will expose the occupation policy, this by means of memoranda and sit-ins opposite U.N. offices and foreign diplomatic missions, and next to the universities and schools, demanding that they be reopened unconditionally. Likewise, it calls on Palestinian academics and educators to prepare comprehensive educational working plans in order to disseminate popular education in all the neighborhoods, villages, towns, and refugee camps in the occupied territories, to counter the occupation [authorities'] policy of inculcating ignorance.

2. Agriculture:

In view of the olive harvest which has just begun, you are called to assist the farmers to collect this fruit. The custom of cooperation is a fine tradition in our popular heritage, therefore let us practice it.

3. Merchants:

We greatly esteem the steadfastness in the nonpayment of taxes and in opening shops between 8:00 A.M. and 12:00 noon, and [in] the boycott of Israeli goods for which there is a local substitute, as carried out by our faithful merchants and our militant masses. We renew our call to adhere to these directives which are published by UNC and urge the merchants' committees to continue on the same path.

4. Internal front:

UNC demands that no leaflets be issued in its name and warns our masses against suspect slogans being written on walls and [about] threatening letters and phone calls which have a hostile source and are directed against the uprising.

5. Popular committees:

These committees are called on to intervene intensively to resolve internal disputes that are liable to arise. They are called on to buttress the internal edifice and to continue to deal with issues pertaining to food. We emphasize the need to complete the formation of the guard committees.

6. Doctors:

UNC insists that all general practitioners and specialists receive patients and wounded from our people throughout the day, this due to the serious circumstances in which the number of casualties is rising. They are also called on to limit the fee for a visit to a maximum of 12 [Israeli] shekels.

7. Lawyers:

Lawyers are urged to coordinate amongst themselves the handling of cases involving detainees, to set up legal committees for their defense, and to convene press conferences which will expose the detention conditions [in the prisons].

8. Resistance to the policy of surprise raids:

The popular committees and the shock squads are charged with responsibility to resist the policy of raids, employing means such as alertness, vigilance, finding new ways to resist, and providing assistance to all persons wanted by the occupation authorities.

O heroic masses of the uprising,

UNC calls on you to carry out the following struggle missions and actions:

—On Friday, October 14, 1988, a general strike will be held to commemorate the Qibya massacre.

—On Wednesday, October 19, 1988, a general strike will be held to protest the unbridled operations of the settler herds, abetted and protected by the occupation forces, against unarmed civilians.

—On Wednesday, October 26, 1988, a general strike will be held to commemorate the Kafr Qassim massacre.

—On Wednesday, October 12, 1988, the olive harvest operation will begin, and will continue until the end of the season throughout the occupied homeland.

—Saturday, October 22, 1988, [will be] a day of solidarity with the regions under curfew.

—Monday, October 24, 1988, [will be] a day of sit-ins opposite U.N. offices, demanding that Israel be forced to accept [U.N.] resolutions relating to the Palestinian issue.

—Saturday, October 29, 1988, [will be] a day of solidarity with the regions under curfew and the struggle against surprise raids.

—Every Friday and Sunday after worship will be days of confrontation, demonstrations, huge mass marches, visits to martyrs' graves, and visits to the wounded.

This uprising will continue until our people gains freedom and independence.

PLO-UNC
The United National Command
October 9, 1988

LEAFLET NO. 28

Communiqué—communiqué—communiqué

No voice will overcome the voice of the uprising
No voice will overcome the Palestinian people—the people of the PLO

Communiqué No. 28

Issued by the Palestine Liberation Organization/
The United National Command of the Uprising

The Independence Proclamation

O masses of our great people,
    At the start of the twelfth month of your uprising; after the failure of all the barbaric Zionist measures of suppression—killing, arrests, deportations, and destruction of property—in an attempt to eradicate and extinguish the flame of the blazing revolution that emanates from your hallowed body; when you, the heroes of the shock squads, the popular committees, and all the sectors of our fighting masses, have decided to continue the blessed popular revolution and, for its sake, to make all the precious sacrifices that are required on the road to liberty, independence, and the crushing of the occupation, until the whole world will be a witness to your courageous blows which have dealt successive political defeats to the Zionist machine of oppression and the fascist executioners in Tel Aviv; when our children are falling in ʿAnabta, Tulkarm, Khan Yunis and Rafah in battles of honor, heroism, and sacrifice, from the gunfire of the usurping Zionists—our National Council is planning to hold its 19th extraordinary meeting, dedicated to the martyrs of the

uprising and the exemplary martyr, Abu Jihad, in "the land of a million martyrs," with the aim of transforming the achievements of our brave and escalating uprising into political accomplishments on the road to freedom, independence, and national liberation and to formulate a clear and realistic political plan which will protect the blood of our martyrs, the torments of our wounded, and the torture of our prisoners in the enemy's jails.

O our heroic masses,

UNC vows to you and to the leaders of our revolution, foremost among them the father and symbol, Abu ʿAmmar, and asks you to continue the popular uprising until the realization of all our inalienable national goals, above all the right of return, self-determination, and establishment of an independent state with Arab Jerusalem as its eternal capital.

Our people's triumphant uprising, which is continuing with a glory unparalleled in the annals of human civilization, is achieving victory after victory every day as it leaves our enemy and all his instruments of oppression frustrated and bewildered. This, after our masses succeeded in implementing their sacred slogan:

—There will be no going back, there will be no retreat and no acquiescence, no matter what the price, despite the processions of martyrs who fall each day on the altar of national independence. The pure blood of our martyrs and their souls that hover in the skies of our beloved homeland, Palestine, will crown the meeting of our National Council with laurel wreaths and symbols of the revolution and the uprising that will continue until victory, God willing.

O our fighting masses,

UNC, the strike force of the PLO, the sole legitimate representative of our people wherever they may be, greets in your name the leaders of our revolution who are taking part in the martyrs' session, the session of national independence, and calls on them to formulate a clear and decisive political plan which will guarantee our people's permanent and inalienable rights, a plan that will conform with the demands of the current stage and will enable action to be taken together with the international community on the basis of our people's fidelity to the establishment of peace in the region, grounded in justice and an honorable solution of our problem.

UNC stresses to the Israeli street that our blessed uprising, launched by our people on December 9, 1987, did not aspire to shed the blood of Palestinians or Jews, but was a revolution against the dispossession, oppression, and fascism of the occupation, and [a manifestation of] national determination to establish a just peace in our region, [a peace] which will emerge only with the establishment of our Palestinian state on our national soil.

Concurrent with our request that our National Council adopt realistic resolutions and plans in order to support our people, put an end to the occupation, and establish our independent state, we are also taking advantage of this opportunity to underscore the recent appeal made by the PLO/UNC to the Israeli street, calling on Arab and Israeli voters to vote for peace forces that support our people's right to self-determination and [the right] to establish an independent state on our national soil.

O our people, O all our people,

UNC greets the U.N. General Assembly, which will meet in extraordinary session to discuss our people's uprising, support our just cause and affirm the Palestinian people's right to self-determination and its right to establish an independent state on the soil of its homeland.

UNC urges the members of the General Assembly to expedite the placing of the occupied lands under international supervision and to protect our defenseless masses against the campaigns of assault, oppression, and deportation being perpetrated by the occupation forces against our people. UNC hopes that the distinguished General Assembly will convene not only in order to condemn the enemy's arbitrary actions but will also act wisely in order to put an end to the violations of Palestinian human rights and to protect both [the Palestinian people's] present and future, so that it can play its part within the framework of human civilization, and place itself at the service of the just causes in the world.

UNC calls on the Security Council, the international community and all freedom- and peace-loving countries to condemn the barbaric bombings that the Zionist enemy's aircraft are carrying out against the [refugee] camps of our people in Lebanon. These acts of gradual annihilation against our people in Lebanon coincide with the acts of violence, the physical liquidation, and the collective arrests which the occupation forces are perpetrating against our valiant people in the occupied lands, since the Zionist occupation forces are trying to escalate the situation on the eve of the elections in Israel in order to win Jewish votes. We call on the General Assembly to bring pressure to bear on the occupation forces to reopen the institutions of higher education and to struggle against Zionist policy which seeks to inculcate ignorance in our people.

UNC condemns the dubious moves by a number of elements in the Lebanese arena who try from time to time to eliminate the Palestinian presence [in Lebanon] in order to assist their masters in the

Pentagon and in Tel Aviv. We urge that all national efforts on the soil of Lebanon be united in order to resist the Zionist occupation and to counter the arrogant actions being committed against our people, against the heroic Lebanese people, and against the national forces who support and are allied with the PLO, our people's sole legitimate representative.

O our heroic masses,

[UNC] greets the U.N. General Assembly, which will meet in extraordinary session to discuss the uprising on Palestine Day, the [anniversary of the] day on which the Palestinian leader, Abu ʿAmmar, the symbol, appeared before the U.N. for the first time in [19]74 and delivered the historic Palestine address from the rostrum of this General Assembly, which encompasses all the countries of the world, as he, the leader of our struggle, held up in one hand the olive branch, the symbol of peace, and in the other the gun, symbol of the struggle. Inspired by [that] speech, our people in the occupied land bears the olive branch in one hand and the sacred stone in the other.

These days mark the anniversary of the day on which the PLO was granted observer status at the U.N. This, despite the attempts of American imperialism, which tried to subvert this recognition and thus diminish its importance.

UNC calls on our people, the shock squads, and the popular committees to escalate the daily demonstrations and stone-throwing against the occupation forces.

O our heroic people, UNC reminds you of the following points:

1. We stress the importance of adhering stringently to the general-strike days declared by UNC in its official announcements and demand their implementation by these groups.

2. UNC reminds you that the partial [commercial] strike [hours] are from 8:00 A.M. until 12:00 noon.

3. UNC calls for an end to all differences of opinion liable to have an adverse effect on our blessed struggle.

4. We stress the unity of purpose and the common destiny of all sectors of our people and its national factions regarding the establishment of an independent state and the right to self-determination, and we urge unity of ranks and that all [our people's] potential be directed toward crushing the occupation.

5. We emphasize the importance of popular education and the need to intensify it and invest the national efforts required to ensure the success of this idea, this in the light of the closure of the educational institutions by the occupation authorities.

6. We must ensure that the schools in Jerusalem and Gaza remain open and not hand the occupation authorities additional pretexts to close them again.

7. We urge the popular committees and shock squads to organize voluntary activity and to join the assistance groups which are helping our farmers with the olive harvest in all regions.

8. UNC [re-]emphasizes everything that was contained in its previous communiqués and the importance of consistently boycotting the offices of the occupation to the degree possible and carrying out the directives of the local commands affiliated with the UNC in this regard.

O masses of the hallowed uprising,

UNC calls on you to implement the struggle missions and actions in the following manner:

—Let Tuesday, November 1, be a general-strike day as the Israeli voter decides between war and peace.

—Wednesday, November 2, a general strike commemorating the accursed Balfour Declaration in the wake of which the Palestinian people was ignored, a total disregard of a people possessing a distinctive identity and of its national right to establish its state. [Simultaneously,] the assumption was refuted that it is a minority with only a few civil and religious rights.

—Saturday, Sunday, and Monday, November 11, 12, and 13, days of escalation to mark the convening of your National Council, the supreme legal body of our Palestinian people, which is engaged in a holy war. On these days, the shock squads and the popular committees will act to escalate the protests and confront the occupation forces wherever they may be on our occupied soil.

—Tuesday, November 15—Independence Day. All our people will take to the streets to celebrate the publication of the Palestinian Declaration of Independence. Streets, houses, and trees will be decorated with Palestinian flags and national slogans, and joy and festivity shall reign everywhere. Independence Day will be peace day.

—Saturday, November 19, the day of the martyr al-Qassam, a day of general strike to commemorate the martyr, Sheykh ʿIzz al-Din al-Qassam and his brothers, who brandished the rifle against the British enemy in the hills of Yaʿbed and Jenin and declared an armed insurrection against tyranny.

Every Friday and Sunday after prayers will be days of confrontation, demonstration, protest marches, and visits to martyrs' graves.

Let the popular uprising be as a fire burning beneath the enemy's feet.

Glory and eternal life to the triumphant martyrs of the uprising.
Insurrection until our people achieves freedom and independence.
We will surely triumph.

The United National Command of the Uprising
UNC / PLO
October 30, 1988

LEAFLET NO. 29

In the name of Allah the merciful and compassionate

Communiqué—communiqué—communiqué

*No voice will overcome the voice of the uprising
No voice will overcome the voice of the Palestinian people—
the people of the PLO*

Communiqué No. 29

Issued by the Palestine Liberation Organization/
The United National Command of the Uprising

The Joy of the Independent Palestinian State Proclamation

O our masses,

Rejoice in your happiness, for it is your happiness and you are the bridegrooms. You are the joy of the independent state and the state is your joy. Delight in the resolutions of the magnificent uprising session [of the Palestinian National Council]. Delight in the declaration of the independent Palestinian state.

Let the mother of the martyr rejoice, she has lifted her voice twice: first on the day of her son's death, and again on the day of the declaration of the state. Let the wounded rejoice who smiled and forgot their agonies after hearing the declaration of the state. Let the prisoners behind bars rejoice, for now, after the declaration of the state, there is no force that can withstand their determination.

Let women, men, children, and the elderly rejoice. Your stones express the will of our sole legitimate representative, as your struggle always did. Through the declaration of an independent state as a step toward practical independence, your furious stones frighten your enemies throughout the world, heighten their isolation and their fear in the face of the fighters' achievement, and delight the friends [who hear via] news agencies the official announcements of [international] recognition of your rights.

O people of the uprising,

In the name of all of you, the United National Command of the Uprising sends congratulations and great esteem to the Palestinian National Council [PNC] and the Executive Committee of the PLO, our sole legitimate representative, for the responsible attitude they have evinced toward our heroic uprising, and their success in translating it—by endorsing the Declaration of Independence—into a document proclaiming an independent Palestinian state and the document of a clear political program. [These documents] express our people's national need to take advantage of this historic opportunity, generated by the uprising, to obtain its right of return, self-determination, and establishment of its independent national state. In this way we will place a new weapon in the hands of your escalating uprising and triumphant revolution.

The resolutions adopted as a result of your glorious uprising, and the need to continue and strengthen it and lend it fresh momentum, expressed the strength of our steadfast national unity internally and externally. Thus our leadership demonstrated responsibility at the moment of turning point and decision wrought by the masses of the uprising and the ongoing Palestinian struggle.

The declaration of an independent Palestinian state underscores the Palestinian identity of our occupied land and the Palestinian people's sovereignty over that land. It affirms that the goal of national independence is an irrevocable goal, whatever the difficulties and whatever the sacrifices entailed. It blocks the way to all the dubious options which were proposed by forces hostile to our people in an effort to liquidate our national cause. It affirms adherence to a different option for which there is no substitute—the Palestinian option. The session of the uprising, the session of the martyr and symbol, Abu Jihad, emphasized the convening of an effective international conference under U.N. auspices with the participation of the five permanent members of the Security Council and all parties to the conflict, [including] the PLO, our sole legitimate representative, on an equal footing with the other parties, on the basis of [Security Council] Resolutions 242 and 338, with the right of self-determination for our Palestinian people. This emphasis proves how sincerely devoted our people is in its aspiration to establish a just and comprehensive peace, this against the background of detente in the international arena and the tendency to resolve regional conflicts on a basis of international legitimacy.

This is not a gratuitous concession as some have described it, but a realistic, revolutionary, and responsible manifestation which has put an end to the Zionist lies regarding our glorious revolution. Likewise, it puts an end to the suffering of our masses both inside and outside, since our future state is a state for all our people.

O our citizens,

The United National Command appeals to a number of fundamentalist elements to prefer the general national interest, our people's national interest, over their basic assumptions and factional interests, and to cease presenting negative stands and manifestations. For they serve the enemy, whether they wish to or not. They must draw the conclusions from the mass celebrations of the struggle marking the declaration of the state, reflecting the deep roots of our legitimate leadership and sole representative, the Palestine Liberation Organization. It is still not too late to fuse all the loyal forces in the melting pot of the uprising and its United National Command.

The PLO/UNC calls on all the Arab states to support their words with actions and to transform the declaration of the state into a practical reality so that their potentialities and resources can be exploited. In this way pressure will be brought to bear on the United States and the Western states to hold an international conference and realize our people's permanent national rights in the spirit of the 19th session of the Palestinian National Council. [UNC] believes that the basic criterion for Arab solidarity is the realization of this noble goal, which serves not only the interest of our people but that of all Arab peoples.

O our masses,

UNC stresses the following:

1. A pledge of allegiance of all sectors of our Palestinian people in the occupied Palestinian state to the Declaration of Independence and the other resolutions of the 19th session of the National Council. In this connection, UNC calls on the shock squads to step up their confrontations with the occupation authorities on the basis of the continuation and escalation of the revolution in order to realize independence.

2. Condemnation of all suspicious leaflets, especially those that vilify people and accuse them of embezzlement. We must denounce all leaflets that slander any national faction and are liable to cause a rift in the

national unity of ranks. UNC warns collaborators against making threats directed at those who raise their voice in support of the resolutions adopted by the PNC. Everyone is urged to lift the Palestinian voice to the heights so it will be heard throughout the world. The continuation of celebrations of support for the [PNC] and its resolutions is the [appropriate] response to all the collaborators who are trying to threaten a number of national personalities via anonymous telephone calls. UNC warns against this.

3. As stated in previous leaflets, the popular committees [should be] supported [so that they can] improve their work and persist in it to assist national industry, ensure workers' rights, and find additional places of employment for [workers].

4. Establishment of cooperatives to market agricultural produce in order to help the Palestinian farmer stand firm in the face of the occupation authorities' pressures and restrictions.

5. Continuation of the struggle in all forms for the opening of the educational institutions, the continuation of popular education, and for resistance to the policy of inculcating ingorance which the occupation authorities are conducting against our sons.

6. In the light of the resolutions of the 19th [PNC] session, UNC welcomes the statement by the national institutions and the trade unions which was published on November 15, Independence Day, declaring the unions, associations, and societies independent Palestinian institutions. It calls on all institutions and all Palestinian sectors to start laying the foundation stone for the new building, the building of the struggle to realize independence.

O our heroic masses,

UNC urges you to go on marking Palestinian happiness through various means and manifestations of struggle and announces the following:

1. November 21, 1988—A day of visits to the wounded of the uprising and families of detainees and martyrs.

2. November 22—A day of escalating the struggle on which marches will be organized and blows delivered to collaborators with the occupation [authorities], and pressure brought to bear on the appointed municipal councils to resign.

3. November 23—A general-strike day in solidarity with the deportees, and a demand to rescind the arbitrary deportation orders.

4. November 24—A day of political information activity to explain the contents of the independence document and the ramifications of the resolutions adopted by the uprising session.

5. November 25–27—Days of confrontation and general escalation against the occupation and its collaborators.

6. November 28—A day of general strike in solidarity with the detainees in the occupation prisons and a demand for their immediate release.

7. November 29—A day of solidarity with the Palestinian people: a day of cohesion between the stone and the olive branch held up by the brother commander, Abu ʿAmmar, who will address the U.N. General Assembly regarding the independent state; a day of escalation and confrontations on which flags will be hoisted everywhere—flags of our independent Palestinian state.

8. November 30–December 4—Days of escalation to show support for our forthcoming state and the PLO's stand at the U.N.

November 30 is also declared a day of mutual social solidarity, on which the popular committees will organize operations to supply food and winter clothing and other necessities to injured families.

9. December 6—A general strike in solidarity with the detainees in Ansar 3.

Let us intensify our devotion, let us enhance our unity! Step up the Molotov cocktails and the sacred stones against the brutal enemy and his henchmen! We shall pursue the struggle on the road of the martyr and symbol Abu Jihad and all our righteous martyrs!

Revolution until victory.

PLO/UNC
November 20, 1988
The 12th month of our people's hallowed uprising

… ..

LEAFLET NO. 30

Communiqué—communiqué—communiqué

*No voice will overcome the voice of the uprising
No voice will overcome the voice of the Palestinian people—
the people of the PLO*

Communiqué No. 30

Issued by the Palestine Liberation Organization/
The United National Command of the Uprising

The Uprising Proclamation

O our masses in our precious homeland,

Your magnificent and hallowed uprising is entering its second year as it achieves victory after victory on the road of liberation and independence and continues with firm steps toward the realization of our legitimate national hopes and our firm and unshakable national rights. As this uprising, launched by the arms of the heroes and the processions of martyrs and the sufferings of our noble people, enters its second year, it is stronger and more acute in suffering, in steadfastness, and in the struggle against the methods of Zionist suppression aimed at liquidating your hallowed uprising. Our masses who have embarked on the road of liberty, glory, and honor will continue on the path to realize their legitimate right and sovereignty over the soil of our independent state, Palestine. On this precious occasion, we send greetings of esteem and honor in memory of our valiant martyrs who fell during the magnificent uprising. We send greetings to those who were wounded by the occupation [forces], and salutations of glory and pride to the processions of prisoners and detainees in the Zionists' prisons. By their [lengthy] struggle they imbue us with a constructive revolutionary spirit to escalate the blessed uprising and ignite the fire of confrontation with the Zionist occupiers, to enable us to declare to the world that the Palestinian people, which launched its uprising a year ago, will not backtrack under any circumstances from its courageous national decision to continue on the road of struggle, self-sacrifice, and martyrdom until the attainment of our firm national rights, including the right of return, self-determination, and establishment of an independent state with holy Jerusalem as its capital.

O our fighting masses,

The voice of the blessed Palestinian uprising has reverberated for a full year throughout the world and has made clear to all forums, currents, and political parties, all friendly and hostile governments, that the Palestinian people is alive and fighting, [is a people] that resists occupation and submission, rejects humiliation and destitution. Therefore, our people endured bitter torments and pains, but on each occasion it bound its wounds with human pride and heightened its responsiveness with each drop of blood of a martyr or a wounded [fighter], the groans and cries of bereaved widows. The unbroken continuity of heroic exploits performed by our generous masses, in defiance of the occupier's strength, tyranny, and wickedness, was a beacon that placed our Palestinian cause at the head of international, Arab, and local interest. The Palestinian issue has become a talking point in every diplomatic and political meeting and discussion in every corner of the world. At the same time, the abhorred occupation has experienced division and political and social schism due to the continuation and escalation of the uprising.

O masses of Palestine, O masses of the independent state! By your strength of will and your noble revolutionary adamance, you succeeded, together with your legitimate representative, the PLO, in striding with agile steps of struggle toward the declaration of Palestinian independence, the dream of every Palestinian and free person on earth, through the notable political success of the uprising session [of the Palestinian National Council] on the soil of Algeria, the session that acceded to the Palestinian call and dream to enable the active national "totality" to converge in the Palestinian arena under the banner of the PLO and its legal institutions and under its constructive national plan, which expresses the wishes of every Palestinian who loves Palestine. Thus, sons of our people, there came about the series of impressive achievements of the uprising from its inception until the proclamation of independence. National sovereignty on the soil of the Palestinian state will inevitably result from the continuation and escalation of the uprising, with stones, Molotov cocktails, knives, and through our powerful national unity and cohesion, and by establishing more and more popular committees together with diverse national actions that are added to the melting pot of the national struggle. We stress that UNC is one and indivisible and that there are no rifts, as hostile information organs have tried to picture it; there was merely a technical hitch. Despite the substantive understanding [reached] regarding every UNC leaflet, the Popular Front, which rejected [U.N. Resolution] 242 as a political stand, believes deeply in national unity and obeys PLO bodies and institutions, including the United National Command.

O magnificent Palestinian masses,

The hated Zionist enemy is pursuing his policy of terrorism against our people by means of raids on villages, towns, and camps. He is pursuing the policy of inculcating ingorance in our pupils in schools, institutes, colleges, and universities. The surrender of the occupation authorities who opened schools under pressure exerted by our Palestinian public is a major achievement which we must preserve. [We must] continue bringing more and more pressure to bear in order to force the authorities to open the institutes and the Palestinian universities. We call on the Council for Higher Education to draw up a Palestinian curriculum, adapting it to the sons of our independent Palestinian state. The persistence of the [Israeli] occupation policy and the use of incendiary materials to repulse demonstrators will not discourage the heroes of the stone and the Molotov cocktail from continuing on the road of the uprising, the road of national independence. Despite the policy of constriction, economic strangulation, and media siege, we call on our valiant masses to go on confronting the occupation authorities and to resist them relentlessly by continuing and expanding the boycott of Israeli products in the realms of agriculture, industry, and food. This requires our masses not to purchase any Israeli goods or merchandise for which a local substitute is available. We also call on the merchants' committees in all locales to boycott Israeli products and not store them in warehouses or [display them] in shops. We demand that the popular committees in all areas conduct an information and national persuasion campaign regarding the boycott of everything Israeli. We call on our workers to boycott work in citrus factories and farms inside Israel, in order to wreak economic damage on Israeli products that compete with our national products.

We urge the masses of our Palestinian people to exercise vigilance and caution in the face of the Israeli intelligence apparatus and its treacherous henchmen, who disseminate false and suspicious leaflets in the name of UNC and the various regional committees. We also call on the shock squads to struggle against the traitors in order to deter them and compel them to change their ways and to struggle against those who write false slogans and attack mosques and houses of loyalists.

We call on the masses to persist in the struggle with a single and united fist against all the Israeli attempts to break into towns, villages, and camps. Everyone must take part in the struggle against these Zionists. We urge the shock squads and our people to be very careful not to fall into the hands of the occupation forces, and [we urge] the guard committees and shock squads to protect the active human element of the uprising.

The United National Command as the fighting arm of the PLO, the sole legitimate representative of our Palestinian people, stresses its adherence to the struggle plan that has been outlined continuously in the leaflets issued since the start of the uprising and reaffirms the pledge of allegiance, the promise and the vow to continue escalating the uprising on the ground and politically until victory.

The political sphere:

UNC renews its vow to the leader of our people and its struggle, the PLO, in adherence to and support of the resolutions [adopted by] the Palestinian National Council in its uprising session, especially the declaration of Palestinian independence and the realization of national unity, pledging to our people not to swerve from this. UNC appeals urgently to all the leaders at the Reagan-Gorbachev-Bush summit to assume their historical and cultural responsibility and [to] support Palestinian national rights, based on international legitimacy, which the Palestinian National Council declared it was accepting as the PLO's part in the attainment of peace and security throughout the world and in the Middle East.

The United National Command expresses its great esteem for the stands of those states that support our just cause and opposed and condemned the U.S. stand, which is hostile to the Palestinian voice, and especially Shultz's arrogant denial of an entry visa to New York to the Brother Commander Abu ʿAmmar to deliver a Palestinian peace address at the U.N. We regard this American stand as an escalation of American hostility toward Palestinian rights and the Palestinian people. We call on all Arab states to reassess their relations and ties with the U.S. We also call on the European states, governments, and peoples to recognize the independent Palestinian state and take a clear stand vis-à-vis Israeli obduracy.

UNC salutes with honor and appreciation the martyrs of the uprising—and their families—whose pure blood has watered the dust of the homeland and enabled the growth of the green plant and the Palestinian olive branch, symbol of peace and justice. At these moments, remembering all our martyrs and the martyr-symbol, Abu Jihad, we say to them: the pledge is a pledge and the vow is a vow, and we shall continue on the road of martyrdom (*shahada*) until the Palestinian flag shall fly above our sacred capital.

O our valiant masses,

As our blessed uprising enters its second year, we call on you to continue your struggle and your boundless responsiveness [in the campaign] against the occupation by strengthening the rule of the people over the soil of Palestine, as a mainstay of our independent state, and as effective steps toward the concrete sovereignty of our Palestinian state. To achieve this, we must devote all our strength to forming more popular committees, expanding their activity, activating strike committees and units, and selecting for them targets that will be more painful to the occupation. We call on our masses to pursue steps aimed at weakening the occupation regime [which operates through] the Civil Administration, taxes, licensing bureaus, and so forth, [and we assert] the need for broad popular participation in the various struggle operations via the melting pot of resilient national unity.

O our masses, we call on you to carry out the following actions:

1. December 6—A day of general strike in solidarity with our brothers and comrades who are incarcerated in the prisons of the Zionist oppression, and especially in Ansar 3, whose heroes are undergoing the torments of hunger [since] the first of the current month.

2. December 8–9—A general strike marking the first anniversary of our people's magnificent uprising.

3. December 11—A special day of escalation to mark the founding of the Popular Front for the Liberation of Palestine. The United Command greets the comrades in the Popular Front.

4. December 14—A day of popular education and activation of the popular-education committees to mark Palestinian Teachers Day. On this occasion, we call on our pupils and teachers to abide by the teaching hours, except on general-strike days, and to continue with popular education.

5. December 18—Jerusalem Day, a day of popular escalation marking the revolution of the masses in our capital and their concrete participation in the defense of their city.

6. December 21—A general-strike day. We greet our Palestinian people inside the Green Line and call on them to declare a strike day for a comprehensive Palestinian peace, marking the anniversary of the strike that was called last year, in order to unite our Palestinian people everywhere.

7. December 22—A day of solidarity with the Palestinian detainees, marking the opening of the al-Dahariya prison. We call on our masses to express their protest and to raise their voice against the methods of Zionist coercion in the fascist prisons.

8. December 24—A day for ringing church bells and calling out *Allah akbar* in the minarets of the mosques, marking the birth of the messenger of peace, the Lord Messiah. We extend felicitations to our Palestinian Christian brothers and urge them to make do with observing the religious rituals.

More struggle until the achievement of victory.

We will surely triumph.

The Palestine Liberation Organization
The United National Command of the Uprising
December 6, 1988

LEAFLET NO. 36

In the name of Allah the merciful and compassionate

Communiqué—communiqué—communiqué

*No voice will overcome the voice of the uprising
No voice will overcome the voice of the Palestinian people—
the people of the PLO*

Communiqué No. 36

Issued by the Palestine Liberation Organization/
The United National Command of the Uprising

The Karameh Proclamation

O masses of our heroic Palestinian people, heroes of honor (*karameh*) on Karameh Day. You whose steadfastness and lengthy struggle have made you a paragon of self-sacrifice and of the noblest sacrifice; you who with your stones, the weapon of freedom and independence, have forged a legend; you who have made your stones into an ideological school of revolutionary struggle; you who with your blood have written the history of a new concept of national liberation.

Today is the anniversary of the Battle of Karameh: marking the armed uprising of the Palestinian giant, marking Palestinian-Jordanian national unity, marking the restoration of dignity to the Arab individual, marking the Palestinian challenge to the Zionists' war machines. This anniversary falls as our glorious uprising intensifies from day to day and underscores the certainty of victory and the establishment of our independent Palestinian state on the soil of Palestine. [This], by deepening the rule of the people, popularizing the uprising and unified activity in the melting pot of the struggle, as the pillar of the Palestinian national movement and as its stable backbone in the struggle and the confrontation [against Israel]. Therefore, the United National Command expresses great esteem for the steps toward unification [taken] within the [workers'] unions, the institutions, and the associations, and reaffirms that the unification drive is considered the spearhead and a bone in the throat of the occupation.

UNC, basing itself on the momentum of the struggle and on the Palestinians' political and diplomatic momentum, salutes the stand of the Peace Now movement and of the forces of progress and democracy in Israel for their latest campaign, expressed in calls for peace and slogans demanding an end to the occupation. On the other hand, our Palestinian masses denounce the stand of Shamir and the members of his government, who oppose our people's rights and are fighting against the voices that are calling for peace and are demanding an end to the occupation. Likewise, [UNC] stresses the continuation of the uprising and its unrelenting escalation—accepting every form of solidarity with our people's uprising— and urges the heightening of the struggle for our people's rights. From this point of departure, UNC asks the Israeli street to respond to the Palestinian calls for peace which truly and sincerely express the hopes and expectations of our Palestinian people for the return [to Palestine], for self-determination, and for the establishment of our independent Palestinian state on the national soil, under the leadership of our sole legitimate representative, the Palestine Liberation Organization.

At a time when the tremendous Palestinian uprising has generated broad changes on all planes—Palestinian, Israeli, Arab, and international— the American administration continues its efforts to employ [methods of] political blackmail, by means of one-sided propaganda about the meaning of terrorism and not distinguishing between [terrorism] and a legitimate resistance struggle in accordance with the international treaties and agreements of Geneva, which affirm our people's right to adopt all forms of struggle. At the same time, UNC and our masses reject and condemn the American stand which is hostile to our people's rights and defends the Zionist terror and its barbarous acts of suppression. These take the form of the murder of individuals and premeditated murder, the wounding of thousands, the demolition of houses, deportation, [and] the incarceration of thousands of our fighters in prisons and detention camps that resemble those of the Nazis. UNC and our Palestinian masses demand that the American administration take courageous steps toward a serious and constructive dialogue with the PLO, and not pursue a method of deceit, blackmail, and vacillation. Likewise, it demands that the European Community play a special role in resolving international conflicts and the problem of the Palestinian Arab people, that it recognize an independent Palestinian state, and that it stress to the international community the need to give international protection to our people, which is suffering under the ugliest forms of suppression and the daily persecution being conducted against it. As regards the Palestinian-Israeli-foreigners dialogue and encounters, whether held inside or outside [the territories], UNC believes that all these political dialogues and meetings must be based on the principle of talks with the PLO, as the sole legitimate representative of our people everywhere, and affirm our people's right to the return, to self-determination, and to the establishment of an independent state on the national soil, while observing fully the resolutions [adopted] by the [Palestinian] National Councils.

UNC stresses that the various forms of Arab cooperation must be based on hostility toward imperialism and Zionism, while firmly rejecting all the solutions and plans that contradict our Palestinian people's aspiration to the return, to self-determination, and to the establishment of the independent state on the national soil, under the leadership of the PLO, the Palestinian people's sole legitimate representative.

We are now in the 16th month of our magnificent uprising. As we mark, in these days, the 21st anniversary of the battle of heroism, self-sacrifice, honor, and giving, the Battle of Karameh, UNC stresses the following:

1. UNC expresses widespread esteem for the struggle of our Palestinian masses, who have inflicted a defeat on the regular army of the [Israeli] occupation, causing its government much anxiety and [leading to] their replacement by the Border Police. Let Yitzhak Rabin know that the masses of the uprising affirm their determination to confront the Border Police with greater violence. They will inflict a defeat on them, and their fate will be no better than that of the regular army.

2. UNC praises and greatly esteems the heroic stand of the inhabitants of Nablus and Gaza, their sacrifices and their heroic resistance to the occupation forces. Intensify your confrontation and your response. O inhabitants of Jabal al-Nar [Nablus], together on the road to freedom

and victory. O our inhabitants in the occupied homeland, step up your struggle and confrontation in order to relieve the pressure on our inhabitants in other locales.

3. UNC stresses that the fall of one of our fighters in the West Bank or the Gaza Strip, and the escalation and the violent clashes with the occupation forces and the settlers' units [that follow in their wake], constitute the giving of true honor to the martyr's spirit. This, in addition to the national activity [and the activity of] the popular committees and the shock squads that will utilize all forms of escalation, such as marches and symbolic funeral processions, without resorting to a general strike.

4. UNC urges those who are still hesitating to resign from the departments of the Civil Administration—and who were called upon to do so by the United National Command in earlier leaflets—to resign immediately, and it views this as a final call, otherwise the shock squads will see to the implementation of this call, and with force.

5. The United National Command views with gravity the cruel behavior [toward] and the inhuman conditions endured by our Palestinian fighters in the detention camps, especially Ansar 3 [in the Negev]. Therefore, it demands that international bodies and organizations intervene, in order to close the detention camps. UNC condemns the campaign of killings of our people's fighters, warns against the continuation of the phenomenon, and stresses that for every murdered martyr, a soldier or a settler can fall.

6. UNC expresses appreciation for the boycott of Israeli products in the West Bank and the Gaza Strip and calls on the brother merchants and our masses in Gaza to intensify the boycott of these products. At the same time, UNC views with gravity the actions of a number of factories and merchants who are marketing Israeli goods under Arab names. It also calls on our heroic merchants to get rid of Israeli goods by March 28, 1989. The inhabitants are not to purchase Israeli goods and are not to go to the Israeli territories to make such purchases.

7. UNC calls on our Palestinian people in Gaza not to affix to their private cars and their taxis stickers permitting their entry into the rest of the territories. Likewise, we call urgently for the resignation of the Arab department heads in the [Israeli] Civil Administration, such as those in the traffic, tax, and customs departments in the Gaza Strip.

8. UNC calls on the authorized chartered accountants not to prepare tax and customs reports, and calls on our masses not to pay fines and taxes, without exception, showing stubborn defiance and confrontation.

9. UNC presents to the teachers sector and our masses the need and necessity for popular and home-based education, and the need to organize committees for popular education among the teachers and students in every neighborhood, village, and [refugee] camp. We view with gravity the closure of educational institutions by the occupation authorities, and we demand that the international bodies, headed by UNESCO, intervene in order to denounce the acts of the occupation [which are designed] to inculcate ignorance in our people. We also call urgently on our academic institutions in the occupied homeland to compensate our students by setting aside financial matters and admitting as many new students as possible.

10. UNC presents the need to solve the labor disputes on a national basis and calls for national mediation committees to be established in this matter.

11. UNC urges our masses to eliminate the phenomena of the peddlers' stalls in the streets and of the wandering money changers and demands their total abolition. An extension is given until March 28, 1989, for the elimination of such phenomena. Likewise, [UNC] calls on our masses to observe strictly the days of general strike and for a stop to the anarchy on the part of the taxis and the private vehicles.

12. The United Command views with gravity the activity of a number of foreign and local elements who are encouraging emigration from the occupied homeland because of the economic pressure which the occupation is wielding against our inhabitants and our people in the occupied homeland. We call on our masses to boycott these suspicious attempts, and we warn these elements firmly against continuing their activity. Let them know that UNC has lists of names in this regard. On the other hand, holding on to the land is a sacred national duty and is one of the foundations of the independent Palestinian state.

The United National Command, the political arm of the PLO, as it continues on the road of the long and difficult struggle to eradicate the occupation and establish our independent state, calls on the masses of the magnificent uprising to carry out the following struggle actions:

*Friday, March 17, the anniversary of the opening of the Nazi Negev camp [Ansar 3], will be a day of going to the offices of the International Red Cross and the [other] international institutions in order to hold sit-down strikes and marches against the continued existence of the detention camps and to demand their total closure. We also call on the progressive Palestinian and Israeli lawyers to work relentlessly to denounce the actions of the occupation [authorities] against our fighters in the detention camps and the Israeli prisons.

★Saturday, March 18, will be a day of confrontation and defiance to protest the actions of the military occupation authorities against our inhabitants in Nablus, in the [refugee] camps, and in the Gaza Strip. On this day the shock squads will carry out their operations with all the means at their disposal. Together, our revolutionaries on the road to the towering victory!

★Tuesday, March 21, will be a day of a protest general strike, marking the anniversary of the decision of the U.S. Congress to close the PLO office in Washington. Protest and condemnation cables and messages should be sent to the American administration abroad [and to its legations] in the occupied homeland.

★Wednesday, March 22, is declared a day of tremendous popular anger and rage, marking al-Karameh. This day shall be a beacon and a torch, serving as an example of the drenching of honor (*karameh*) in pure blood on the soil of our dear homeland.

★Thursday, March 23, is designated a special day for popular and home-based education. UNC urges all the educational institutions, university administrations, the Council for Higher Education, and the teachers and students, to work together for the success of popular education.

★Friday and Sunday, March 24 and March 26, will be days of prayer in the mosques and churches for the repose of the souls of the martyrs of the popular uprising and the martyrs of our Palestinian revolution, and these days shall be filled with marches.

★Monday, March 27, will be a day of a general strike in order to turn to the land, to work, till, and prepare it for planting, and to work for the development of home-based manufacturing enterprises and the establishment of agricultural cooperatives among the inhabitants in the neighborhoods.

★Tuesday, March 28, a special day for settling accounts with those who distribute Israeli merchandise and with the phenomena of the peddlers stalls and the wandering money changers. UNC hails all the arms of the shock squads that will act on this day to punish the distributors of these goods.

Long live our heroic uprising.
Long live the Palestinian Karameh Day.
Glory and victory to our masses.
Glory and eternity to our immaculate martyrs.

The Palestine Liberation Organization
The United National Command in the Occupied Homeland
State of Palestine
March 16, 1989

LEAFLET NO. 41

In the name of Allah the merciful and compassionate

Communiqué—communiqué—communiqué

*No voice will overcome the voice of the uprising
No voice will overcome the voice of the Palestinian people—
the people of the PLO*

Communiqué No. 41

Issued by the Palestine Liberation Organization/
The United National Command of the Uprising

The Defiance and Continuity Proclamation

O our masses, O our masses of steadfastness and the national struggle, determined to triumph.

After more than a year and a half since the outbreak of your heroic uprising, our national struggle is today witnessing a grave and critical juncture, since the enemy has turned to the idea of eradicating the uprising by political means, having become convinced of the failure of all his salient methods of oppression to quell it. Their imperialistic mentality [i.e., of the Israeli authorities] has engendered a horrific plan—even as compared with the notorious Camp David—bearing the name of Shamir and Rabin, which takes the form of the holding of local elections in order to elect a small representative body that will conduct bilateral negotiations with the enemy in order to establish autonomy. This [autonomy regime] will be of five years' duration and will be based on the continuation of the occupation and the oppression. The proposed plan is accompanied by a heightening of the official repression, the insane attacks by the settlers, an exacerbation of the belligerent declarations by Rabin and others, [this in order] to intensify the oppression in the event the plan does not get a positive response. They are spinning in a vacuum, as it were. If the methods of oppression have failed thus far to eradicate the uprising, how will they succeed in bringing about acceptance of a plan that is not serious and that is intended merely to halt the uprising and prettify the face of the Zionist entity in the eyes of the world? At this moment of the uprising, we face the mission of convincing the enemy, before the friend, that the Palestinian giant that has been liberated, will not return to the pre-December 9, 1987, situation, and that the fate of the Shamir scheme will be the dustbin of history, alongside the autonomy plot, the Reagan plan, the territorial compromise, the functional division, and others. At the start of the uprising, Rabin set himself the challenge of [seeing] who will get tired first, and now he admits that we are bearing all the torments tirelessly, whereas in them the weariness is clearly visible.

The Palestinian people has become acquainted with the way of the haven and will not return from it until its objectives are attained—the return [to Palestine], self-determination, and establishment of the independent state on the [occupied] soil, under the leadership of the PLO, the sole legitimate representative of our Palestinian people. [In this way] it stresses to the world and to the Arab masses that the way of liberation and victory is not the way of the regimes that suppress their people and bend before their enemy, but the way of steadfastness, struggle, and sacrifice, until the enemy desists from his aggression and lets us live in peace.

O our heroic people, the United National Command commends the Arab summit meeting, which dealt with the Palestinian problem and which placed the emphasis on the latest session of the [Palestinian] National Council and its resolutions pertaining to the national program. [UNC] calls on the Arab regimes to translate their resolutions into deeds, while undertaking to support the uprising, both morally and materially, and calls on the Arab masses to hold marches and demonstrations of support for the Palestinian uprising. At the same time, UNC [expresses] esteem to the Palestinian groups of the PLO, the Palestinian national liberation movement—Fatah, the Popular Front for the Liberation of Palestine, the Democratic Front for the Liberation of Palestine, the Arab Liberation Front, the Palestinian Communist party, the Palestine Liberation Front— for their unified stands. All of them are considered to represent the United Command of the Uprising. The resolutions adopted by the Arab summit regarding our cause do not contradict the Palestinian stand. But our people, groaning under the occupation, needs more than public verbal stands. The suffering we have endured for more than twenty years is a direct result of the deep-rooted Arab failure and impotence. Let them translate their decisions into deeds and utilize all their political and economic weight in order to pressure the United States, which is aiding our primary enemy, to cease its foot-dragging and its step-by-step methods, and to recognize our legitimate rights as a true opening toward peace and security in the region. The United States must know that every procrastination in raising its level of representation in the dialogue with the PLO, in taking it seriously and practically, and in recognizing our legitimate rights, will merely fan the flame of the uprising.

UNC calls on all persons of conscience and supporters of human rights in the world to visit the State of Palestine,[1] in order to see firsthand the terrible conditions in which our Palestinian people is living under the occupation and in order to pressure their governments and get them to recognize our legitimate rights of return [and] self-determination in an independent state on our soil like other peoples.

O our resolute masses, an insane escalation has occurred in attacks by the army and the herds of settlers who rampage through our cities and villages, thinking that this is how they will put an end to the heroic uprising. We have chosen the way of the triumphant uprising and we shall not deviate from it no matter how costly the sacrifices. The racist Zionist authorities are trying to combat our masses, members of the Palestinian working class, [by affecting] their livelihood. They are repeating the acts of the Nazis and the fascists by obligating the wearing of an identity tag, in order to differentiate between us and the Zionist laborers at places of work, and by their attempts to compel our workers and our people in the steadfast Gaza Strip, the strip of heroism and defiance, to accept a special identification card which enables its bearers to go to their places of work. Our masses have no other choice but to stand up to and clash with these racist measures by realizing worker and public solidarity in the struggle against the racist actions. Let all the forces of the people be unified and let all the loyal nationalist forces in the garrison of the uprising unite. Let the intensification and strengthening of the uprising continue [and thus it will attain] an ever higher level, as it continuously brandishes the slogan of martyrdom (*shahada*) or freedom and independence, victory or death.

1. Referring to the occupied territories.

O our steadfast masses, UNC greets our heroic masses in Gaza, Nahalin, Kifl Kharith, Tamun, Qalqilya and Sinjil, and elsewhere, for their firm stand in the face of the enemy's insane attacks, and stresses the following:

1. Our people's blood shall not be shed in vain, for every day we face cold-blooded slaughter. It is our legitimate right to defend ourselves, and our blood is no cheaper than their blood.[2]

2. UNC eulogizes with pride and esteem the martyred prisoner, the fighting Palestinian, our comrade ʿUmar al-Qassim, a member of the Central Committee of the Democratic Front, who was martyred after twenty-one years' imprisonment in which he did not bend. UNC imputes full responsibility for our comrade's death to the Zionist occupation forces, since they neglected his treatment and killed him in cold blood. [UNC] asserts that the crime of his killing will remain a perpetual stigma on Zionism.

3. Committees should be set up in every city for the protection of the captive [i.e., prisoner], and a day in the period covered by each leaflet should be devoted to holding press conferences and information assemblies in order to expose the depressing conditions in which our captives live in the Zionist detention camps and particularly in the liquidation camp, Ansar 3, where dozens are suffering from a situation of endangered health. [UNC] calls on all the humanitarian institutions throughout the world to act for their release in order to save their lives.

4. Diligent action should be taken to unite the popular committees into united committees in all the cities, villages, and neighborhoods, to entrench them, to stiffen their backbone, and to expand their ranks, so they will form the basis for the rule of the people in the independent State of Palestine. This should be regarded as a basic mission which cannot be ignored, in order to intensify the uprising. Additional shock squads should also be established, [for they are] the magnificent arm of the uprising and its weapon in withstanding the enemies of the people, soldiers, settlers, and infiltrated agents.

5. More blows should be brought down upon the collaborators, and a national settling of accounts with them should be undertaken. The focus [should be] on those against whom there is proof and a national consensus for their denunciation, and a distinction should be drawn between them as regards the level of punishment, according to the scale of their crimes against the people and the measure of their readiness for a true return from their evil ways.

2. "Their blood" refers to the Israelis.

6. The unity of the national ranks must be strictly maintained, while coping with the problems that are liable to crop up in the people's ranks within the framework of the national interest to continue the uprising and realize the unity of the Palestinian people wherever they may be. [UNC] calls on the members of the Palestinian people in the areas of 1948[3] to close ranks in support of the uprising and to act against racial discrimination.

7. UNC commends the establishment of the Supreme Students Council, and affirms it as the authority that decides on all student matters in the independent State of Palestine, and calls on all the academic institutions to cooperate with it.

8. UNC calls for an absolute boycott of work in the settlements and for the creation of committees of solidarity with the workers who respond to the boycott call and for providing them with the essential means of subsistence.

9. UNC stresses, in the economic realm, the supreme importance of building a local economy according to the principles of popular development through the establishment of productive cooperatives in agriculture and industry which do not require large capital and are based on improvement of the soil and an autarkic economy. It further stresses the strengthening of the boycott on Zionist industrial and agricultural products for which [local] substitutes exist and calls for the establishment of economic committees in order to examine the economic situation and to make proposals for projects with the potential to succeed.

10. UNC calls on all the owners of wells to lower the price of water, so that small farmers can continue to exist and develop their national agricultural produce.

11. UNC calls on the bakery owners not to turn the bakeries into grocery stores, and to undertake to sell only bread and biscuits.

12. UNC warns the price-gouging merchants and calls on the merchants committees and the popular committees to set a list of prices and to ensure that there are no deviations.

13. UNC calls on the Chartered Accountants Association in Gaza to dismiss those of its members who are continuing to submit tax reports to the Civil Administration and calls on all chartered accountants to avoid fulfilling this despicable role.

14. UNC urges the masses in Gaza not to spoil the agricultural produce, such as watermelons, etc., arriving from the Jordan Rift Valley to heroic Gaza.

3. Namely, the Israeli Arabs.

15. UNC calls on the judiciary not to comply with the military orders, issued by the occupation, numbered 1271 and 1274, relating to the law of property owners, renters, and court registration fees.

On the way to the escalation of the uprising and its intensification until the long-awaited victory, UNC calls on our masses to carry out the following actions:

Sunday, June 18—A general strike to demand that the U.S. administration convene an international conference possessing full authority, as an instrument capable of bringing about the establishment of peace in the region.

June 18, 20—Two days of escalating the struggle and a heightened war of knives and petrol bombs against the enemy soldiers and the herds of settlers.

Wednesday, June 21—A general strike in solidarity with our working population in the Gaza Strip and as a response to the measures of the fascist enemy against them.

June 21–27—Days of activity, struggle, and escalation of the struggle against the neofascists.

June 28—A day of activity, struggle, and condemnation of the annexation of Jerusalem, on which Palestinian flags will be flown in the capital of our independent state and throughout our beloved homeland.

Friday, June 30—A general strike to protest the attacks by the herds of settlers against our masses.

July 1—The day of the Palestinian heritage. Marches, heritage exhibitions, and bazaars will be held, with the emphasis on our people's devotion to its heritage and safeguarding it from attempts at forgery.

July 2–3—In the light of the policy of [inculcating] ignorance which the occupation authorities are conducting by closing our academic institutions, we stress the importance of denouncing the enemy's behavior by appealing to international institutions to exert pressure on the occupation authorities for the opening of the schools and universities to our pupils. On these days, struggle activities will be held, such as sit-in strikes and marches. At the same time, [UNC] calls on the private schools in Jerusalem not to dismiss teachers and to grant them all their rights.

We will surely triumph.

Long live the PLO, the sole legitimate representative of our Palestinian people wherever it may be, long live al-Quds [Jerusalem], capital of our State of Palestine.

The Palestine Liberation Organization
The United National Command in the Occupied Homeland
State of Palestine
June 13, 1989

LEAFLET NO. 45

In the name of Allah the merciful and compassionate

Communiqué—communiqué—communiqué

*No voice will overcome the voice of the uprising
No voice will overcome the voice of the Palestinian people—
the people of the PLO*

Communiqué No. 45

Issued by the Palestine Liberation Organization/
The United National Command of the Uprising

The September and the Shahada Proclamation

O our heroic masses, people of the *shahada* and the victory,

We greet you as you are inscribing your glory by means of your struggle and your sacrifices in order to attain your sacred rights of freedom and independence, for life with honor like other peoples. Greetings to the people of the martyrs and the heroism, who withstand Israeli oppression which increases from day to day. [This] oppression only heightens [the people's] determination to continue its legitimate struggle for the elimination of the occupation. A special greeting to our fighting workers and their families in valiant Gaza, who are showing steadfastness for the third week in the face of the oppression and the starvation. Greetings to our persecuted heroes in the wadis and in the hills, who are withstanding the treachery of the authorities [and the danger of] immediate execution at their fascist hands.

Our fighting masses, mothers and wives, children of the martyrs and the detainees, elderly and heroes, workers and merchants, forgers of the glory, the nobility, and the honor. UNC, which is fulfilled in each of you, in every prisoner, martyr, male and female fighter wherever they may be, in every youngster who has raised his arm to defend the honor of his homeland and his nation, in every worker and merchant who has taken part in the struggle plan of the uprising and has done his duty according to the imperative of his nobility—[UNC] affirms to you that the key to your strength is your unity, your mutual surety, your standing in one rank, in one line, in directing the fire of your struggle against a single enemy, the occupation, for a single goal, independence. If your unity is the key and the stable basis for the continuation of your struggle and its escalation, now it constitutes a target for the occupation authorities, who will not succeed, no matter how clever and diversified their satanic fascist methods, in quenching the fire of your surging uprising. The occupation authorities are trying to execute their mission by means of an extensive campaign, which includes rumors and "planted" leaflets, by exploiting and fanning clan and personal disputes and by sullying the reputation and honor of personages across the length and breadth of our occupied state. [This] in the hope that you will be consumed by frustration and will preoccupy yourselves with personal and local disputes and will deviate from your principal mission and your sacred goal; and then the uprising will begin to collapse from within, after Israel has failed to destroy it from outside.

O masses of our magnificent uprising: Try as he may, all the enemy's plans and technological methods, as promised by [Central Command Chief, Maj. Gen. Yitzhak] Mordechai, are bound to fail, with God's help. This, thanks to your unrelenting awareness and alertness in the face of [the enemy's] despicable attempts to sow discord and to split the ranks; thanks to aiming the fire of the surging uprising at the enemy; and thanks to the attacks on him everywhere, and the escalation of your struggle against the occupation, and the use of new methods which you invent in your militant revolt against its apparatus and through diligent work to entrench the unity of our people, and doing constructive action in establishing committees and united public institutions, including defensive guard committees to withstand the enemy's suppression attacks on our villages, and his repellent attempts to pursue those who are wanted and liquidate them on the spot, or arrest them. Therefore, let the September Proclamation be a call for unity and cohesiveness of ranks. The activity to establish united committees and an apparatus, and the struggle against the occupation with stones and slingshots, should head the many missions of your struggle, which have succeeded in inflicting defeat on the enemy's most technologically advanced means of suppression.

O our heroic masses,

Even as we stand on the brink of a new reality, imposed on the political map by your uprising and your sacrifices, namely, the reality of the declaration of the independent Palestinian state and the call for a just peace, we find that there has been a regression in the American stand in the dialogue meetings with the Palestinian leadership and greater extremism as regards embarking on the road to the peace process. This raises serious questions among our people as to the usefulness and purpose of this dialogue. We also find insane opposition to Palestine's co-optation as a member to U.N. institutions, and we condemn this. As we face these temporary obstacles, we are a people that believes that the continuation and escalation of the uprising is our people's sole option to attain freedom and independence.

The [UNC] leadership, relying on the PLO's long-term strategy, stresses the following:

1. Collaborators:

We reassert that the cadres of the shock squads and the popular committees must exercise discipline, for fear of anarchy, which is liable to afford the enemy the opportunity to exploit this phenomenon in the field and in the media. Therefore, act with moderation and be certain before hurling hasty accusations, and then approach the supreme ranks before executing sentence, or send warnings and threatening letters. Opportunity for repentance and for a mending [of ways] should also be given. Before meting out punishment, choose surveillance [of suspected collaborators].

2. Official contacts with Israelis:

UNC reiterates the need to boycott all political contacts with officials of the Israeli administration. UNC further stresses that the Israeli street is a legitimate and supplementary arena in the plan of the uprising and its implementation. Therefore, the guided information activity, sanctioned by the PLO, which seeks to expand the circle of those who support the justice of our struggle against the occupation and [those who] recognize our right to self-determination and the legitimacy of the PLO to represent our people, is a necessary activity and an integral part of our struggle to bolster the independence of our state which was declared in the resolutions of the Palestinian National Council in Algeria.

3. Studies:

The thrust for education is an integral part of our struggle. Therefore, UNC calls on all our pupils to be present during the school hours and to differentiate between this part of their struggle and their other missions, which can be carried out after school hours and outside the school yards. This, in order not to afford the enemy opportunities and pretexts to close the schools and carry out his policy of inculcating ignorance in our people. School strikes must take place only on officially declared general-strike days. Do not accede to spontaneous calls by certain persons for school strikes.

4. The united popular committees:

UNC calls for action to be taken urgently, with a united perception on a revolutionary democratic basis, for the integration of all the cadres of the battalions (*kata'ib*) and the companies (*fasa'il*) of the popular army into the united array of the shock squads in order to prevent the enemy, who exploits the disintegration and the schisms, from attaining his purposes. It also calls [on all the cadres] to desist completely from issuing any leaflets bearing various signatures which are not signed by UNC. This, in order to block the enemy's attempts to issue leaflets bearing forged signatures and intended to split the national ranks and sow confusion and mutual suspiciousness among the inhabitants.

5. Boycotting the enemy's apparatus and products:

UNC salutes the struggle of its members in Gaza against the magnetic cards [for entry into Israel]. It hails our people which has fought and sacrificed by boycotting the enemy's apparatus and offices, his taxes, and his products; and it renews the cry to our masses to press forward their struggle of disobedience and boycotting the enemy's products, each according to his ability and conditions. In this connection, UNC reasserts its call to those working in the apparatus of the Civil Administration to resign, with the exception of [those in] the health and education systems. It also repeats its call to boycott and hound those employed in the tax departments.

6. UNC urges our fighting masses to observe strictly the days of general strike, to uphold their sanctity, and to refrain from making trips and journeys on strike days.

7. UNC appeals to our masses to refrain from bringing gifts liable to customs duties across the [Jordan River] bridges, as this affords the [Israeli] occupation the opportunity to rake in huge sums that bolster its economy.

8. UNC calls on the UNRWA administration to show fairness to its workers [in the West Bank] and place them on an equal footing [regarding conditions of employment] with their colleagues in Gaza. UNC further calls on UNRWA workers to evince moderation as regards mea-

sures liable to be detrimental to the interest of UNRWA students and of those who receive its services. The matter should be referred to the PLO for further study and a decision.

O our heroic masses, our eyes fill with tears as Black September approaches,[1] the September of Sabra and Shatila and of the massacre of Palestinians across the length and breadth of the land, but [our eyes] are filled with confidence for the future. We can only dedicate this month to the memory of the martyrs, whose blood was shed in the struggle for liberation and national independence. UNC salutes your unwavering spirit, your effort, and your response and asks you to carry out the following struggle actions:

1. Saturday, September 9—A day of a general strike marking the start of the 22nd month of the uprising.

2. Tuesday, September 12—The birthday of the Prophet. On this great day, UNC sends greetings and salutations to our fighting masses and calls for marking the day by intensifying the clashes and confrontations with the occupation forces and the herds of settlers.

3. Friday, September 15—Winter time of the Palestinian state will begin: set your watches and clocks back one hour.

4. September 13, 14, 15, 16—The days preceding the massacre of the hundred and twenty, the massacre of Sabra and Shatila, will be dedicated to mobilization, preparation, and firing up [the population] with a view to the black day. The shock squads and the popular committees and the fighting forces must be fully prepared.

5. On September 17, 18, and 19, black flags that will be flown from the roofs of houses and buildings, [and from] electricity and telephone poles, will fill all the squares. Palestinian flags will also be flown, and marches will be held throughout our occupied state. Clashes and confrontations should be conducted, and let the ground split open under the feet of the occupying army.

6. On September 17, at 10:00 A.M. Palestine time, all traffic shall cease for one minute throughout the occupied state. Vehicles shall stop and their passengers exit [to observe a minute's silence]. At the same time, our sons the pupils and their teachers in the classrooms shall rise for a minute of silence in honor of our martyrs and to perpetuate their righteous memory. This will be followed by the reading of the Palestinian national anthem.

---

1. Black September refers to the bloody war that broke out in Jordan in September 1970 between the Palestinian organizations and the Jordanian army. The war ended in July 1971. Following the war, the Palestinian organizations moved from Jordan to Lebanon.

7. Monday, September 18—A day of a general strike in solidarity with the heroic workers in Gaza. [On this day] all the workers' movements are urged to support our workers in their struggle against racism and the oppression.

8. Friday, September 22—A day of a general strike in solidarity with our valiant detainees in all the prisons and detention centers of the occupation and with the deportees.

9. September 23, 24—Days of confrontation [with the Israeli army], social activities, and mutual social assistance.

Together on the road of the triumphant uprising until victory

The United National Command
PLO, State of Palestine
September 5, 1989

LEAFLET NO. 48

In the name of Allah the merciful and compassionate

Communiqué—communiqué—communiqué

*No voice will overcome the voice of the uprising
No voice will overcome the voice of the Palestinian people—
the people of the PLO*

Communiqué No. 48

Issued by the Palestine Liberation Organization/
The United National Command of the Uprising

The Proclamation of Independence

O our heroic masses, the soldiers of the stone and the Molotov cocktail, you who have restored to the Palestinian and Arab person his national dignity, you have stood up against the most powerful military force in the Middle East, you have made tremendous achievements, you have broken the military strength of the hated occupation army and have raised the standard of the revolution and national liberation—acclaim to you and glory to your martyrs, forward on the road to freedom and national independence.

O our fighting masses, in these days our Palestinian people is celebrating an important national holiday, that of the declaration of independence of the State of Palestine. The first anniversary of the declaration of independence is approaching at a time when our people's will is heightening its fortitude and its steadfastness and its defiance [and at a time when] the magnificent uprising—thanks to our people's struggle, its sacrifices, its awareness and its cohesion around its united national leadership and around the PLO, its sole legitimate representative—has succeeded in thwarting all the scheming policies and plans which are bent on bypassing our national and legitimate right of return, of self-determination, and of establishing an independent state, and above all [thwarting] the plan of the Zionist Shamir, the Baker points, and the American flanking attempts. Our people's uprising has demonstrated the possibility of triumphing and of realizing our people's national aspirations on the basis of its national plan, which was approved in the 19th meeting of the Palestinian National Council and gained inter-Arab and international support, and [which] is based on developing and escalating the uprising, and on continued adherence to the Palestinian peace initiative.

O masses of our popular uprising, UNC shares in the joy of the independence celebration of our Palestinian people wherever they may be and stresses its determination and the determination of our masses to hold fast to our legitimate rights of return, of self-determination, and of establishing the independent state. Our masses will never forgo these rights and will not agree to half-solutions. [UNC] affirms the continuation and escalation of the uprising, while drawing all the lessons gleaned from our people's struggle experience. It emphasizes its support for the resolutions of the latest Palestinian Central Council meeting in Baghdad, and for the exclusive right of the PLO to determine and announce the Palestinian delegation for any preparatory negotiations toward the convening of an effective international conference.

O our proud masses, together with you UNC marks the independence holiday and the day of world solidarity with our Palestinian people and stresses that our war with the occupation is long and difficult and obligates a high level of steadfastness and habituation to the struggle, and it issues the following call:

First: In the Palestinian sphere:

1. Strengthening national unity and improving the situation of the popular, national, and sectorial committees [and] completing their establishment in the various locales, since they are the revolutionary form of the popular government and the primary organizer of the mass movement and its struggle. On the occasion of the independence holiday, UNC calls on our masses to decorate the walls of the cities, villages, and [refugee] camps with uniform slogans and posters bearing the signature of UNC only.

2. UNC is proud of the [exemplary] instances of civil disobedience that our masses carried out in Beit Sahur, in Nablus, and in the Gaza

Strip and calls on our masses in other places to take their lead from these examples, which demonstrate the tremendous forces of struggle which our people possesses and the possibility of realizing the all-encompassing national revolt despite the policy of starvation, despotism, and bloody suppression. UNC stresses that these locales would not have achieved what they did without the deep-rooted national unity in which they excel and without the immense progress they made in the realm of the organized building of the apparatus of the uprising. Likewise, [UNC] affirms that our victory requires that we escalate the struggle against the Zionist enemy, inflict losses in his ranks, and ridicule and foil his various plans.

3. Intensifying the boycott of Israeli goods and support for all forms of national production, by strengthening and expanding the role of the productive cooperatives and the household economy, cultivating the land, and guidance in consumption. On this occasion, the [UNC] leadership calls on our heroic merchants in Jerusalem to boycott the remaining Israeli goods for which a national substitute is available, and not to trade in goods whose source of manufacture is unidentified.

4. UNC calls on our masses in the homeland and the diaspora to strengthen the forms of solidarity and mutual surety with the families of the martyrs, the wounded, the detainees, and all the injured.

5. UNC affirms the importance of providing every type of aid and support to the fighters and to those designated as wanted [by the Israeli authorities]. You must supply their needs, give them shelter, and help them continue their heroic struggle against the occupation.

6. UNC calls on all our high-school pupils to behave responsibly and to ensure discipline in the [classrooms] during the period of the examinations.

7. UNC salutes the inhabitants of Beit Ṣaffa for the restraint they showed during the recent events and calls on all to eliminate factional, communal, and family disputes and to invest all efforts in strengthening national unity and consolidating it in our ranks.

Second: In the inter-Arab and international sphere:

1. UNC calls on the Arab masses and their national forces to establish a very broad Arab popular front in order to aid and support the uprising, to designate November 15th [the date of the declaration of a Palestinian state] as a national holiday on which popular marches will be held, and to implement the role of the fighter abetting our people's struggle.

2. UNC calls on the Arab regimes to support our people's struggle and its magnificent uprising and to provide the needs of the steadfast-

ness by diligently fulfilling all the commitments and resolutions that were adopted by the summit meetings in Casablanca and Algeria; to work for the formation of a force that will pressure the American stand which is unilaterally predisposed in Israel's favor, as was recently seen in the use of the power of veto to foil a draft resolution of the Security Council condemning the barbaric actions of the occupation authorities against our inhabitants in Beit Sahur.

3. UNC demands that the Syrian regime rectify its relations with the PLO on the basis of a joint struggle against the Zionist enemy, strengthen and improve the state of the Arab national steadfastness, and take an active part in supporting our people's uprising.

4. UNC calls on all our people's allies and friends in the world, and first and foremost in the Soviet Union and the socialist bloc, and on the world liberation movements, to invest additional efforts and to press for the convening of an effective international conference with the participation of the rest of the parties, including the PLO on an equal footing, and to support our people's right of return, of self-determination, and of establishing its independent state.

5. UNC welcomes the stand of Pope John Paul II, who supports our people's just cause, and deeply appreciates the declarations by President Mitterrand to the European Parliament at Strasbourg, and requests that the states of the European Community aid and support our people's legitimate rights and exert pressure on the U.S. and Israel to accept the international will.

6. UNC calls on the international community and on the U.N. and its secretary-general to send a permanent international supervisory committee in order to gather first-hand knowledge about the daily crimes [being committed] against our people and to work to place the occupied lands under temporary international supervision.

O our heroic masses:

On the road to freedom and independence, UNC vows to continue the struggle until the removal of the [Israeli] occupation and the realization of [Palestinian] independence and calls on you to carry out the following struggle actions:

1. November 12, 13, 14—Days of preparations for celebrating the first anniversary of the independence holiday, on which Palestinian flags will be flown, mass marches will be organized, the national anthem will be sung, songs and national calls will be voiced, and fireworks set off. November 14 shall be a day of honor to our people's martyrs, on which visits will be paid to the martyrs' families and to their graves, and to the families of the detainees, the wounded, and the

deported, and [on which] military marches and various struggle activities will be organized.

2. November 15 will be a national holiday on which the institutions, the companies, the factories, and the local newspapers will be closed. There will be assemblies, debka [dance] circles, children's parades, and balloons. The shops will remain open until 5:00 P.M. Palestinian flags will be flown in all the cities, villages, and [refugee] camps of our Palestinian state, and the women of our people will adorn themselves in Palestinian dress.

3. November 16, 17, 18—Clashes [with the Israeli army]. While they are taking place, the lands of the State of Palestine will be declared liberated lands by loudspeakers and by the muʾazzins, with all the manifestations of insurgence this entails: erecting barricades, hoisting flags, writing slogans, and organizing military marches.

4. November 19—A general strike, to protest the enemy's measures and policy against our holy places, and his repeated actions to enter the Temple Mount and build the illusionary [holy] temple in al-Aqsa square; and to commemorate the fall of the Palestinian commander Sheykh ʿIzz al-Din al-Qassam.

5. November 20, 21—Two days [devoted] to higher education, on which various actions will be undertaken to pressure the occupation [authorities] to reopen the universities and institutes. Likewise, UNC calls on international educational institutions and organizations, and on UNESCO, to aid and support this demand.

6. November 22, 23, 24—The functional committees[1] will monitor the implementation of the decision to boycott Israeli goods for which a national substitute is available, will supervise prices, and will ensure that there is no price-gouging.

7. November 25—Diverse activities will be held in solidarity with our detainees and against the actions of the oppression administrations [in the prisons] and to protest the arrest campaigns and the establishment of the fascist detention camps.

8. November 27—Shall be designated as a day for carrying out special struggle actions against the occupation, the collaborators, and the herds of settlers.

9. November 28—A general strike to express our people's rejection of all the liquidation plots and plans, which seek to sidestep our people's legitimate rights.

---

1. The functional committees were established by Intifada activists at the local level to deal with various day-to-day matters. These committees were intended to serve as a substitute apparatus to the Israeli Civil Administration.

10. November 29—The day of world solidarity with the Palestinian people. On this day sit-down strikes will be organized opposite the building of the International Red Cross and opposite foreign consulates in Jerusalem, and memoranda will be sent demanding that the international institutions intervene to stop the violations of Palestinian human rights.

11. December 1, 2, 3—Days of escalation and clashes with the Zionist invasion army.

We swear that we shall avenge the martyrs' blood. We swear that the uprising shall continue until victory. Hand in hand, we shall thwart all the scheming plots. Together, on the road to freedom and independence.

Long live the uprising and our fighting masses.

The Palestine Liberation Organization
The United National Command
State of Palestine
November 10, 1989

LEAFLET NO. 55

In the name of Allah the merciful and compassionate

Communiqué—communiqué—communiqué

*No voice will overcome the voice of the uprising
No voice will overcome the voice of the Palestinian people—
the people of the PLO*

Communiqué No. 55

Issued by the Palestine Liberation Organization/
The United National Command of the Uprising

The Proclamation of Jerusalem, Eternal Capital
of the Independent Palestinian State

O masses of the uprising,

It is essential to begin in the heart of Palestine, the holy of holies, which is subject to insane attacks of maltreatment in the sphere of taxes and by the armed settlements and their provocations, and whose inhabitants, Muslims and Christians, are making common cause against the evildoers. Therefore a greeting [is sent] to the *murabitun,* and a vow to continue until the establishment of freedom and peace in the city of peace [Jerusalem], and from the heart of Palestine to the Arab world. The UNC condemns the insane attack against the sister [state], Iraq, and condemns the attack that preceded it against the sister [state], Libya, declaring its full solidarity with them.

O our fighting masses,

There is no doubt that every cruel and harsh confrontation requires innovation [and obligates] changes in the means of confrontation against the enemy [Israel], in order to confound him and not give him the opportunity to adapt and get used to the struggle activity against him. At this time, after you have succeeded, like miracle makers, in defeating 29 months of oppression and tyranny, it is only natural that our enemy has already begun to revive himself and to launch his attempt to quench the erupting fire of the uprising. This obligates us to refocus our struggle efforts on the vital and creative aspects of this sacred revolution, and to introduce appropriate tactical changes in order to regain the initiative and sow confusion in the enemy's ranks.

O masses of the martyrs, masses of the sacrifice and the response,

Our basic goal in the field and the guideline of our confrontation continues to be the boycott on the apparatus of the occupation, in the realm of the administration, the economy, and taxation. At the same time, we must act to develop and organize the Palestinian national government, in the knowledge that the revolt and the building are two sides of the same coin and in the knowledge that we cannot attain our objective, which takes the form of civil disobedience, as long as we do not act diligently to develop our alternative government. Our political goal continues to be the heightening of world support for our legitimate demand for freedom and independence and to deepen the conflicts within the Israeli society, increasing the numbers [of Israelis] who support our people's right of return, of self-determination, and of establishing an independent state and actuating the political movement that supports these goals, under the leadership and guidance of our legitimate leadership, the PLO.

With this as a starting point, and out of the need to reorganize this sweeping popular revolution, and in order not to allow its forces to be wasted, or their diversion from the correct course of the struggle with the enemy, or from the building process which aims to broaden and implement the apparatus of our independent state, UNC reaffirms the following points:

Popular activity:

UNC calls on all our people, irrespective of age or place of residence, to work diligently and seriously to establish neighborhood committees in every neighborhood, street, and district. These committees will serve as a tool of struggle of the popular participation in the spheres of life of the uprising, and will constitute the hard core of the popular committees, and the security, education, training, and agriculture committees, and so forth.

UNC further calls on the shock squads to ensure full coordination with the neighborhood committees, with the aim of ensuring security and protection for the residents of these neighborhoods. In this sphere, UNC demands that all personnel of the shock squads refrain from using facial covering in contacts with the public, unless absolutely necessary, and to confine the use of facial covering to confrontations with the enemy authorities. This, in order to prevent the enemy from making use of this phenomenon to sow confusion and foment a civil war among the public.

Strikes:

UNC stresses that the strikes are a manifestation of protest that has psychological and information usefulness, but in order to ensure that they do not become a means that will bring satisfaction to the enemy [and enable him], due to their routine nature, to combat them, and to ensure that they should not become a means of self-strangulation, UNC announces that it will replan the strike program in different and innovative ways. Likewise, UNC stresses that the strikes do not mean staying at home. The strike hours should be used to carry out various actions, including protest marches and confrontations with the occupation authorities, and also to deepen the meaning and implementation of Palestinian independence, under the supervision of the neighborhood committees and the shock squads.

Mutual social surety:

On the brink of the holy ʿId al-Fitr, which Allah, may He be exalted, shall bring for the good of the Islamic nation, UNC emphasizes the necessity for the neighborhood committees to fulfill their obligations toward the needy families. Every committee must bear full responsibility for the people of its neighborhood or district. Our forces should be deployed to build bridges of trust and love between the members of our one people.

In addition, UNC appeals to our people regarding the need to assist the wanted [by the Israeli authorities], the vanguard and heroes of the uprising, and to grant every assistance to them and to their families, and to assist the families of the detainees and the martyrs and give them preference, together with the bearers of the green cards [who are forbidden to work in Israel], in employment and aid. The leadership also requests factory owners and those with the means to organize a program to adopt needy families.

The internal killing:

The enemy has succeeded in exploiting for propaganda purposes the phenomenon of Palestinian internal killing, at the personal, family, and clan level, by encouraging the kindling of the fire of these disputes through his collaborators. It must be understood that many of these events, and the fertile ground on which they occur, have their origins in the inability of the surging popular forces to hit the true target, namely, the occupation regime—leading to an eruption of inner mental frustration. UNC appeals to our masses, entreating them to be very careful of letting themselves be dragged into the tangle of marginal conflicts. From this day onward, UNC declares a national covenant and a sacred historical undertaking, not to shed Palestinian blood by a Palestinian hand, and not to allow personal differences to assume an organizational or political guise.

In this matter, UNC further asserts the sanctity of its unity and the unity of all the groups and activists, both those operating independently and within a framework, who stand with [UNC] on the national line [of defense] in the confrontation with the occupation [regime] and in the escalation of the independence revolution. On this occasion, UNC urges all factions to intensify national unity, and stresses the need to eliminate the tendentious rumors against honored national figures, such as those that were disseminated in Beit Sahur.

Collaborators:

The enemy has also succeeded in exploiting the phenomenon of the liquidation of collaborators [with Israel] and the abuse of their bodies. In addition, the executions of collaborators has not, to date, solved the [problem] of the existence of these collaborators and their shameful deeds. Therefore, the [UNC] leadership, with its operational branches—namely, the shock squads—stresses that executions are not to be undertaken without an order from above. The shock squads will continue to keep these collaborators under surveillance, organize a social boycott against them, and determine the appropriate punishments for their level of deviation. In cases of essential self-defense, the masses and the personnel of the shock squads can kill the assailants.

On this occasion, UNC announces that it is issuing of an order for the execution of Mardus Matussian[1] and others. Their names will be made public, but the implementation of the verdict will be postponed until a new announcement is made.

Monitoring the implementation of the Leadership's directives:

UNC announces that the shock squads will monitor the implementation of its directives. In this connection, UNC reasserts to the prop-

---

1. Matussian sold a building in Jerusalem's Christian Quarter to ʿAteret Cohanim yeshiva. The sale triggered a public furor, and was strongly opposed by the Greek Orthodox church.

erty owners, particularly in the central regions, not to raise rent and exploit the housing shortage. At the same time, the leadership urges the renters to honor their obligations to the property owners.

In addition, UNC warns the group of exploiters among the merchants and the factory owners, who manufacture local products, not to continue raising the prices of their goods. It also calls on the pharmacies—with the exception of the duty-pharmacies—to uphold strictly the strike dates set for the commercial sector. It warns the bakery owners who are turning their bakeries into small grocery stores and calls on them to sell only bakery items.

In addition, it warns the merchants, particularly in Jerusalem, against selling Israeli goods for which [local] substitutes are available. In this season we will mention especially watermelons. The shock squads will strike with an iron fist against whoever dares to practice deceit regarding these orders or to dilute them.

The shock squads:
The shock squads will operate in the field in a united manner to intensify the confrontation with the occupation authorities and against the stands of these authorities and [against] their property. They will also see to the inhabitants' protection and security, particularly on the days of the intensification of the phenomenon of the liberated villages and the bolstering of the independence concept. UNC notes, in this regard, the stress on the united slogans and leaflets, [calls on you] to avoid writing slogans on the walls of private houses, and to make sure before throwing stones at passing or parked cars.

O masses of the magnificent uprising, O you who realize a victory with the fall of each martyr,

UNC, which lauds the steadfastness and sacrifices of our heroic people, especially in Khan Yunis, Rafah, Gaza, Jerusalem, Kafr Malik, ʿAyn Yabrud, Jalazun, Beit Furiq and Salim, calls on you, on the road of the planned escalation and actualization of the revolt, and the realization of our independent state, to carry out the following actions:

★Saturday, April 21—[Shops will be] opened for a full day, until 5:00 P.M.

★Sunday, April 22—Jerusalem Day, a general strike, with the emphasis on Christian-Islamic solidarity, in the capital of the Palestinian state, in the face of the aggressors.

★Monday, April 23—The day of the liberated villages, a general strike. Flags will be flown, the entrances to the villages and the residential areas will be blocked with stone barriers. The shock squads will ready themselves to defend the liberty of the village and block the charging soldiers.

The neighborhood committees will organize mass marches and popular assemblies in the village and city squares and in the residential areas, and the alternative national rule will be organized.

★Tuesday, April 24—Holiday eve, [shops to be] opened for a full day.

★Wednesday, April 25—The blessed ʿId al-Fitr. Opening [of the shops] until 1:00 P.M. On this occasion, the leadership greets our Islamic masses and calls on our masses to visit the martyrs' graves and their families.

★Thursday, April 26—The day of mutual surety, opening [of the shops] until 1:00 P.M. The neighborhood committees will render assistance and services to the needy in their neighborhood.

★Friday, April 27—The day of solidarity with the uprising and with Jerusalem. A general strike. The Arab and Palestinian masses inside and outside the state [of Palestine, i.e., the occupied territories], are called on to organize mass actions, protest marches, sit-down strikes, symposia and lectures.

★Saturday, April 28—The day of the deportees. Opening [of the shops] until 1:00 P.M. At precisely 1:00 P.M., all pedestrians and private and public vehicles will stop, and the passengers will alight, this for five minutes only, during which the horns of the vehicles will be sounded and all will cease work during these minutes.

★Sunday and Monday, April 29–30—Two days of opening until 1:00 P.M.

★Tuesday, May 1—The worldwide workers' holiday. The factories, companies, and institutions will give their workers paid leave. On this occasion, the [UNC] leadership sends a special greeting to the masses of our workers in honor of their world day. The leadership urges the companies, factories, and institutions to show solidarity with our workers sectors and to assist the unemployed among them. The national companies and factories will improve their living conditions and raise their salaries. In addition, the [UNC] leadership draws the attention of those responsible to the need to solve the Waqf[2] personnel problem with all speed. Commercial enterprises will be open until 1:00 P.M.

★Wednesday, May 2—A day of opening [of the shops] until 1:00 P.M.

★Thursday, May 3—The meeting of the tenth national conference of the General Union of Students. The Leadership sends special greetings to those taking part in the conference. It also takes the opportunity to appeal to the student public in our occupied state to curb the phenomenon of cheating in examinations, as this has begun to threaten a basic Palestinian treasure, namely, the correct educational process. Opening [of the shops] until 1:00 P.M.

2. Religious trusts.

*Friday, May 4—The day of our martyred children under ten. Prayers for the repose of their souls should be said in the mosques, and marches organized. Opening until 1 p.m.

*Saturday, May 5—The day of solidarity with the closed schools and universities. Opening [of shops] until 1:00 P.M. Solidarity actions should be organized, and diligent attention paid to popular education. At 8:00 P.M., all the lights in the houses should be shut off, and the youngsters will go into the neighborhoods in order to express their resistance to the policy of inculcating ignorance.

*Sunday, May 6—The memorial day for the heroes in the [Israeli] prisons and for their suffering. A general strike. UNC greets our heroes in the prisons and calls on them to continue their laudable activity to strengthen the unity of the prisoners' movement and to do away with disputes and to employ reason and dialogue.

*Monday and Tuesday, May 7–8—Two days of partial opening [of the shops] until 1:00 P.M.

*Wednesday, May 9—A general strike marking the start of the 30th month of the uprising.

*Thursday and Friday, May 10–11—Two days of full opening [of the shops].

*All the days are considered days of activity and struggle [against the Israeli occupation] using all means, especially after school hours.

We will surely triumph.

The United National Command of
the Uprising/PLO
State of Palestine
April 19, 1990

LEAFLET NO. 68

In the name of Allah the merciful and compassionate

Communiqué—communiqué—communiqué

*No voice will overcome the voice of the uprising
No voice will overcome the voice of the Palestinian people—
the people of the PLO*

Communiqué No. 68

Issued by the United National Command of the Uprising

The Unity Around the PLO Proclamation

O people of martyrs and fathers, o people of the uprising which continues with unabated vigor and resolution toward achieving victory, despite all the measures of suppression and harassment and the tightening of the siege and the curfew orders in all the towns and Palestinian refugee camps. O our heroic Palestinian people, throbbing heart of the Arab nation, which never accepted the day of disgrace and humiliation.

O our people that is fighting with all its strength and with every means of struggle,

Sister Iraq remains steadfast in the face of the most brutal attack [ever carried out] on a people in modern history. Its courageous people and army have succeeded in thwarting, boldly and in the twinkling of an eye, the attempts to destroy Iraq's ability, its liquidation at the hands of the Zionist imperialist interests in the region, and its absolute subjugation as an American satellite. Every additional day of the gallant stand by heroic Iraq brings renewed devastating attacks by the hostile Allies and increases their determination to bring about its submission, and this after its declaration on the removal of its forces from Kuwait. The aggression continues, and the attempts to destroy and subjugate [Iraq] continue despite the unity of the Iraqi army and its heroic stand. That stand was what forced the Allies' hostile leadership, led by the criminal Bush, to declare a halt to the hostilities against Iraq and the start of contacts with it in order to bring about the arrangements required for the continuation of the ceasefire.

O heroic people of the uprising,

O people that has been able to repulse and foil the plots at every turn. The reactionary Arab Zionist imperialist alliance seeks to take advantage of the Iraqi withdrawal from Kuwait and of the illegal presence of the invading forces in parts of Iraq to sow despair and dismay among our struggling masses and within the Arab national movement in order to bring about its surrender to the Zionist imperialist plots and force it to submit to those plots from a position of weakness. Our experience with the Zionist imperialist enemy shows clearly the intention of the enemy alliance to set in motion liquidation plans after the appropriate conditions are created. These plans are aimed at reaping the fruits of the Allies' achievements against the Arab or Palestinian liberation movements, as occurred in the aftermath of the 1967 aggression.[1] At that time the Zionist enemy awaited the declaration of surrender and the acceptance of the Israeli terms by the Arab liberation movement led by [Egyptian President] ʿAbd al-Nasser, or the obliteration of the achievements of the Palestinian revolutionary liberation movement, as occurred following the '73 war. [In the 1973 war] the Arabs scored an important achievement, but the Allies exploited it to impose an enforced liquidation solution, which found expression in the Camp David accords which were agreed to by the traitor [President] Sadat. The same occurred following the failure of the aggression in '82[2] which sought to put pressure on the Palestinian revolution and the Lebanese resistance movement in order to make the revolution and the region submit by imposing the plan of [President] Reagan. This also happened after the blow dealt to the occupation with the outbreak of the magnificent popular uprising in beloved Palestine, when the [Israeli] enemy tried to thwart our people's heroic struggle by means of an imposed solution in the form of the Israeli government plan, known as the Shamir Plan, to hold elections

1. The reference is to the Arab-Israeli war of 1967.
2. That is, the Lebanon War, which began in June 1982.

[in the territories for] an administrative council. Now, after the enemy Allies' failure to subjugate the Iraqi people and army, to eliminate the spearhead of their struggle and compel them to declare a cessation of hostilities in the Gulf region, talk is heard about the [character of the] desirable arrangements in the region to ensure security and peace, as they claim. The truth is that [these arrangements] are intended to ensure the imperialist interests in this region. They are also meant to ensure, directly or indirectly, a solution of the Palestinian problem in the spirit of the American-Zionist outlook, which would apply the Camp David model in the region, to be followed by a devastating offensive against the PLO and against the abiding rights of the Palestinian people, [namely] self-determination and independence.

The road to this process leads through the occupiers' attempt to apply curfew, which is one of the Israeli measures imposed on our people in the occupied territories, and the tightening of the ring of suffocation on the masses in an effort to suppress the uprising and resuscitate the dead apparatus of the occupation and its affiliated local arms. [These measures are] the overture to local proposals for a solution which are consistent with the occupiers' intrigues and which blend with the plot of the self-government [plan] and with every [other] proposed solution which does not meet the aspirations of our people, namely, liberation from the occupation, self-determination, and the establishment of a Palestinian state. Therefore, the next stage in our people's struggle demands heightened alertness and caution, opposition to the occupation's plans and means of suppression, and resistance to all those faint-hearted people who would take part in them. Above all, what is needed now is greater unification around the PLO and support for it as the sole legitimate representative of our Palestinian people everywhere.

The United National Command, unified on the road of liberty and independence, which is leading our people in the struggle, reiterates the following:

Support must be given the Palestinian peace initiative and a solution in the spirit of the resolutions of the Palestinian National Council and the [PLO's] Central Committee, and a warning given to all the cowards who have begun coming out of their holes to back the [Israeli] occupation plans and the American solutions which mean accepting something that is less than absolute independence and less than the establishment of [the Palestinian] state in the spirit of the demand of the U.N. and its institutions. Action must be taken to restore the credibility [of the U.N.], which the Uunited States bent to its service [in the campaign against Iraq]. Speedy [action] must be taken to bring about the withdrawal of the enemy forces from the Gulf region and to negotiate firmly with Israel in order to force it to act in accordance with the legal international resolutions pertaining to the Palestinian problem. Until then, we request the application of the international protection required by our people which is standing steadfast in its homeland against the unilateral Israeli measures. We ask all those who identify with and support us [throughout] the world to assist our people to develop its economic and productive capacity. We ask the European Community to extend aid to our people through the PLO and the national institutions, and we reject every effort to ignore the PLO as our people's exclusive representative.

We appeal to the Arab peoples and to the Arab solution states[3] to act against the American interests in the region and to declare a boycott on American goods, transport planes, and freighters, and those belonging to their allies, until they withdraw their troops from the Gulf region.

In the name of our people in the State of Palestine, the PLO congratulates the Iraqi people and its courageous army for the responsibility shown by the Iraqi leadership in its decision to withdraw from Kuwait in order to preserve the strength and resources of the Iraqi people, enabling it to be a bone in the throat of imperialism, its allies, and its tails[4] in the region.

O masses of the heroic uprising,

UNC, aware of the difficulties being caused to our people throughout the region as a result of the imperialist aggression against Iraq, and certain of its ability to overcome the difficulties [by] finding effective methods for the struggle against the measures [imposed] by the unilateral occupation and for breaking its orders, and as an expression of the uprising's continuation and its preservation as a lever in our people's struggle for freedom and independence, calls on you to carry out the following actions:

March 5—Demonstrations in the homeland [Palestine] and outside it, as a mark of solidarity with the heroic Iraqi people and as a demand to evacuate the enemy army from the Gulf region.

March 8—World Women's Day. UNC greets the Palestinian woman on her holiday and requests that women hold marches, organize sit-down strikes, and brandish posters with slogans on the occasion of this day.

March 17—A general strike marking two months since the start of the aggression against the Iraqi sister [state].

3. "Arab solution states" refers to Jordan, Algeria, Sudan, and Yemen. In the Gulf War, these states worked for a compromise solution entailing Iraq's withdrawal from Kuwait, to be followed by talks to resolve the conflict over oil sources between the two countries.

4. *Tails,* a Palestinian euphemism for collaborators.

March 21—Karameh Day, a struggle day in which Palestine flags will be flown and the resistance intensified against the Israeli occupation forces.

March 30—Land Day, [to be devoted] to the cultiuvation of our land, to planting trees, and to sparking acts of rage and violence everywhere in our homeland, including occupied Palestine of 1948.[5]

The United National Command
State of Palestine
1 Adhar 1991
[March 1, 1991]

5. That is, the State of Israel in its pre-1967 boundaries.

• • •

LEAFLET NO. 70

In the name of Allah the merciful and compassionate

Communiqué—communiqué—communiqué

*No voice will overcome the voice of the uprising
No voice will overcome the voice of the Palestinian people—
the people of the PLO*

Communiqué No. 70

Issued by the United National Command
of the Uprising in the State of Palestine

The Building Proclamation

O masses of the magnificent uprising,
    Forty-two months and the glorious uprising is forging ahead, sounding to the whole world the voice of our people, which is erupting and bursting forth with great power despite the number of victims and the evil of the brutal Zionist attack and the campaigns of harassment and suppression to which [our people] is exposed. Our people proclaims its determination to continue the struggle until the attainment of its objectives: freedom, victory, and the establishment of an independent state on its national soil. The role of our Palestinian people has been manifested in the magnificent uprising and through the unflagging Palestinian activity in the political and diplomatic [arena], [the people] acting with conviction and relying on many international calls for adherence to the legal international resolutions on a solution to the

conflict[1] in order to force the United States to treat [our people] on the basis of criteria based on equality. All this has placed our problem at the head of the international agenda and given it urgency and imperativeness. The cumulative contribution of our magnificent uprising in its legendary proportions [to the Palestinian problem], the sacrifices that were made, and the steadfastness of the Iraqi people and army against the gigantic enemy[2] have borne fruit. [All these] have carved out a path and opened new strategic horizons for our Palestinian cause and have caused it to be addressed at the diplomatic level.

Notwithstanding the political ideas which reverberate inside and outside the occupied land, relating to the rapid political shifts in the region, and especially the trips of the American leapfrogger[3] James Baker—which steel all the arms of the PLO—in an attempt to impose a Pax Americana on the Palestinian problem, there is agreement on the urgent need to act to preserve the PLO's place as the sole legitimate representative of the Palestinian people. [Likewise, we insist on the need] to protect our people's unity, inside and outside, and to turn aside every plot aimed at eradicating the idea of [our] inalienable and unassailable national rights, which are the right of return, self-determination, and the establishment of an independent state with Jerusalem as its capital. As long as the deviation from these goals persists, we must work to consolidate the democratic base and the unity of political outlook by means of a responsible debate which will be dominated by constructive and substantive criticism, while cultivating an awareness of the nature of the [current] stage. All this in order to ensure that all the arms taking part in the Palestinian struggle agree on the current stage with the aim of following the right road, which is the continuation of the uprising and strengthening its prevalence inside and outside [Palestine], escalating its activities, and committing its most vital and dynamic forces to the task of reinforcing the link between [these] matters and foiling the gamble of those who were convinced they could douse or weaken the flame of [the uprising].

---

1. The reference is to the U.N. resolutions pertaining to the Arab-Israeli conflict, such as those of the General Assembly and Security Council on the return of refugees and the establishment of peace arrangements based on the return of territories captured by Israel in 1967.

2. In this Palestinian perception, the results of the Gulf War constituted a political victory for Iraq and a catalyst for a political solution of the Palestinian problem. The "gigantic enemy"—*Atlasi*, in the original Arabic—has two meanings: one, the giant of mythology; the other, geographic, alluding to the North Atlantic Treaty Organization.

3. A sarcastic term indicating a negative approach to the shuttle diplomacy of former Secretary of State James Baker.

UNC understands well that the overall, just solution to the Palestinian problem cannot be realized through future talks or negotiations which will be divorced from the street struggle which represents the spearhead of political action. Likewise, the street struggle alone cannot bring about this solution without taking part in building the political campaign. Both directions are interwoven in an organic dialectical bond.[4]

UNC commends the resolutions of the Palestinian Central Council and stresses its adherence to the fixed Palestinian principles, which are at odds with [the formula of] the regional conference and the like, [notions] which are not based on legal international resolutions. [UNC favors] positive and active participation in the political efforts, with adherence to the Palestinian peace initiative, and readiness to work for the creation of broad public support [for the establishment of] an Arab and international front which will mobilize to correct the route of political action [leading to] a solution of the Palestinian problem. [This will be done] through the convening of an international peace conference with the participation of the sides involved, including the PLO and the five permanent members of the Security Council.[5]

UNC deplores the continuation of acts of dispossession and harassment by criminal gangs against our [Palestinian] people in Kuwait, actions which are carried out with the knowledge and before the eyes of the Kuwaiti authorities. UNC appeals to the Arab publics to show solidarity with the Palestinian people and establish permanent bodies to support [the Palestinians]. Likewise, UNC turns to the international community, which is now showing "humane sensitivity" toward the Kurds in Iraq, to show responsibility and work for the protection of our people in Kuwait in the face of the suppression and intimidation campaigns. UNC greatly appreciates the PLO's readiness to demonstrate a constructive approach and take part in the current [inter-Arab] efforts to end the Lebanese crisis, resolve the issue of the armed Palestinian presence in Lebanon in a manner that will maintain the bonds of Palestin-

---

4. The leaflet's authors believe it is necessary to integrate the PLO's political struggle with the popular struggle waged by UNC, together with the Palestinians in the territories, against Israeli rule.

5. The Palestinians consistently opposed the idea of a regional conference in which the Soviet Union and the United States would host the sides to the conflict—Israel, Syria, Jordan and the Palestinians—without the participation of the United Nations, the permanent members of the Security Council, and the PLO. Finally, the regional conference idea was accepted, after Israel agreed to a Palestinian delegation comprised of residents of the territories, though formed with PLO coordination. The result was the Madrid Conference, which convened in October 1991.

ian-Lebanese fraternity, and ensure the protection of the [refugee] camps of our [Palestinian] people in Lebanon as well as their political rights and their rights of struggle within the boundaries of sovereign Lebanon.

UNC is mosty appreciative of the enlightened French stand regarding the Palestinian problem and the meeting which recently took place between President [of the "State of Palestine"] Yasir Arafat and French Foreign Minister Roland Dumas. [UNC] sees this as a step in the right direction by Europe and one which should be followed by additional steps [which will contribute] to the formation of an independent, active European stand toward the [Lebanese] crisis.

UNC, including all its arms and members, condemns the criminal murder of the French tourist in Bethlehem and emphasizes that doubtful actions of this kind are meant to harm the Palestinian national movement and tarnish our people's religious, cultural, and historical image. We stress that the sacred uprising is a revolution against the [Israeli] occupation and is leading to a just peace which will ensure that our people realize their objectives of freedom and independence.

O masses of the magnificent uprising, the uprising is our fundamental alternative [to the present situation]. It is the true guarantee that we will attain our national goals. It is the ship of redemption to which we must cling. It is the natural form of reaction to the plots being hatched against our cause and to the brutal actions being perpetrated against our people. As the uprising entered its fourth year, the Zionist enemy stepped up his attempts to bring about the eradication of our economic and human existence, and his organized efforts—including economic boycott, moves to starve our people, and the closure of the universities and colleges—to destroy our economic and educational infrastructure. The natural reaction to these measures is to devote this year to mobilizing all our reserves of energy to the resumption of the building and development of our economic, educational, and social institutions, and to begin working in this sphere according to a national criterion for the benefit of all our people.

UNC greets our brave workers on the workers' world holiday, May Day, and calls on the owners of the factories and companies to make employment possibilities available to the greatest possible number [of workers] by broadening the production base, raising wages, and canceling arbitrary dismissal decisions. UNC simultaneously renews its call to our working public to return to the land, increase agricultural output, and give expression to our ability to stand steadfast on our soil in the face of the insane settlement initiatives of the extreme right-wing government in Israel.

It is essential to take the public pulse every so often in order to ensure harmony between the demands made by the struggle and the public's economic needs. UNC serves the economic interest by diligently assuring harmony between the struggle programs and the public's ability and responses. If the basic criterion [guiding the activity] is the degree of discipline our people is showing and its trust in its leadership, any change in the struggle program should follow a careful examination based on an understanding of the public's demands. This should be publicized through UNC leaflets and not by means of gossip, the dissemination of rumors in the streets, and material broadcast by the Zionist enemy's media.

O our people's masses,

1. While [the Israelis] prevent our workers from working [in Israel], UNC sees fit to stress [the need to adhere to the instructions of] the boycott on Israeli goods for which a national substitute exists [and] to encourage [the purchase of] local goods. [UNC] asks our masses everywhere to abide by the boycott [instructions] and to punish violators accordingly.

2. UNC calls on the teachers' organizations to act for the opening of private courses to compensate highschool students who were unable to meet the demands of the curriculum due to the existing circumstances. UNC also warns against the phenomenon of cheating on highschool final exams and against the use of masked people in the schools during the exams. Anyone who cheats or instigates or utilizes a mask should be seen as violating the national consensus. UNC calls for the establishment of teachers' and parents' committees to set right this negative phenomenon.

3. UNC reiterates that the general-strike days are set in UNC and Hamas movement leaflets, conditional on their not clashing with festive events. [UNC] demands that the people comply with them alone and not with other leaflets calling for a strike. UNC further emphasizes that a strike for the sake of martyrs shall be a one-day commercial strike only, to be held in the area where the martyr fell, and irrespective of the number of that day's martyrs.

4. UNC warns the frivolous who are trying to harness the political activity to family or clan interests, and calls on them to prefer the supreme national interest over personal accounts.

5. UNC warns all those who are making use of the name of the uprising to raise funds on its behalf by means of threats. By doing so, they cause it to lose stature in the eyes of the public.

6. UNC congratulates the Arab Liberation Front on the first anniversary of its embarking on the road to liberation and victory.

O masses of the magnificent uprising,

UNC calls on you to carry out the following actions: May Day is a day of solidarity with our courageous workers on which festivals and other activities will be organized.

The first week of May [will be used] to organize struggle actions against the campaigns of the insane settlers on our Palestinian soil, with processions and resistance to be organized against the settler herds.

May 9, a general strike marking the start of the forty-second month of the uprising.

May 9, 12, and 19, shops will open during the day.

The second week of May, a week of struggle and solidarity with our prisoners in the Zionist detention camps, [to be marked by] processions and sit-in strikes at the Red Cross offices in opposition to the enemy's measures against the Palestinian prisoners.

May 15, a separate day of struggle commemorating the taking of Palestine by force.

May 18, the day of the renewal of the alliance with the [Palestine] Liberation Organization and the underscoring of our people's unity inside and outside [Palestine], by flying Palestinian flags from the rooftops.

May 20, a commercial strike and popular rage to mark the first annual memorial day for the massacre perpetrated against our workers at ʿUyun Qara.[6] It is essential that the transportation arrangements serving the educational system function properly on that day.

Long live the magnificent popular uprising

Long live the PLO, our people's sole legitimate representative

The Palestine Liberation Organization/
The United National Command
1 Ayar 1991
[May 1, 1991]

---

6. ʿUyun Qara is the Arabic name for the area where the Israeli city of Rishon Letzion is located, and where a young Israeli gunned down seven Palestinian workers from the territories. The incident occurred on 20 May, 1990.

Leaflets of the Islamic Resistance Movement (Hamas)

LEAFLET NO. 1

In the name of Allah the merciful and compassionate

The infidels "will not cease from fighting against you till they have made you renegades from religion, if they can. And whoso becometh a renegade and dieth in his disbelief such are they whose works have fallen both in the world and in the Hereafter. Such are rightful owners of the fire: they will abide therein."[1]

O *murabitun*[2] on the soil of immaculate and beloved Palestine: O all our people, men and women. O our children: the Jews—brothers of the apes, assassins of the prophets, bloodsuckers, warmongers—are murdering you, depriving you of life after having plundered your homeland and your homes. Only Islam can break the Jews and destroy their dream. Therefore, proclaim to them: Allah is great, Allah is greater than their army, Allah is greater than their airplanes and their weapons. When you struggle with them, take into account to request one of two bounties: martyrdom, or victory over them and their defeat.[3]

In these days, when the problem is growing more acute and the uprising is escalating, it is our duty to address a word to the Arab rulers, and particularly to the rulers of Egypt, the Egyptian army, and the Egyptian people, as follows: What has happened to you, O rulers of Egypt? Were you asleep in the period of the treaty of shame and surrender, the Camp David treaty? Has your national zealousness died and your pride

---

1. Surah of The Cow (2), 217. The translations from the Qur'an are taken from Mohammed Marmaduke Pickthall, *The Meaning of the Glorious Koran* (New York: Mentor Books, 1953).
2. Muslims who settled in outlying areas during the initial period of the Muslim conquests in order to defend the borders.
3. In Islamic tradition, one of two bounties are requested from Allah: victory or martyrdom in battle.

run out while the Jews daily perpetrate grave and base crimes against the people and the children? And you, O army of Egypt, O descendants of Salah al-Din al-Ayyubi,[4] Qutuz[5] and al-Zahir Baybars,[6] what has happened? Have the rulers paralyzed your movement and stripped you of your power, making you so impotent that even the usurpers are no longer frightened of you?[7]

And you, O defeated Egyptian people, which is incapable of doing anything, God will help you and us. We greet you through the pioneer Muslims who have come out of al-Azhar and all the universities in order to express their solidarity with their brethren in Palestine, strengthen their hands, and cry out to the usurpers that their end shall come in the morning—is the morning far off—is it not near? [Know] that God does not abandon but gives respite.

Let the whole world hear that the Muslim Palestinian people rejects the surrender solutions, rejects an international conference, for these will not restore our people's rights in its homeland and on its soil. The Palestinian people accuses all who seek this [solution] of weaving a plot against its rights and its sacred national cause. Liberation will not be completed without sacrifice, blood and *jihad* that continues until victory.

Today, as the Muslim Palestinian people persists in rejecting the Jews' policy, a policy of deporting Palestinians from their homeland and leaving behind their families and children—the people stresses to the Jews that the struggle will continue and escalate, its methods and instruments will be improved, until the Jews shall drink what they have given our unarmed people to drink.

The blood of our martyrs shall not be forgotten. Every drop of blood shall become a Molotov cocktail, a time bomb, and a roadside charge that will rip out the intestines of the Jews. [Only] then will their sense return.

You who give the Jews lists containing the names of youngsters and spy against their families, return to the fold, repent at once. Those who deal in betrayal have only themselves to blame. All of you are exposed and known.

To you our Muslim Palestinian people, Allah's blessing and protection! May Allah strengthen you and give you victory. Continue with

---

4. The victorious commander over the Crusaders in the Battle of Hittin (1187).

5. Mamluk Sultan of Egypt (1259–1260), who defeated the Mongols in the Battle of ʿAyn Jalut, near Nablus, in 1259.

6. Mamluk Sultan of Egypt (1260–1277), who fought in the Battle of ʿAyn Jalut.

7. Salah al-Din, Qutuz, and Baybars vanquished the empires of the time. By implication, Israel, another empire, can also be defeated.

your rejection and your struggle against the occupation methods, the dispossession, deportations, prisons, tortures, travel restrictions, the dissemination of filth and pornography, the corruption and bribery, the improper and humiliating behavior, the heavy taxes, a life of suffering and of degradation to honor and to the houses of worship.

Forward our people in your resistance until the defeat of your enemy and liquidation of the occupation. Then the mark of Cain shall be erased. O our people of clean conscience! Spare no efforts [to fan] the fire of the uprising until God gives the sign to be extricated from the distress. Invoke God's name plentifully, for "lo! with hardship goeth ease, / Lo! with hardship goeth ease."[8]

The Islamic Resistance Movement
January 1988

8. Surah of Solace (94), 5–6.

LEAFLET NO. 2

In the name of Allah the merciful and compassionate

The Blessed Uprising

"Make ready for them all thou canst of [armed] force and of horses tethered, that thereby ye may dismay the enemy of Allah and your enemy, and others beside them who ye know not."[1]

Our people the *murabit* on its soil in which they have mingled their blood with the blood of their ancestors, fighters of the holy war among the immaculate Companions of the Prophet (*sahaba*), and their righteous and merciful descendants.

O patient mothers, righteous fathers, youth who are fighting a holy war, splendid lion cubs, O men, women, elderly, and young! Because of the distraction of our people which was scattered among small states embroiled in conflicts, enemies placed rulers in them with loyal troops and reliable guards. As a result, the first section of precious Palestine was handed over in 1948.[2] Following twenty years of turning away by the nations and blows sustained by the Islamic movement everywhere—for desiring to eliminate the true danger posed by the enemies of Allah in general and tyrants in particular—the remainder of Palestine, above all the blessed al-Aqsa mosque, was lost in 1967. The Jews believed they had triumphed. Their pride rose and their arrogance surged, "their effort is for corruption in the land."[3] Thus it was in the savage Israeli attack on the land and on man alike.

1. Surah of the Spoils of War (8), 60.
2. Blame for the 1948 military defeat is imputed to the Arab regimes.
3. Surah of The Table Spread (5), 64. The reference is to the Jews. "The Jews say: Allah's hand is fettered. Their hands are fettered and they are accursed for saying so. Nay,

This took the form of the expropriation of most of the lands in Palestine from their legal owners forcibly and with violence, by fraud and corruption. In this way hundreds of settlements were established, fruit trees were cut down, orchards were plowed under with bulldozers, building permits were revoked, they fought against farmers with their depraved methods, and did everything in their power to lay waste the land and empty it of its inhabitants.

The inhuman policy against a defenseless people was expressed in the arrest of thousands of men, women, and children, who were beaten and tortured with abuse and invective against the name of God and Muhammad, His messenger, in the form of base expressions. Curfew was imposed on [refugee] camps and cities, customs were levied, administrative detention [was employed], universities and educational institutions were shut down, fire was opened indiscriminately with intent to kill, relatives were prevented from attending martyrs' funerals, and they were buried in the dead of night under guard. These and other actions are in the nature of the cowardly, weak, assassinating, villainous, resentful ruler. His henchmen thought our people had indeed sunk into a state of despair and helplessness and was asking for mercy on bent knee and with hand extended to the dwarf rulers!!!

But nothing could prevent the outburst. And then [the Jews] asked themselves: Is a defenseless people capable of raising its head? Will these people act without outside support? They expected the generation that grew up after 1967 to be wretched and cowed, a generation brought up on hashish and opium, songs and music, beaches and prostitutes, a generation of occupation, a generation of poisoners and defeatists. Yet what actually happened?

What happened was the awakening[4] of the people. The Muslim people is avenging its honor and restoring its former glory. It refuses to concede a centimeter of its land, is opposed to the Camp David accords, objects to an international conference and a humiliating peace, rejects arrests and deportations, opposes surrender of any kind. Thus there came about the mass outburst in the refugee camps, cities, villages, and deserts throughout Palestine. The escalation in these locales reached a level that led the news agencies to describe the centers of the events as war fronts.

---

but both His hands are spread out wide in bounty. He bestoweth as He will. That which hath been revealed unto thee from thy Lord is certain to increase the contumacy and disbelief of many of them. And we have cast among them enmity and hatred till the Day of Resurrection. As often as they light a fire for war, Allah extinguisheth it. Their effort is for corruption in the land, and Allah loveth not corrupters."

4. In the original, *sahwah*—religious awakening.

Every day the earth absorbs the blood of the righteous. Kneels in front of the graves and bows before the martyrs of grace. This is part of the price of pride and honor, liberation and salvation. This is the dowry of those with "lovely eyes,"[5] a substitute for paradise. "Allah is Knower, Wise. Lo! Allah hath bought from the believers their lives and their wealth because the Garden will be theirs."[6]

Everyone opposes the occupation and rejects the existing situation. Each day the escalation becomes more acute, despite the usurping occupier and his crimes, expressed in breaking into mosques, ruthless arrests, throwing ingenious bombs to suppress the blessed movement,[7] sending in thousands of troops to extinguish the flame, breaking into [refugee] camps with tanks, preventing the press from reaching the scene to block their coverage of the events.

Despite all this, the resistance movement asserts the following:

O plundering occupier, violence on your part will only bring about an escalation of the outburst. What has taken place so far is a prologue to what is yet to come, and the land will not be able to bear the oppression.

O Arab rulers, who invest efforts for the sake of the false peace, who kneel before the world, who entreat Israel to agree to a "just" peace, who implore the Security Council, who pretend to support the uprising but in fact are immersed in a deep sleep. We hope you will fight at least once [in order to prove] that you partake of Arab boldness or Muslim strength.

Forward our *murabit* people who stand steadfast until God's salvation will come. "And say [unto them]; Act! Allah will behold your actions, and [so will] His messenger and the believers."[8]

Know that victory demands patience and God is on the side of the righteous. "So have patience [O Muhammad]! Allah's promise is the very truth, and let not those who have no certainty make thee impatient."[9]

And finally: No to the Zionist existence! No to the Jewish occupation! No to deportation! No to detentions! No to tyranny! No to concessions, [not] even of a grain of dust from the soil of Palestine.

---

5. Surah of The Mount (52), 20. In the emblem used here, the pure type of chaste womanhood is figured. Such women are chaste, and their eyes are big with wonder and beauty.

6. Surah of Repentance (9), 110, 111, which continues: "they shall fight in the way of Allah and shall slay and be slain."

7. Referring to the Islamic Resistance Movement (Hamas).

8. Surah of Repentance (9), 105.

9. Surah of The Romans (30), 60.

Let the uprising continue with strength for the sake of right, freedom, heroism, and pride.

The Islamic Resistance Movement
Palestine
Jumadi al-Awwal 1408
Qanun al-Thani [January] 1988[10]

---

10. Most of the Hamas leaflets use the Muslim (*hijri*) as well as the European calendar. 1408 is the *hijri* year, i.e., the year since the immigration of the Prophet Muhammad from Mecca to al-Madina (A.D. 622).

• • •

LEAFLET NO. 4

In the name of Allah the merciful and compassionate

"If ye are suffering, lo! they suffer even as ye suffer and ye hope from Allah that for which they cannot hope."[1]

O our Muslim people on our soil purified with the blood of the Companions of the Prophet and their followers, and all who pursued their path of truth, strength, and liberty.

O descendants of Abu ʿUbayda, Maʿad Bin Jabal[2] and Salah al-Din [al-Ayyubi]!

O brothers of the *mujahidun*[3] and *murabitun* from generations past unto—Judgment Day! An army equipped from head to foot is fighting our chained and weaponless people. Tanks, armored vehicles, and airplanes pursue the inhabitants. Ingenious toxic bombs are hurled at our masses, sometimes from airplanes and sometimes by soldiers. Curfew is imposed on towns, villages, and camps; houses are broken into by day and by night, and all the furniture smashed; women are intimidated and children are terrorized; they are pursued, arrested, and tortured; mosques are invaded and tear-gas bombs thrown at worshippers and kneelers; youths are murdered in their houses and at road junctions and their bodies thrown between the trees; children are kidnapped and their feet broken; universities, schools, and scientific institutes are closed. The plunderer has revealed his malice and unmasked his true face, wielding his iron fist to impose a death sentence on the liberty and honor of our people.

1. Surah of Women (4), 104.
2. Abu ʿUbayda Ibn al-Jarrah and Maʿad Bin Jabal were numbered among the *sahaba* (Companions of the Prophet). They were killed in a battle fought on the soil of Palestine in 639.
3. *Mujahidun*, fighters of the *jihad*, the holy war.

These criminal methods are clear proof of the Jews' hatred and despotism. They break youths' teeth with riot batons, beat them senseless, arrest and torture youngsters, and prison administrators refuse to admit them.

Despite the brutality and violence, despite the plunder and terror, despite the tanks, the armored vehicles, and the airplanes that seek to terminate the uprising, [our people has been ready to] make sacrifices and demonstrate heroic steadfastness. The steadfastness and the defiance of the enemy reflect belief in Allah and confidence in our victory engendered by absolute faith. "How many a little company hath overcome a mighty host by Allah's leave!"[4] The cry of "Allah is great" has overcome the sound of the bullet and the grenade, and thus the processions of martyrs continued to the high heavens. May their present place be pleasant, for "they are living. With their Lord they have provision."[5] Greetings of honor and esteem to our people, our whole people, which is standing firm: workers, merchants, students and clerks, mothers, fathers, elderly, and children. God bless your efforts and your heroism on the road to honor and liberty.

The Islamic Resistance Movement takes pride in you and salutes your stand and hopes you will undertake the following:

Devotion to Allah: Whoever fights so that the word "Allah" shall be above all, will devote himself to Allah irrespective of the loss in life or property, for Allah's sake.

"Lo! We suffer not the reward of one whose work is goodly to be lost."[6]

Deployment: The settlers are trying to attack our villages and camps in order to strike terror into our hearts. We draw no distinction between settler and soldier, both are Jews. Today's settler is tomorrow's soldier and all are enemies who sow hate. To cope with these evildoers, avail yourselves of the following directives:

Do not open your doors to them, fortify yourselves in and above your houses. Organize guards on a shift basis above the houses and in strategic locations. Equip yourselves with stones, sticks, axes, and knives. Go up to the roofs, little children as well as adults, and call "Allah is great," and remember the words of Allah: "Fight them! Allah will chastise them at your hands, and He will lay them low and and give you victory over them, and He will heal the breasts of folk who are believers."[7] Protect yourselves and the honor of your wives and children. Do

---

4. Surah of The Cow (2), 249.
5. Surah of The Family of ʿImran (3), 169, which begins, "Think not of those who are slain in the way of Allah, as dead."
6. Surah of The Cave (18), 31.
7. Surah of Repentance (9), 14.

not surrender to cowards. God will strike fear and terror into their hearts and they will turn tail, beaten.

Caution: Beware of planted leaflets filled with hatred and irresponsible declarations. Some are trying to exploit the events by climbing on the bandwagon. Likewise, suspicious leaflets are being circulated to achieve particular goals. For example, the communiqué signed by the Palestinian Communist party, which expresses fear at the rising power of religious reactionaries, fundamentalists, and clerics. And another [leaflet] signed in the name of the Islamic [Resistance] Movement, calling for a halt to the uprising and trying to split our Muslim people. This in addition to declarations casting doubt on the Muslim nature of the uprising. Beware of such irresponsible behavior.

Patience: Patience, patience, stand firm, stand firm, in the face of [the Jews], the most cowardly and pusillanimous of people. Hundreds of them are refusing to join their military units, "and thou wilt find them greediest of mankind for life."[8] In the Knesset there are increasing voices maintaining that "the uprising will bring disaster to our country." Therefore, forward our steadfast *murabit* people with God's help and His providence. The Prophet tells you: "A *ribat*[9] of one day for the sake of Allah is better than this world and all its goods."

Let the blessed uprising continue and its slogan shall be: Allah is great in His whole being and God be praised for every state. "Verily Allah helpeth one who helpeth Him. Lo! Allah is Strong, Almighty—"[10]

The Islamic Resistance Movement
Hamas
Palestine
Jumadi al-akhira 1408
Shubbat [February] 1988

---

8. Surah of The Cow (2), from 96. The passage refers to sinners, and continues: "And to live [a thousand years] would by no means remove him from the doom. Allah is Seer of what they do."

9. The *ribat* is the safeguarding of the frontiers of the world of Islam. The term is derived from the Qur'an (8:60), and is applied by the jurists to one particular aspect of the *jihad*. The authors of Hamas leaflets perceive Palestine as *ribat* land.

10. Surah of The Pilgrimage (22), 40.

• • •

LEAFLET NO. 6

In the name of Allah the merciful and compassionate

"Do not humiliate yourselves by suing for peace, for you are better than your enemy."[1]

A general strike against the new American conspiracy.
Shultz in the footsteps of Kissinger and Rogers.
O Muslims on the soil of the *ribat!*
With the intensification and continuation of your blessed uprising, with your steadfastness and determination, with your sacrifices and your martyrs, with additional wounded and detained—the Zionist onslaught increases and the American political lobby tries to scuttle your uprising and take it over as a service to its ally, especially after the exposure of [Israel's] ugly face before the world, for it has exceeded the Nazis in burying people alive and has outdone South Africa in its racism and in the crimes of the settlers against our people which outdo those of Hitler and Nero.

O Muslims on the soil of *al-Isra' wal-Mi'raj*.[2] Tomorrow the American Secretary of State Shultz, with the Zionist face, arrives in the region in order to divert the world's gaze from your uprising and

---

1. The authors of the leaflet meant to quote verse 139 in Surah 3 (The Family of 'Imran): "Faint not nor grieve, for ye will overcome them if ye are [indeed] believers." Instead, they produced a garbled version of verse 35 of Surah 47 (Muhammad): "So do not falter and cry out for peace when ye [will be] the uppermost."
2. *al-Isra'*: the night journey of the Prophet Muhammad who according to Muslim tradition journeyed, whether in a daydream or a night vision, to Jerusalem and thence ascended to heaven astride a horse that came down from the skies accompanied by the angel Gabriel. The night of the Prophet's ascent to heaven is the Night of Virtues (*al-Mi'raj*). The journey is mentioned in Surah 17 in the Qur'an, and thus one of the names of Palestine is the Land of the Night Journey and the Ascent to Heaven.

suffering to the miserable surrender initiatives, so that the cowed ones from our nation will run after them and then will return empty-handed and disappointed because the only thing they will get from the United States and its policy is illusion. This is because the United States supports Israel with money and arms, and opposes us in everything, even in the Security Council when it condemns the Zionist occupation policy against our unarmed people. And why not? After all, it is the United States that supplies Israel with every bullet and shell that is fired on our Palestinian people in every place. And what face will this ugly American present? And how will he be received by those who wish to meet him and who are urging surrender?

O Muslim people!

Some are trying to turn your uprising into a bridge [by which] to reach autonomy or an international conference, or for American recipes that are designed to liquidate the Muslim Palestinian cause. They are running and panting after Shultz and his envoys. We warn everyone who is thinking about meeting with him and completing these wretched deals behind the scenes.

O descendants of Khalid [Ibn al-Walid]³ and Salah al-Din [al-Ayyubi]!⁴

Greetings of pride and esteem to our patient merchants, our *murabitun* workers, and our insurgent pupils who have sacrificed what is most dear to them for the sake of their liberty and honor.

This is your day! Let us work together against the Zionist occupiers, against American policy in the region, against those who run and pant after solutions aimed at liquidating our sacred cause. Wednesday and Thursday will be days of full general strike, the movement of vehicles and of workers will cease—whoever violates this will have only himself to complain to. People must remain in their houses. In the mosques, prayers will be said for the missing, following the Friday service.

Our slogan will be:

In the name of Allah, Allah is great. In the name of Allah, the hour of Khaybar⁵ has arrived.

---

3. Khalid Ibn al-Walid, called by Muhammad the Sword of God. In 632, following Muhammad's death, he was sent by the Caliph Abu Bakr to subdue rebels against Islam, and in 634 he took part in the Battle of the Yarmuk against the Byzantines.

4. See leaflet no. 1, n. 4.

5. Khaybar—a desert oasis in Arabia populated by Jews. Muhammad accused the inhabitants of treachery and the Muslims conquered the site in 628. To Muslims, Khaybar symbolizes the treachery of the Jews.

Allah is great, death to the occupiers.

The Islamic Resistance Movement
Hamas
Palestine
6 Rajab 1408
February 23, 1988

LEAFLET NO. 7

In the name of Allah the merciful and compassionate

"*Fight them! Allah will chastise them at your hands, and He will lay them low and give you victory over them, and He will heal the breasts of folk who are believers.*"[1]

March 7, a day of confrontation and defiance against the occupation.

O Muslims on the soil of the *ribat*,[2]

Despite the ugly Zionist oppression and despite the policy of the iron fist and the thick club, despite the continuing procession of martyrs, the broken hands and legs that fill the hospitals, despite all this your blessed uprising continues and today enters its fourth month, declaring to the world, to friend and foe, that our people is opposed to the occupation and refuses to forgo its right to Palestine.

O descendants of Khalid [Ibn al-Walid] and Salah al-Din [al-Ayyubi]!

History repeats itself. In 1936, our Palestinian people held a six-month strike that shook the ground beneath the feet of the English occupiers, but the British conspired to foil the strike by making promises to Arab leaders and monarchs. Our people was led astray by these promises and the strike ended without accomplishing anything. Today the American conspiracy reappears to foil the Muslim uprising through Arab monarchs, presidents, and rulers, under false slogans such as "land for peace" and "the umbrella of an international conference," but this is no more than a mirage, deceit, and the usurpation of your uprising and feelings.

O Muslims, O *mujahidun*, O *murabitun*,

Monday, March 7, the anniversary of the Jews' withdrawal from the Gaza Strip in 1957, will be a day of defiance and confrontation. Let this

---

1. Surah of Repentance (9), 14.
2. See leaflet no. 4, n. 9.

be a day of defiance and confrontation until [the Zionists] leave our lands and our homeland, and an Islamic Palestinian state is established on the pure soil of Palestine.

O Muslims,

The uprising continues, to flinch from it is death, the Zionist occupiers torture and humiliate the people at every opportunity. Let the stone be our strong weapon against the occupiers! Let Palestinian flags fly! Down with the wretched defeatist conspiracies! Our slogans shall be:

In the name of Allah, Allah is great, in the name of Allah the hour of Khaybar has arrived, Allah is great, death to the occupiers!

The Islamic Resistance Movement
Hamas
March 4, 1988

LEAFLET NO. 8

In the name of Allah the merciful and compassionate

al-Isra᾽ wal-Mi ʿraj escalation of the blessed resistance

"And We decreed for the Children of Israel in the Scripture: Ye verily will work corruption in the earth twice, and ye will become great tyrants. So when the time for the first of the two came, We roused against you slaves of Ours of great might who ravaged [your] country, and it was a threat performed. Then we gave you once again your turn against them, and We aided you with wealth and children and made you more in soldiery. [Saying]: If ye do good, ye do good for your own souls, and if ye do evil, it is for them [in like manner]. So, when the time for the second [of the judgments] came [We roused against you others of Our slaves] to ravage you, and to enter the Temple even as they entered it the first time, and to lay waste all that they conquered with an utter wasting. It may be that your Lord will have mercy on you, but if ye repeat [the crime] We shall repeat [the punishment], and We have appointed hell a dungeon for the disbelievers."[1]

Our *murabit* Muslim people on our blessed soil, O people of the precious uprising, O patient ones who resist all the forms of oppression, humiliation, and surrender.

Your uprising is moving into its fourth month to celebrate the Day of *al-Isra᾽ wal-Mi ʿraj* on the eve of the 27th of the month of Rajab. The appearance of *al-Isra᾽ wal-Mi ʿraj* in these historic days has placed in the hands of our Muslim people the heritage of a fragrant gift of memory comprised of three principal elements:

The first: The place of the Temple and Palestine among Muslims.

Is there a place after Mecca and al-Madina for which the hearts of Muslims on the soil of Allah throb more than the Temple? The first

---

1. Surah of The Children of Israel (17), 4–8.

house of worship for Muslims toward which passersby from all ends of the earth turn to pray and to be close to God. (Passersby make pilgrimage to three mosques only: al-Haram mosque, this mosque, and al-Aqsa mosque).² Prayer in al-Aqsa is the equivalent of five hundred prayers [in other mosques] with the exception of the mosques of Mecca and al-Madina [al-Haramayn], which is where the prophecies descended and the prophets took refuge. In the event of *al-Israʾ wal-Miʿraj*, God placed the crown of the prophets' seal as the master of all men on the soil of Palestine. In no other capital and in no other city on earth but Jerusalem did an event like *al-Israʾ* occur, so that it might become the sister of Mecca in history, and so that the Muslims might know that the abandonment of Jerusalem is tantamount to the abandonment of Mecca and al-Madina.

—[The mosque] which is surrounded by our blessing: Whole Palestine shall not be divided.

North and south, its coasts and its hills, its sea and its rivers, all cojoin into a single elevating perfection with the blessing of God and His prophets and the angels of God. It was blessed by the Qurʾan which will be read unto the end of days—a blessing on the soil, a blessing on the tree and its fruit, a blessing of the air and the rain, an immeasurable, unexampled blessing.

The second: The corruption of the Israelites:

"Ye verily will work corruption in the earth twice."³ The corruption of the government and the regime in the blessed land. Where is there corruption greater than this government and its domination? If they murder even their prophets, how shall they pity and take consideration of us? They say: "We are not to blame for the ignorant," that is, it is no sin to strike at them and massacre them.

—They corrupt economically: monopoly, fraud, and interest are their handiwork and are ingrained in their nature, the various taxes, the customs, the material decrees imposed on the inhabitants until they collapse. [They] are corrupt—they arrest, beat, curse, use weapons prohibited throughout the world, strike women, children, and the aged, lie, inform, cheat, and deceive. This is the Jewish identity.

The third: There is no liberation and salvation except through Islam: The blessed land that was honored by the night journey of Muhammad was conquered by ʿUmar⁴ and the *sahaba*⁵ who are noble in their purity

2. Al-Haram mosque is in Mecca; "this mosque" refers to the mosque in al-Madina.
3. Surah of The Children of Israel (17).
4. ʿUmar Ibn al-Khattab, the second of the first five caliphs following the death of the Prophet Muhammad, was killed in 644.
5. In Muslim tradition, the Companions of the Prophet are considered religious authorities.

and righteousness, was liberated by Salah al-Din, who restored it to Islam, was lost by the most foolish rulers in history in an act of forgetfulness and withdrawal, and will be restored only by pure hands and good souls. This is a historic religious belief:

The faith states: "If ye help Allah, He will help you,"[6] "We roused against you slaves of ours of great might."[7] And in history: when was our nation victorious without religion? When did it have pride without faith?

And when did it gain unity without Islam? Our situation is the best proof: Arab public relations likes to screen films about our wounded, our funerals, the breaking of our bones, the pursuit of our women and children. They count the number of martyrs who fall every day in the Zionist-occupied land, while at the same time they [the information dispensers] meet with [the Zionists], are loyal to them, and keep guard around them.

O our *murabit* Muslim people: Arab saliva flows at the sound of the words, a just and durable peace, the American initiative and so forth. Their supreme ambition is an international peace conference which, whatever fruit it bears, [they] will devour every word and be satisfied with every statement. They make do with the word "peace"—even its first half.

We declare before our people and the world our stand regarding peace, and our response to those who long for and dream of the convening [of an international conference]. It is: "No to peace with the Zionist entity":

1. Because they are prone to foot-dragging and are greedy. An example of foot-dragging is Taba. Years of negotiations, and the results—bubbles. And the delegations continue to meet... Taba will not be returned in negotiations.

2. Allah did not vouchsafe them peace in the land "and [remember] when thy Lord proclaimed that He would raise against them till the Day of Resurrection those who would lay on them a cruel torment."[8]

And where is the durable peace?

Where is justice as long as they still retain land on the shores of Haifa and Acre while the owners reside in a [refugee] camp in Lebanon, in the West Bank, in the Gaza Strip, and in Jordan. What kind of justice is it when the rightful owner flees and the plunderer takes over? Let any

---

6. Passage from verse 7 in the surah of Muhammad (47).
7. Passage from verse 5 in the surah of The Children of Israel (17).
8. Surah of The Heights (7), 167.

hand be cut off that signs [away] a grain of sand in Palestine in favor of the enemies of God and our enemies who have seized the soil of *al-Isra' wal-Mi'raj*, the blessed land.

O our heroic people!

Greetings of appreciation and esteem for your steadfastness, your sacrifice, your patience, and your staying power in the precious and blessed uprising. We hope you will carry out the following:

1. Compassion: let compassion prevail between people, between neighbors, rich and poor, buyer and seller, let this be the slogan: "Have pity on those who shall be pitied on earth and in heaven."[9]

—This is a call to the directors of the Muslim Waqf[10] and to all municipalities. In view of the difficult economic situation, tenants must be exempted from paying the rent they owe. We remind you that this is the quality of mercy . . . and the quality of mercy is nationalism, and the nation derives from Islam . . . Our people will never forget this act of mercy, "and God will help man as long as man helps his brother."[11]

—To all leasers: whoever is in a good [economic] situation should release tenants from the burden [of paying rent] to the extent possible, and your conscience is the guarantee of your judgment in these matters.

—To tenants: Whoever can afford it should not delay a payment due to the owners . . . Do not rob people of their money with a lie.

2. Production and prohibition of exploitation—To all our factories, firms, and exporters: Stand firm and increase production so that our industry can compete with the products of the plundering enemy. Take heed not to exploit your patient brothers.

To importers and consumers: Our whole people must refrain from purchasing any products from the grudge-bearing Jews. Every penny we pay them is another bullet aimed at our throat and a gas grenade that chokes our children and wives. God asks everyone "about his capital and how he earned it and on what he spent his money." And it is to you that the following *fatwa*[12] applies:

"Prohibit every Muslim to purchase merchandise from Jews if he can find a national substitute in its place. We must combat the hated Jewish market." We must reduce our expenditures and make do with essentials.

---

9. One of the sayings attributed to the Prophet (*hadith*).
10. Waqf—properties dedicated to religious purposes.
11. One of the sayings attributed to the Prophet.
12. Islamic legal opinion.

3. Beware of the policy of inculcation of ignorance: the plundering enemy has shut down the educational institutions in order to disseminate ignorance among our people. Everyone must know that activity against the occupation does not conflict with education but is parallel to it. We must be armed with education. We must believe in a return to our study institutions, universities, and schools of teachers and pupils ... Otherwise, the educators must go to the mosques in order to teach and to prepare a curriculum for the leaders of the future.

4. Fast day: Let next Thursday, 29th Rajab, or March 17, be a fast day for Allah, a pilgrimage throughout Palestine in commemoration of *al-Isra' wal-Mi'raj*.[13] We shall entreat Allah to relieve the suffering of the nation. Then will we know that the supplication of the fast is not in vain.

On the occasion of *al-Isra' wal-Mi'raj* we proclaim: no to the false peace, no to conceding even an inch of land from the soil of Muslim Palestine, no to Jewish merchandise, no to the policy of [inculcating] ignorance. Yes to compassion between people, yes to tolerance and steadfastness on the road of the blessed uprising, yes to unity and cohesiveness.

With the words Allah is great, praise to God, Allah is great, our call shall be: In the name of Allah, Allah is great. In the name of Allah the hour of Khaybar has arrived.[14]

The Islamic Resistance Movement
Hamas
Palestine
25 Rajab al-Khayr 1408
Adhar [March] 13, 1988

13. Muhammad's night journey to Jerusalem and his ascent to heaven.
14. See leaflet no. 5, n. 2.

LEAFLET NO. 11

In the name of Allah the merciful and compassionate

Call to students, teachers, responsible officials, and opinion molders among the public

"Read: In the name of thy Lord who createth, /
Createth man from a clot. /
Read: And thy Lord is the Most Bounteous, /
Who teacheth by the pen, /
Teacheth man that which he knew not."[1]

The end of the fourth month of the uprising is at hand, and our courageous pupils have taken an active part in escalating the uprising, devoting to it all their efforts and time. They were fired with the spirit of revolt against the occupation, the plundering, and the oppression. With chest bared they met the armed forces, determined to attain their freedom and to expel the usurpers of their land and homeland. They sacrificed martyr after martyr. Their spirit did not falter. They did not show weakness and they had no fear of the Jewish nazism.

Today, as the end of the school year approaches, and examinations are about to be held, we strengthen the hands of our heroic students—may God bless them and may they succeed—and we whisper to them: return to your studies on the days on which there are no disturbances. You must be courageous and study diligently to compensate for the loss of classes.

Do not cease attending the schools, colleges, and universities, except on those days on which you are called upon not to attend. Be certain that the uprising will not end until the cowardly Jews leave our land and

---

1. Surah of The Clot (96), 1–5.

our holy places. Know that the road with the Jews is long and will not end soon. Accustom yourselves to patience and steadfastness, and ready yourselves for a protracted effort in studies and achievements. When obligations increase, one must organize one's time. One must devote time to studies and afterward take part in resistance to the occupation. We are convinced that you are not evading your duty.

By organizing your time, you will be able to continue until the defeat of the wicked Jews.

National and religious duty obligates teachers at all levels of the educational system to redouble their efforts and to show understanding for the situation of their pupils, for the sake of their pupils, and to focus primarily on the important subjects. The schoolteacher is a pioneer and a paragon of the society. All of them must be loyal and make every effort, and manifest a desire for sacrifice, for seriousness and for giving, with a constant view to the words of the Prophet, may he rest in peace, "If one of you commits an act, God loves it to be done perfectly." Parents should send their children to the schools, colleges, and universities, and draw the children's attention to the importance of not absenting themselves from studies. They must monitor the situation in cooperation with the various educational institutions.

Preachers, notables, and opinion molders must do their duty and make every effort to ensure their pupils' interests. The mosques must fulfill their mission by intensifying education and raising the level of the pupils, in order to compensate for and supplement what is missing. The Islamic Resistance [Movement] issues this call and will punish whoever tries to hold a school strike on days when there is no strike, or who throws stones at educators. His name will be inscribed as an enemy of the people.

Greetings to our courageous students and faithful educators.

"Allah and His messenger and the faithful will act and see your conduct, and ye will be brought back unto Him who knoweth the invisible as well as the visible, and He will tell you what ye used to do."[2]

The Islamic Resistance Movement
Hamas
Palestine
Friday, April 1, 1988

---

2. Garbled and partial quotation from surah of Repentance (9), 94.

• • •

LEAFLET NO. 13

In the name of Allah the compassionate and merciful

The massacres by the Nazi Jews are continuing
in the manner of the Deir Yassin massacre

O Muslims on the soil of *al-Isra'*,

On April 9 [1948], the Jewish butchers perpetrated the massacre of Deir Yassin, killing the aged, women, and infants, and ripping open the bellies of pregnant women in order to destroy the seed of our people that persecutes them night and day until they have been scattered to the four winds and obliterated.

On April 9, the blessed uprising entered its fifth month. It will break the impudence of the Jewish butchers, their arrogance and violence, and will declare to the whole world that the will of our believing people on the soil of Palestine is stronger than their tanks, airplanes, and bullets. It will not cease to exist and to wait patiently, and to escalate [the struggle] from day to day, until the irrevocable expulsion of the occupiers from our sacred soil.

O Muslims,

The uprising continues in its fifth month with violence and force, and proclaims the foiling of plots aimed at liquidating our cause—the cause of Palestine and the Palestinian people—and tramples all the plots, from Camp David to the Shultz and international conference plans.

O successors of Ja'far and Abu 'Ubayda,[1]

---

1. Ja'far Ibn Abu Talib was a Mulsim military commander. He fought against the Byzantines in the Battle of Mu'tah in 629. Muslim tradition relates that when one of his hands was chopped off during the battle, he seized the standard with his other hand. When his second hand was chopped off, he pressed the flag against his breast, and then he was killed. On Abu 'Ubayda Ibn al-Jarrah, see leaflet 4, n. 2.

Our Muslim people in its homeland knows well that the Zionist crimes constantly increase as long as our people's uprising and revolution continue. Their generals are behaving insanely, they do not understand what they are doing or wreaking. Their shooting has failed and the thick club has failed, their economic pressures have failed along with the starvation [tactic]. Our people are removing themselves from [their clutches] from day to day. Every type of collective punishment and political and media stifling which is intended to obscure the truth about their crimes against our people and our relatives in the occupied homeland is doomed to failure. The virulent publicity which their agents are disseminating among our people in order to weaken its [determination] and will power and to generate despair about the [still] unclear future—will fail.

O *murabitun*,[2]

The uprising continues to escalate, torrents of blood flow daily in our villages, our refugee camps, and our towns. The butchers think they can proceed confidently, but they have forgotten that the hand of God is mighty, and the day will inevitably come when they will pay the price of the slaughter and the price of the brutal Nazi racist crimes they are perpetrating.

O patient *murabitun*,

The inhabitants are accustomed to visiting prisons through the Red Cross, but they [the Israeli authorities] want everyone to obtain a permit from the military authorities in order to visit a detention center. We know that what is behind this plan is [a desire to] obstruct us and to exert the heaviest pressures. Therefore everyone should refuse to visit the Ansar 3 detention camp in the Negev except through the Red Cross, and not by obtaining individual permits.

Let Saturday be a day of general strike and provocation in order to wear down the Jewish occupier enemy. Let traffic cease. Let us hoist Palestinian flags. Let our slogan be: In the name of Allah, Allah is great, in the name of Allah, the hour of Khaybar has arrived.[3]

Allah is great, death to the occupiers.

The Islamic Resistance Movement
Hamas
Palestine
April 7, 1988

2. See leaflet no. 1, n. 2.
3. See leaflet no. 5, n. 2.

LEAFLET NO. 14

In the name of Allah the merciful and compassionate

I am at your command O Palestinian prisoner

"And they will not cease fighting against you until they have made you renegades from your religion, if they can."[1]

The month of Ramadan approaches, the month of beneficence and compassion, the month in which the fiendish Jewish human beings who spread corruption in the land die [or] are imprisoned. Now they intend to expel a new group of inhabitants from their own land and their own native city to Lebanon—and they are killing and blowing up houses everywhere, particularly in the suffering village of Beita in which settlers sowed corruption—and aged and children fall martyr to the gas bombs that are hurled at them indiscriminately in houses and in every place.

O you Muslims on the soil of beneficent Palestine,

Today you encounter the destiny of God, may it be realized at your hands. Greater brutality by the Jews will hasten their end. On this day you shall encounter the might of God and the strength of angels, stones, and trees, and say: O Muslim, behind me is a Jew, come and kill him, but you Jews [are] imbued with greater cruelty! And you, Muslims, increase your faith and penitence—and the pledge shall be upheld.

O you *murabitun* on the soil of Palestine.

At the start of the month of Ramadan we mark the Day of the Palestinian Prisoner who languishes under Zionist oppression, the prisoner who endures torments in solitary confinement, the prisoner whose hand is bound by Nazi Zionism, [who] has spent all or most of his life in prison.

---

1. Surah of The Cow (2), 217.

Greetings to all the believing prisoners on the day of solidarity, the Day of the Prisoner, which falls on Sunday, April 17. Let this be a day of protest and demonstrations against the occupation forces.

The Islamic Resistance Movement, the powerful arm of the Muslim Brothers, salutes the steadfastness and confrontation of our Muslim people. It calls on the inhabitants to undertake the following:

1. To respect the month of Ramadan, refrain from eating in public and from violating the laws of God.

2. Sunday will be a day of strike, confrontation with the Jews, and solidarity with the prisoners and detainees.

3. Cessation of traffic on declared strike days, with the exception of ambulances and doctors' vehicles—whoever violates the order will be exposed to danger along with his vehicle.

4. Boycott all Zionist soft drinks (Crystal, Tempo, Schweppes). The Resistance Movement will punish merchants who import these items—the inhabitants must make do with national products.

Jihad in God's way until victory or death.

Let our battle slogan be: In the name of Allah, Allah is great.

In the name of Allah, the hour of Khaybar has arrived,

Allah is great and death to the occupiers.

The Islamic Resistance Movement
Hamas
Palestine
Nissan [April] 15, 1988

∙ ∙ ∙

LEAFLET NO. 16

In the name of Allah the merciful and compassionate

"Allah had already given you the victory at Badr, when ye were contemptible. So observe your duty to Allah in order that ye may be thankful."[1]

Tuesday, Ramadan 17, a day of remembrance of the great Battle of Badr,[2] a day of *jihad* and resistance.

O Muslims, the month of Ramadan falls in the shadow of the oppression and occupation and the escalation of the actions of the tyrannical Zionists: restriction of worship, restriction of the Islamic giant, which had begun to pour out of the mosques and turn this battle into a war of religion and faith, in order to eradicate this cancer which is spreading through the soil of *al-Isra' wal-Mi'raj* and is threatening the entire Islamic world. Behold him murdering, wounding, and smashing hands and feet, behold him strangling towns, villages, and camps by imposing curfew, behold him suffocating the Muslims in the occupied land by closing markets and destroying property. Behold them demolishing homes, expelling people from Palestine, wave after wave. Behold them filling the prisons with thousands. Behold them confiscating identity cards in order to force the inhabitants to pay taxes, or seeking to make us perish through unemployment. Behold them imposing heavy fines on vehicles, behold them permitting the herds of settlers to attack everywhere without any consideration, behold them cutting off power and water to camps and towns, uprooting fruit trees, and confiscating amplifiers from

---

1. Surah of The Family of 'Imran (3), 123.
2. In the Battle of Badr, fought on March 16, 624, Muhammad and his forces defeated the people of Mecca. It was here that the rules regarding spoils of war had their origin, as well as the concept that Muhammad's theocratic authority is unassailable. See surah of the Spoils of War (8).

mosques in order to prevent reading and prayer and to silence the voice of "Allah is great." But they do all this in vain, and their hope is dashed. For the uprising continues to escalate despite the claims of the collaborators and the defeatists who try to disseminate an atmosphere of despair and frustration among our people. To them we say: the uprising goes on. Our people, inspirited, attacks repeatedly, like waves of the sea without end. Our people, which has foiled all the programs to settle the refugees and the American liquidation plans, is capable with God's help of foiling all the Jews' attempts to eradicate the blessed uprising.

O fasting *murabitun*,

The month of Ramadan teaches us forbearance in tribulation and in encounters with the enemy. Our capacity to endure is greater than what the enemy imagines. We shall divide the loaf of bread amongst ourselves, we shall make all the sacrifices, we shall remain steadfast on our path and we shall sidestep the enemy's plots. We shall pay no heed to the economic strangulation, the restrictions, and the barbaric measures.

In the month of Ramadan the unity and cohesiveness of the Islamic nation is manifested. Muslims must be alert to all the attempts of Israeli intelligence to foment disputes and differences among the inhabitants by writing lying slogans or distributing leaflets full of falsehoods.

The Islamic Resistance Movement emphasizes the need for unity, and announces that it is not responsible for the leaflet signed in its name dated April 24, 1988. This is part of the attempts of [Israeli] intelligence to stir up quarrels between the currents [among the Palestinians]. This policy too is doomed to fail.

O Muslims,

After the night comes the dawn, after the hardships comes relief. Let us be patient and help each other and thus stand firm, as did the Prophet and his companions in the Battle of Badr. God brought them victory—despite their [small] numbers and little equipment in the face of their enemies' multitudes and vast strength—because they were God-fearing. This is the key to victory.

Let us make Tuesday, Ramadan 17, into a day of *jihad,* a day of resistance to the occupation, so that the occupiers will know that our people has ousted them irrevocably. Our people will not give up its homeland and its right to Palestine, no matter how long the road, and however precious the sacrifices.

Let our war slogan be:

In the name of Allah, Allah is great, in the name of Allah, the hour of Khaybar has arrived.³

The Islamic Resistance Movement
Hamas
Palestine, May 3, 1988

3. See leaflet no. 5, n. 2.

LEAFLET NO. 18

In the name of Allah the merciful and compassionate

"O ye who believe! Endure, outdo all others in endurance, be ready, and observe your duty to Allah, in order that ye may succeed."[1]

O masses of Muslim *murabitun!*

Today you meet the might of Allah, praise be to Him, which affects the Jews and their henchmen. Moreover, you are part of the might which will uproot their entity sooner or later, with the help of God, exalt and bless Him.

The hundreds of wounded and tens of martyrs who sacrificed their lives during the week for the sake of Allah and for the sake of the pride and honor of the nation, for the sake of restoring our rights in the homeland, for the sake of hoisting the banner of Allah over the land—are a correct expression of the spirit of sacrifice and selfless devotion with which our people is imbued, and which has left the Zionists sleepless, jolted their very being, and demonstrated to the world that a people that is ready to sacrifice its life will not die.

The Jews must understand that despite their restrictions, their prisons, and detention camps, and despite our people's suffering in the shadow of the criminal occupation, and despite the torrents of blood that flow daily, despite the wounds, our people is great in the capacity to suffer and to be steadfast in the face of their arrogance and despotism, greater than their patience. Let them know that our sons and youngsters will stand firm in the face of the policy of violence, for they love [the promised] paradise more than our enemies love the life of this world.

The uprising of our *murabit* people in the occupied land is an act of defiance against the occupation and the pressures, against the policy of

---

1. Surah of The Family of ʿImran (3), 200.

dispossession of the land and the planting of settlements, against the Zionist policy of oppression. The uprising is meant to arouse the conscience of those who run after the anemic peace, after empty international conferences, after bad unilateral compromises like Camp David. Let them know well that Islam is the solution and the alternative!

Let the contemptuous settlers know that our people is set in its way—the way that entails martyrdom in a holy war and the way of sacrifice.

Our people is known for its self-sacrifice. The policy of the military and of the settlers will be of no avail, and all their efforts to eradicate our people will fail, despite their bullets, their agents, and their humiliations.

Let them know this: violence begets violence, murder breeds murder, and he was right who said:

"The drowning person is not afraid to get wet."

And to the criminal Zionists!

Remove your hands from our people, our cities, our camps, and our villages! Our struggle against you is a struggle of faith, existence, and life.

Let the world know that the Jews have perpetrated Nazi crimes against our people, and that they will yet drink from the same cup.

"And ye will come in time to know the truth thereof."[2]

The Islamic Resistance Movement
[undated]

2. Surah of Sad (38), 89. The context is Allah's warning to infidels.

* * *

LEAFLET NO. 21

In the name of Allah the merciful and compassionate

"This is a clear message for mankind in order that they might be warned thereby."[1]

Communiqué No. 21

"If ye have received a blow, the (disbelieving) people have reached a blow the like thereof. These are (only) the vicissitudes which We cause to follow one another for mankind."[2]

"If ye are suffering, lo! they suffer even as ye suffer and ye hope from Allah that for which they cannot hope."[3]

The Battle of ʾUhud[4]—Remembrance of Sacrifice and Devotion
O Muslim brothers!
Today is the anniversary of the Battle of ʾUhud which put the Muslims to the test and taught them an unforgettable lesson, it was a campaign of sacrifice and determination, a campaign of absolute discipline toward God and His messenger, otherwise they would have been defeated in the same way that our nation is suffering today. The Qurʾan

---

This is Hamas' first numbered leaflet. We collected 19 of the previous, unnumbered, leaflets, but there may have been more.
1. Surah of Abraham (14), 52.
2. Surah of The Family of ʿImran (3), 140.
3. Surah of Women (4), 104.
4. The Battle of ʾUhud was fought in 624 between supporters of the Prophet Muhammad and the Quraysh tribe which sought to avenge the Muslims' victory at the Battle of Badr. Muhammad himself was wounded in this battle.

discusses what happened to the Muslims at ʾUhud, and reminds them that the enemy is suffering as they are suffering and is paying the same price they are paying. The Muslims ask from God things that the plundering enemy does not ask. If today the enemy rules—tomorrow you shall rule. Today we say to our people, the Muslims in occupied Palestine, that the uprising continues despite the rumors being spread by doubters that it has already accomplished its task. The goals of the uprising will not be realized until the occupation is eliminated. The positive aspect is immense, immeasurable. Those who ask what the uprising has accomplished, let them ask themselves what they accomplished in the period of their torpor and running to fill their bellies.

O immaculate Companions of the Prophet (*sahaba*),

The natural situation is that an occupier knows no rest and does not stand stable, and perpetual confrontation prevails between him and the plundered people which fell prey to international Zionist conspiracies and the negligence of the Arabs across the border. Today our people adamantly seeks to realize its goals and obtain its right, despite the long road and the scale of the sacrifice. Palestine is precious, and only the righteous blood will purify it. Our people has not yet paid the price—the price is steep and the way is long, but rain begins with a single drop, and the road begins with a single step.

The Islamic Resistance Movement turns to you in this communiqué, in remembrance of the Battle of ʾUhud, in order to stress the following:

1. [The movement] is grateful to parents and children for their commitment to studies and to the examinations and emphasizes the obligation to pursue the studies until the sons turn to fulfilling their sacred duty in the uprising.

2. Our people whom the authorities are burdening with high taxes and fines are urged to refrain from paying taxes and fines.

3. Every defeatist and submissive call originates with the initiative of the Jews and their collaborators.

Friday and Saturday, May 27–28, 1988, shall be days of confrontation and rejection of the policy that assails the mosques and prevents the inhabitants from worshipping and from fulfilling their religious duty. We stress the continuation of the uprising and the foiling of all the Zionist plots to liquidate the uprising.

Allah is great—death to the occupiers.

The Islamic Resistance Movement
Hamas
Palestine
Friday, May 27, 1988

LEAFLET NO. 22

In the name of Allah the merciful and compassionate

"This is a clear message for mankind in order that they may be warned thereby."[1]

Communiqué No. 22

"And what though ye be slain in Allah's way or die therein? Surely pardon from Allah and mercy are better than all that they amass. What though ye be slain or die, when unto Allah ye are gathered?"[2]

Saturday and Sunday, June 4, 5, will be days of confrontation and a general strike.

O Muslims on the soil of *al-Isra' wal-Mi'raj,*[3] you who underscore by your bold stands the Islamic cause, after it was revealed to the whole world that the Arab nation had collapsed and been severely enfeebled in the contemptible June defeat. Our nation is today experiencing the anniversary of the defeat, while continuing to run breathlessly after the surrender solutions that arrive from the West and the East.

O descendants of Khalid [Ibn al-Walid] and Salah al-Din [al-Ayyubi][4]

Already you have proved beyond a doubt that you are stronger than all the Zionist and international conspiracies that are being hatched against you, from Camp David to Shultz's visits and his liquidation plans. Israel has failed to subdue our people even though it made use of all the oppression tactics, from shooting to [limiting the supply of]

1. Surah of Abraham (14), 52.
2. Surah of The Family of 'Imran (3), 157–58.
3. See leaflet no. 6, n. 2.
4. See leaflet no. 1, n. 4, and leaflet no. 6, n. 3.

food. Today, it is making every effort to break your resolve by means of political plots. It has forgotten that our people defeated it in every one of its battles, especially in Lebanon, when it humiliated [the Israelis] at this time in 1982 and broke its resolve. Thus [Israel] withdrew, dragging its tails of failure and ignominy. Our people has the ability to foil all the conspiracies that seek to liquidate its just cause, its full right in Palestine.

O Muslims, the greatest of the sons of Satan have met in Moscow in order to finalize their deals—resolution of the conflicts between the two superpowers, liquidation of the cause of our people here in Palestine [and the cause of] the Muslim people in Afghanistan, who humiliated the Soviet bear into the dust and forced him to retreat. At the same time, Shultz returned to the region in order to complete the deal regarding which our people has [already] announced in the clear[est] manner its rejection and opposition. In the meantime, the Arab summit conference will soon convene in order to discuss our people's uprising, and it sees that the support of these rulers for the uprising is inconceivable unless a stand is taken against surrender and unless the way of the blessed *jihad* is pursued.

It was in this month that the Companions of the Prophet thwarted the plot of the clans (*al-ahzab*) that gathered around the city of the Prophet, may he rest in peace, seeking to eradicate Islam and the Muslims.[5]

Today, with Allah's help, our Muslim people is capable of continuing on this road and destroying all the conspiracies of the clans and the sons of Satan in this generation.

The Islamic Resistance Movement thanks all the sectors of our people who are standing fast against the enemy and sacrificing martyr after martyr. It declares its solidarity with al-Shati [refugee] camp in Gaza, in which the occupation authorities are employing every means of pressure on the inhabitants who are suffering from a lengthy siege and the sealing of the camp's windows. [Hamas] strengthens their hands until the breaking of the siege and the defeat of the enemy, and stresses:

1. Its condemnation of attacks on [local] vehicles on days when no strike has been declared, and announces that it will punish violators.

2. Disclaims responsibility for threats made against the girls and the women teachers in a number of schools. [Hamas] regards this action as incommensurate with its method [of drawing people closer] to Allah by wise means and preaching the pleasant path.

---

5. The clans were idolatrous tribes that formed an alliance with Jewish tribes and fought together against the Prophet. In the fifth year of the *hijra* they attacked and laid siege to al-Madina, where Muhammad resided. See Surah of The Clans (33).

3. Saturday and Sunday, June 4–5, days of general strike and confrontation with the usurping occupiers.

For our war is a holy war for the sake of Allah unto victory or death. Allah is great and death to the occupiers!

The Islamic Resistance Movement
Hamas
Palestine
Huzayran [June] 2, 1988

LEAFLET NO. 28

In the name of Allah the merciful and compassionate

"This is a clear message for mankind in order that they may be warned thereby"[1]

Communiqué No. 28

"but Allah [also] plotteth; and Allah is the best of plotters."[2]
"Allah will vouchsafe, after hardship, ease"[3]

Islamic Palestine from the sea to the river

Praise to God Who honors believers and gives victory to warriors, shatters usurpers, and humiliates infidels. Prayer and peace to the commander of the warriors, a paragon for humanity, Muhammad, may he rest in peace.

Our *murabit* people: If we peruse the file of the Palestinian cause of forty years ago, we shall find that the intervention of Arab rulers [in the 1948 war] prevented the holy war from advancing, on the claim that Palestine would be liberated by the Arab armies, and that this was [an Arab] national problem and not a territorial problem. The first conspiracy was the relinquishing of the entire Palestinian coast to the abased ones who had angered God. For twenty years the confrontation states[4] safeguarded the Zionist entity and helped it build itself up and strengthen

---

1. Surah of Abraham (14), 52.
2. Surah of the Spoils of War (8), 30.
3. Surah of Divorce (65), 7.
4. The Arab states.

its forces, until the second conspiracy encompassing the remainder of Palestine, which was relinquished cheaply in 1967. Thereafter, the three no's [no to peace, no to negotiations, no to recognition of Israel] were published in Khartoum. For forty years the Palestinian problem was exploited to bolster the Arab rulers politically and to embezzle the funds earmarked for the steadfast stand and the confrontation. The eruption of the uprising in the form of a blessed *jihad* was unavoidable, as the only means to liberate Palestine, and to humble the pride of the Jews and curb their arrogance. People near and distant saw that the stone bests the airplanes, missiles, armored vehicles, and cannons which are utilized for ceremonies of [Arab] monarchs and presidents and are aimed at the heart of the people, to destroy cities and hammer the inhabitants. Israel failed to quell the uprising, despite all the means it employed and despite all the advice it received from interested parties.

At this time the Jordanian king has announced his [July 1988] decision to sever the administrative and juridical ties between Jordan and the West Bank, and has decided to hand over the land to its legal owners. Although this decision, Palestine for the Palestinians, generates astonishment at first glance, we describe it as a pitiful phenomenon externally and an agonizing one internally.

Our patient people, the dispute about who will receive Palestine [and who] will administer its affairs will have a purpose only after the enemy is ousted and those hostile to it are scattered far and wide, and after the liberation of Acre and Jaffa, in addition to Gaza, Jenin, and the Night Journey of the messenger of Allah [to Jerusalem] in the heart of Palestine. Then there will be a place to discuss who will receive the land, which is not now the case when the enemy is pressing down, murdering and destroying, arresting and confiscating. [To hold this debate now] would mean suffocation and confusion, and giving pleasure to Jacob.[5]

Furthermore, since when are schism and rift an expression of nationalism, especially if the decision emanated from the land of conciliation and consensus?!![6] Part of our people accepts this decision gladly on the pretext that it is assent to confrontation and regards it as the greatest fruit of the uprising: a free Palestine, a Palestinian government. The arrangement will be the establishment of a government-in-exile, Israel will proclaim its wrath and threaten liquidation, and people will start thinking about how to bring the officials of the state-to-be from outside

---

5. Referring to the Jews.
6. The reference is to the Arab summit conference held in Amman in November 1987.

and inside [the territories], and diplomatic activity will be launched around what is known as the Middle East problem. After the resolution of the Afghanistan issue and the Gulf War [between Iraq and Iran] will come the turn of the Palestine problem, and the political solution, and negotiations in an international conference, and thus [they will force] the Palestinians to sign to the Jews' ownership of the land of the forefathers, and this will be a mark of ignominy on the brow of the Muslim Palestinian people.

O people, what shall we say to the martyrs who fell in the course of the years for the liberation of Palestine? And how shall we reply to the Muslim peoples when we sign [a peace agreement entailing the ceding of] al-Jazzar mosque [in Acre] and al-Istiqlal mosque [in Haifa], or the internationalization of Jerusalem, or consent to the settlements scattered [in our midst]? And how shall we explain to the peoples of the world our voluntary ceding of our rights?

O our Muslim people, the Islamic Resistance Movement, Hamas, declares the following:

1. Unity is one of the elements of victory: dispute, rift, and schism are the basis of defeat and surrender.

2. Israel understands only the language of force and believes neither in negotiations nor in peace. It will persist in its evasiveness and in building the military entity, in exploiting the opportunity for attack, and in breaking the Arabs' nose.

3. Every negotiation with the enemy is a regression from the [Palestinian] cause, concession of a principle, and recognizing the usurping murderers' false claim to a land in which they were not born.

4. The Arab world is not so weak as to run after peace, and the Jews are not so strong as to be able to impose their will. The rulers are mere clerks, and the situation cannot continue as it is. How did Iraq cope with eight years of a savage war which consumed people and capital? How long can Israel withstand all the forces?

5. The Muslims have had a full—not a partial—right to Palestine for generations, in the past, present, and future. This is not only the right of the Palestinians or the Arabs alone, and no Palestinian generation has the right to concede the land, steeped in martyrs' blood.

6. A Palestinian state is not a rhetorical flourish in a political plan, and it is not a proclamation for circulation or positions for dispensing, but the fruit of a protracted effort and boundless sacrifice.

7. Sunday, August 21, 1988, the anniversary of the burning of the blessed al-Aqsa mosque—the platform of Salah al-Din al-Ayyubi—by the Jews in 1969. On this day a general strike will be held.

8. Monday the tenth of the month of Muharram. The fast day of which Allah's messenger, may he rest in peace, said, "it atones for the year that has passed," will be observed on August 22. This is [also] the day of the martyrdom of the hero Ahmad ʿAbd al-ʿAziz, commander of the *mujahidun* of the Muslim Brothers, in 1948 while defending the soil of Palestine and the holy places. This day shall be a day of fasting and supplication.

9. You must continue the uprising and stand up against the usurpers wherever they may be, until the complete liberation of every grain of the soil of *al-Israʾ wal-Miʿraj*, Palestine, all Palestine, with God's help. And when you are asked, When will this come to pass? Answer: Soon it is hoped.

"And Allah was predominant in his career, but most of mankind know not."[7]

The Islamic Resistance Movement
Hamas
Palestine
August 18, 1988

7. Surah of Joseph (12), 21.

• • •

LEAFLET NO. 30

In the name of Allah the merciful and compassionate

"This is a clear message for mankind in order that they may be warned thereby."[1]

Communiqué No. 30

In memory of the massacre at Qibya and at Kafr Qassim

The Jews killed the Prophets . . . slaughtered the innocents . . . arrested the God-fearers . . . There can be no peace with the murderers.

Praise to God, eradicator of the usurpers, prop of the dispossessed, prayer and peace to the Prophet Muhammad, who fought against heresy and despotism until the right road was revealed to him, to his Companions (*sahaba*), their followers (*tabiʿun*), and the *mujahidun,* unto the Day of Judgment.

Our *murabit* Palestinian people, all the signs are that the wicked enemy has lost his head and self-control due to the continuation of the blessed uprising. The enemy has escalated his unbridled assault against our lives, our honor, our intelligence, our liberty, and our property. He is employing diverse tactics in order to suppress the uprising:

—Launching surprise attacks on towns, refugee camps, and villages, and besieging them while cutting off the water and electricity and blocking the roads leading to them.

—Bursting into homes in the dead of night and at dawn, beating adults, youngsters, children, and women.

—Imposing a clampdown on mosques, carrying out searches in them, confiscating the loudspeaker systems, arresting hundreds of preachers,

---

1. Surah of Abraham (14), 52.

imams, and young people coming to worship. Forcing the inhabitants to go to a public square in the middle of the night and attacking them barbarically in a manner commensurate with the Jews' dirty nature.

—Massive use of gas bombs containing chemical elements, which are fraught with great dangers, both immediate and future, and this before the eyes of the Arab world and international organizations.

—Intensive and concentrated use of live fire and plastic bullets—which has raised the number of fatal casualties and the number of wounded and maimed. Because of this, infants have lost their sight.

—Continuing intelligence activity—interrogation, threats, [empty] promises, appropriation of Arab vehicles from their owners in order to pursue youngsters and for spying and espionage against our people day and night.

O patient people, ten months have passed since the beginning of the uprising, which has worn down the enemy materially and morally, until he himself has declared that the achievements of the uprising exceed those of all the Arab armies during tens of years. Our people continues to stand firm and to sacrifice victims, with the help of Allah. The responsiveness and self-sacrifice are growing and are expressed in the convoys of wounded, detainees, and casualties.

The anniversary of the [Battle of] Khaybar, on September 26, 1988, which the Hamas movement declared a day of all-out confrontation [against the enemy]—is overwhelming proof of our people's resistance to the occupation. The number of martyrs and wounded and the number of disturbances increased on that day.

Greetings to the people, in the villages, [refugee] camps, and towns for its patience, its untiring efforts, its extraordinary responsiveness and its confrontation with the despotic occupier. "Nor gain they from the enemy a gain, but a good deed is recorded for them therefor. Lo! Allah loseth not the wages of the good."[2]

Our generous people, the Jews and their supporters are striving to split our ranks and generate disputes by spreading rumors that Hamas is competing [with other movements] or seeking to replace them: in reaction to these virulent rumors, we call on the people to peruse the covenant of the Islamic Resistance Movement [Hamas] in order to acquaint themselves with it and learn its goals. The competition will consist of confrontation against the enemy and inflicting grave damage on his camp. We reiterate that we are for unity of ranks, against schism, and for everyone who works faithfully for the liberation of Palestine—all of Palestine.

2. Surah of Repentance (9), 120.

We are against conceding so much as an inch of our land which is steeped in the blood of the Companions of the Prophet and their followers. We emphasize to all that we shall not change our way, namely: war on the occupation. We shall prosecute [this war] with trust in Allah, in His ability and His succor. The source of our strength is every believing Muslim wherever he may be . . . this is our broad prop. Of this we are convinced. With Allah's help we shall triumph. "Verily Allah helpeth one who helpeth Him. Lo! Allah is Strong, Almighty."[3] In our view, the uprising is [only] the beginning—not the end. The start of a lengthy struggle for Allah (*jihad*), the vanguard of the army that shouts: "Allah is great." Our aspiration is for power steeped in blood . . . even if it takes time.

Our dear people, in the light of the continuation of the courageous uprising, the sacrifices, and the self-sacrifice, Hamas makes the following call:

1. Underscoring adherence to comprehensive unity of all [factions] of our people notwithstanding their different names and places. Our stand against the tyrannical enemy will be united and uniform. Let the world know that the enemy's most dangerous weapon is his policy of "divide and rule."

2. There is an urgent need to renew studies in the schools and universities. Let us work earnestly to close the gap in this [realm], based on two principles: first, activity to open the educational institutions and denying our enemy pretexts for further closures. Studies will be held in parallel to the struggle against our enemies and will not conflict with that struggle. Second, a call to fathers, mothers, educators, and the educated to ensure that students will make use of their time as gainfully as possible to study [according to] the curriculum to the best of their ability. The focus should be on the elementary school level.

3. A call to the entire public to render whatever assistance they can to casualties, families of martyrs, detainees, and the unemployed.

4. Intensifying the uprising in reaction to the surging wave of arrests and provocations. We stress that the violence and pressures of the Jews will only imbue our people's enthusiasm and awakening with greater strength and courage.

5. Adherents of Islam in the country and abroad shall be Hamas's information envoys, in view of the murkiness that prevails in the information realm both locally and internationally.

6. Friday, October 14, 1988, will be a day of general strike to mark the massacre at Qibya by the murderous Jews.

3. Surah of The Pilgrimage (22), 40.

Saturday, October 29, 1988, will be a day of general strike to mark the massacre at Kafr Qassim and the triple aggression against Egypt, Islam, and Arabism.[4]

7. We shall mark the Prophet's birthday by making visits of solace and consolation to families of martyrs, detainees, and the wounded.

We shall continue the uprising on the road to the liberation of our whole land from the contamination of the Jews (with the help of Allah). Even if the number of victims multiplies, we will heighten our trust in Allah.

"Allah's are the hosts of the heavens and the earth, and Allah is ever Mighty, Wise."[5]

The Islamic Resistance Movement
Hamas
Palestine
24 Safar 1409
October 5, 1988

---

4. The military cooperation between Israel, France, and Britain in the 1956 Suez Campaign against Egypt.

5. Surah of Victory (48), 7.

LEAFLET NO. 31

In the name of Allah the merciful and compassionate

"This is a clear message for mankind in order that they may be warned thereby"[1]

Communiqué No. 31

The martyr al-Qassam: No to the Balfour Declaration, yes to the blessed uprising.

Praise to God, Master of the believers, Vanquisher of the tyrants, peace and prayer to our faithful prophet and to the righteous, unto the Day of Judgment.

Our Palestinian people, the series of barbaric Jewish actions is continuing out of a desire to seize control of the stormy situation in our land of Palestine. It is [our] duty to stress [these actions]: arrests, particularly of clerics, preachers, sermonizers, university lecturers, [and the use of] torture against them, breaking into mosques to carry out searches; opening fire in them and closing some of them, [with all this] being totally silenced; insistently disrupting the educational process and studies by closing educational institutions; a harsh economic assault on the farmers in general and on olive-grove owners in particular by imposing heavy taxes on olive presses, a move fraught with implications for the farmers; imposing curfew on all villages in order to prevent the inhabitants from reaping the harvest; prohibiting and restricting exports so that produce accumulates and prices fall, with the result that [farmers] will not be able to cover the effort [they invested] and their expenses; olive trees being damaged in assaults by

---

1. Surah of Abraham (14), 52.

tractors which carry out a death sentence against them and smash them to pieces; earlier they undermined the grape harvest by barring exports, causing frustration among farmers; persecuting merchants and confiscating their vehicles and their identity cards in order to force them to pay insane taxes.

The Jews' behavior should come as no surprise, because history repeats itself. It was in this very month that Banu Nadir plotted against our Prophet may he rest in peace. They tried to roll a boulder on him when he was their guest and after signing contracts with him.[2] This is not surprising, since they are the tribe of treachery and deceit. The proof is in the Qur'an: "So learn a lesson, O ye who have eyes!"[3]

Our patient people, frequently the *shirk*[4] and unbelief operate hand in hand against the faith. A [good] example is the Balfour Declaration, that black page in contemporary history, when Britain worked to realize the Zionist aspiration on the basis of the saying they liked to repeat, "We are a people without a homeland who want a homeland without a people," and thus Britain forsook all its pledges to Hussein Bin Ali, "he of the first bullet,"[5] the greatest Arab traitor of our time. After the British forces conquered the port of Gaza, Lord Arthur James Balfour published his statement [known as] "the Balfour Declaration" on November 2, 1917, regarding the establishment of a national home in Palestine for what he termed "the Jewish people," and promised that the British government would make efforts to accomplish this goal. The Jews in Palestine were called a people even though they constituted no more than 8 percent of the inhabitants of Palestine. Whereas the Arabs, who were 92 percent, were called communities!!! Thus we are more convinced [than ever] that the *shirk* and infidel states, whatever their names, are faithful to the Zionist enemy, as it is written: "[O ye who believe! Take not the Jews and Christians for friends.] They are friends one to another. He among you who taketh them for friends is [one] of them."[6]

---

2. The Banu Nadir were a Jewish tribe residing near al-Madina. According to the Qur'an (Surah 59), the tribe violated its covenant with Muhammad, causing the Prophet to exile them and confiscate their property.

3. Surah of Exile (59), 2.

4. *Shirk* means a partnership of polytheism and Allah and worship of all of them. This is an unforgivable sin, but "He [Allah] forgiveth [all] save that to whom He will. Whoso ascribeth partners to Allah, he hath invented a tremendous sin." (Surah of Women (4), 48).

5. The sharif of Mecca in 1916.

6. Surah of The Table Spread (5), 51. The section in parentheses was omitted from the leaflet.

Our *murabit* people, on 19th Tishrin Thani [November], 1935, the *mujahid,* man of religion and Azhari teacher, Sheykh ʿIzz al-Din al-Qassam, inscribed a new page of heroism when he fell martyr, together with a group of his companions, after inflicting heavy losses on the British, sacrificing his soul to Allah on the morning of that day in the groves of Yaʿbed near Jenin.

This sheykh was a teacher in the Islamic school in Haifa and an imam and preacher in al-Istiqlal mosque [in Haifa] . . . al-Qassam, symbol of self-sacrifice, al-Qassam the spark of the [Arab] revolt of 1936!

Our dear people, your movement, the Islamic Resistance Movement (Hamas), salutes you in your outposts for your resolute stand against the usurper, and calls on you as follows:

1. To preserve the unity of the people. Pay no heed to the enemy's attempts to cause a rift in families, clans, currents of thought, and ideas.

2. [We must] denounce the leaflets being planted in the name of Hamas, which the occupier circulated in order to split the ranks and cast aspersions on the [various] currents. We call on the entire people, including all its factions, not to give the usurper an opportunity and to fight him.

3. We must protect the educational institutions and ensure that they fulfill their mission. We commend the role of the teachers and parents who are tending to the education of our sons, in reaction to the occupier's policy of suppressing education.

4. Hold on to the land. Do not emigrate to satisfy momentary interests such as studies, commerce, security, and flight from the iron fist. Do not give the enemy's emigration policy a chance.

5. Efforts [must] be made toward mutual aid during the olive harvest in the West Bank, in order to foil the enemy's plan.

6. We stress the strike on Saturday, October 29, the anniversary of the Kafr Qassim massacre and the English-French-Israeli aggression against Egypt, Arabism, and Islam.[7]

7. Wednesday, November 2, marking the anniversary of the wretched Balfour Declaration, will be a day of general strike.

8. Wednesday, November 9, a day of general strike marking the start of the twelfth month of the blessed uprising.

9. A general strike on Saturday, November 19, marking the fall of the man of religion and *mujahid,* Sheykh ʿIzz al-Din al-Qassam, and his companions.

---

7. The reference is to the Anglo-French attack on the Suez Canal and Israel's simultaneous Sinai Campaign in 1956.

Let the blessed uprising continue in the struggle against the occupiers. Let us burn the ground under their feet with fire.

"Those who do wrong will come to know by what a [great] reverse they will be overturned!"[8]

Allah is great, praise to God.

The Islamic Resistance Movement
Hamas
Palestine
16 Rabiʿ al-Awwal 1409
Tishrin al-Awwal [October] 27, 1988

8. Surah of The Poets (26), 227.

• • •

LEAFLET NO. 32

In the name of Allah the merciful and compassionate

"This is a clear message for mankind in order that they may be warned thereby"[1]

Communiqué No. 32

The partition of Palestine in 1947 was rejected by the Palestinian people [and] the Islamic and Arab governments and peoples—and today?!

Praise be to God, Master of the universe, prayer and peace to the commander of the *mujahidun,* the Companions of the Prophet (*sahaba*) and those who follow in their footsteps.

Our Palestinian people, forty lean years of suffering and patience, martyrs and blood, treachery and conspiracy, have ended with a year of hope and revolution, the year of the uprising against the occupation. The uprising which has eliminated any argument regarding possible life together or good-neighborliness between the two peoples, and has buried the hopes for coexistence in the sands of the humiliation, despotism, and brutality against people, animals, vegetation, and inanimate things. At the same time, the world was witness to the heroism, self-sacrifice, and patience [of] the Palestinian child, father and mother, man and woman, adult and young. They added new honor to the brow of the Palestinian people, which fought the British army, redeemed with its life the whole Arab nation, assumed responsibility for the defense of al-Aqsa mosque and the Temple Mount and its courtyards, rose up against the

---

1. Surah of Abraham (14), 52.

Jews, revived inner pride, and evoked [the deeds of] heroism and the battles of the *mujahidun,* [which are written] in the pages of history.

At the end of the first year of the uprising, elections were held for the 12th Israeli Knesset. Arab circles followed [the campaign] with great interest in the hope that the political arena would undergo change and the wagon of peace would get a push forward. However many were dumbfounded, because the results were disappointing and entailed the following ramifications:

1. Elections are a slap in the face to all Arab regimes, which are involved in a power struggle, irrespective of the differences between them.

2. The Jewish majority reveals the substance of the Jewish face that supports extremism. Some demand the annexation of the occupied lands and some call for the transfer of the Palestinians.

3. The appearance of the religious camp [in Israel] as a [political] force toward which all adopt a hypocritical attitude. At the same time, a war is waged against Islam in the Arab world and its adherents are imprisoned and killed because it is the only [force] that brings about the denunciation of the regimes and cuts the ground from under the feet of the tyrants.

On the other hand:

How can anyone who knows the Jews claim that some of them are disposed toward the good of the Arabs or call for peace? The Jew, whatever his political affiliation, will not concede anything unless he encounters strong force. "Or have they even a share in the Sovereignty? Then in that case, they would not give mankind even the speck on a date-stone."[2] All the endeavors toward peace are a waste of time and [result in] the persistence of the humiliation.

Then came the American elections, and [Arab] hearts appealed to them to express loyalty [to the elected president]. But the equation that has repeated itself since the establishment of the State of Israel [is]: the elected president is quick to declare his loyalty to the Jews and America embraces its infant and the apple of its eye.[3] Nevertheless, [the United States] continues to be a place of pilgrimage for [Arab] rulers.

Our patient people, within a few days we will mark the blackest day in the history of the Palestinian cause, the anniversary of the partition of Palestine. Its roots go back to July 7, 1937, when the Peel Commission proposed the creation of a Jewish state and an Arab state on the soil of

2. Surah of Women (4), 53.
3. Referring to Israel.

Palestine. In the London Conference, which was held from September 10–October 2, 1946, Britain proposed to the Arabs the "Union Plan" (*al-mashruʿ al-ittihadi*) [according to which] Palestine would be divided into two states, Arab and Jewish. Then, on Saturday morning, November 29, 1947, the U.N. General Assembly voted on the plan to partition Palestine, and the plan gained a majority. Thus was born Resolution 181. But no Islamic or Arab state voted for it. At the same time, the infidel states, including the United States and the Soviet Union, employed all the means and pressures at their disposal to ensure the victory of the resolution, and this is what happened.

At that time the Palestinian people [and] the Arab governments and peoples regarded the partition resolution as a treasonous resolution which must be adamantly rejected. And then came 1948, and Arab armies advanced [into Palestine] in order to prevent the Palestinian people from defending its rights, and, in a conspiracy with the infidel states, relinquished the Palestinian coast to Israel so that it could establish a state. The United States recognized it immediately, followed by the Soviet Union. The Arab regimes turned the expelled Palestinian people into a problem of refugees who found shelter in several [Arab] states. The latter used them as an excuse to collect vast funds to stabilize the disintegrating throne. It fell to the lot of the Palestinians in Lebanon to bear the brunt of the tragedy, the killing, and the tortures. The [Arab] states deluded their peoples into thinking that the Palestinian problem was the problem of all the Arabs. The upshot was the show of 1967, in which the [remaining] part of Palestine was relinquished; [and] the Golan and Sinai. When Sadat dared to hold negotiations with Israel, the Arab peoples and governments were outraged, and he was stigmatized as a collaborator, and he received his just reward at the hands of the *mujahid* hero Khalid al-Islambuli from the Islamic Movement.

In short order, the situation changed and all the Arab states began advocating peace and negotiations with Israel. [They] encouraged the Palestinians to give up their right with their own hands and to bury the era of struggle, arms, and liberation in the martyrs' cemeteries. The Arabs forgot that it was Israel that destroyed the nuclear reactor in Baghdad, invaded Tunis, and destroyed Palestinian headquarters there. Afterward, [Israel] assassinated the deputy general commander of the revolution [Abu Jihad] and still continues to threaten the nation's existence. Today, the Arabs are at a nadir [as regards their readiness] for concessions, and the Jews are at the height of overweening arrogance.

Our *murabit* people:

Your movement, Hamas, salutes your steadfastness and the continuation of your uprising, and calls on you as follows:

1. Full vigilance regarding the Jews' repeated attempts to split the united Palestinian ranks at this perilous stage, and regarding disputes at all levels. Let us deny them the opportunity and work together, and stand as one in the face of the common enemy.

2. Be alert to the consequences of the virulent propaganda against Hamas in the Israeli media, and the insertion of lying reports about mourning and strikes, and the publication of false leaflets which are full of vilifications. An example is the leaflet dated November 17, 1988.

3. To hold a general strike on Tuesday, November 29, 1988, the anniversary of the 1947 [U.N.] resolution to partition Palestine.

4. To hold a general strike on Thursday, December 8, the first anniversary of the uprising.

5. To hold a general strike on Friday, December 9, the day on which the uprising enters its second year.

6. To continue the resistance to the occupation and inflict damage on it.

7. Pay no attention to enfeeblers of the will and disregard all talk that is liable to dampen the fervor and stop the uprising.

This is the uprising on the way to the liberation of all Palestine, whoever the victims and however long it takes. Despite the barbarism and the hard hand of the usurper and despite the enervation and disarray.

"And whoso [taketh Allah and His messengers and those who believe for friend will know that], lo! the party of Allah, they are victorious."[4]

Allah is great, praise to God.

The Islamic Resistance Movement
Hamas
Palestine
Friday, 16 Rabi^c al-Thani 1409
Tishrin Thani [November] 25, 1988

---

4. Surah of The Table Spread (5), 56.

LEAFLET NO. 33

In the name of Allah the merciful and compassionate

"This is a clear message for mankind in order that they may be warned thereby"[1]

Communiqué No. 33

"Fight them! Allah will chastise them at your hands, and He will lay them low and give you victory over them, and He will heal the breasts of folk who are believers."[2]

On December 25 (Qanun al-Awwal) of 1947 the battalions of the sacred *jihad* were established by the hero ʿAbd al-Qadir al-Husseini, as a concrete reaction to the Partition Resolution, No. 181, of 1947.

Praise to God, Who gives victory to the believers and defeats the infidels and their henchmen, the enemies of religion. Prayer and peace to the imam of the *mujahidun,* paragon of the world, Muhammad, may he rest in peace, and on all his Companions, and all who follow in his path, unto the Day of Judgment.

O sons of our heroic Palestinian people,

A year has passed since the [start of] the war against the occupation and the victory over its army in the defense of this homeland and preservation of its identity. The masses of this precious Muslim people have paid for this with their blood and their sons [to the point where from the] blessed dust of the homeland grass has sprouted with an aroma like the blood of the martyrs and like

1. Surah of Abraham (14), 52.
2. Surah of Repentance (9), 14.

the tears of the patient mothers who are concerned for their children [who behave like] men.

A year has passed of pride and exaltation, [a year] filled with far-reaching changes in the way of life and habits of this people. Its sincere supplication to its God and its faith was expressed in the slogans, calls, and day-to-day behavior [during] this blessed uprising.

A year has passed which was as a new dawn in a situation [previously] fraught with despair, and has eliminated that weakness. [Despair and weakness] have vanished, and in their place have arisen the principles of self-sacrifice and martyrdom. A mighty generation has arisen, heroic and stubborn, which has imbued our cause with legitimacy and honor in all Arab and international circles, and has dispelled the fear of the occupation and its military apparatus.

Our patient people,

Despite the plunder and the Zionist tyranny, despite the force of its despotism and violence against the tremendous uprising, despite the harsh conditions, the abandonment by [the Arab] brothers [and the acts] of deception by enemies and the [sense of] helplessness, you have pushed the enemy of Allah and your enemy into a difficult situation. [The enemy] is utterly bewildered and is considering plans to liquidate the blessed uprising whose continuation God desires. It will continue, God willing, with His help and assistance, until [our] will and justice triumph over the apparatus of oppression and force. Victory will come with patience, and God helps the patient.

Our *murabit* people,

The latest political developments regarding the Palestinian problem demand of us awareness, vigilance, and understanding, lest [we find ourselves] taken by surprise at the loss of our homeland and its borders in a world which believes only in the rule of force and self-interest.

The blessed uprising which is symbolized by the *takbir*[3] generation and by the stone, warns against [the danger of] being swept up by soothing hopes, dreams, and words. It stresses that a realistic policy necessitates great momentum and an outstretched arm so that the quiver of arrows will not be emptied and to ensure the burning of all documents [dealing with a possible peace settlement], otherwise all the borders of the homeland, its shores, and Jerusalem will remain in the hands of the oppression and occupation. History teaches that a policy of force and resolute defiance preserves the claim of those who are in the right, restores the land to the dispossessed, and protects his honor.

3. *Takbir* is a call of *"Allah akbar."*

Your movement, the Islamic Resistance Movement, Hamas, will continue to raise the flag of *jihad* without retreating and without being lured by the policy trap and its labyrinth. It will maintain strictly the precepts of religion and will follow the way of all the *mujahidun* whose blood drenches this precious homeland, with utmost determination and adamance, until the restoration of the great right and the plundered homeland.

Our mujahid people,

Your movement, Hamas, is proud of you for rallying around its Islamic flag, and stresses the following points:

a. The continuation of the blessed uprising is the true guarantee for securing our just rights and is the way to victory and triumph with honor and with international standing.

b. A constant emphasis on the Islamism of the Palestinian cause and the important and cardinal role of the Arab and Islamic peoples in the war of liberation.

c. The right of the Palestinian people to establish an independent state on all the soil of Palestine. Do not heed the U.N. resolutions which try to accord the Zionist entity legitimacy over any part of the soil of Palestine, since the U.N. has no right to behave [as it pleases] regarding the land of Palestine, for it is the property of the Islamic nation and not of the U.N.

d. Constant emphasis on unity of ranks and unity of word, a healing of the rift and [resolution of] differences.

e. Do not give a chance to the intervention attempts of the [Israeli] ruling apparatus which disseminate [rumors] with the aim of stirring up hatred amongst the members of the single [Palestinian] people.

f. Maintaining the educational process and devoting all possible efforts toward the opening of all the educational institutions, and forging a proper educational atmosphere, so that the [young] generation will draw on the wellsprings of knowledge and flourish in original educational hothouses.

g. The affront to the mosques is an affront to this nation's symbol of faith. The struggle against [that affront] is a religious duty and a legitimate right. We shall not make light of the Zionist enemy's attempts to violate their sanctity by arson (as occurred in Ibtan) [or] by closure or by confiscating loudspeakers and intimidating worshippers.

O inhabitants of the *ribat,*

1. Struggle and confrontation on Sunday, December 25, 1988, to mark the anniversary of the founding of the sacred *jihad* battalions on

the soil of Palestine under the command of the hero martyr ʿAbd al-Qadir al-Husseini.

2. Friday, December 30, 1988, is declared a day of solidarity with the mosques in Palestine, the place where the uprising broke out, and the wellsprings for its continuation. On this day, worshippers will call out "Allah is great," will read from the Qurʾan in the turrets of the mosques and from the roofs of houses, and will pray for the repose of the martyrs' souls following the Friday prayers.

3. A general strike on Saturday, December 31, 1988, in solidarity with the prisoners and detainees and to protest the policy of deportation and the cruel arrests.

4. A general strike on Monday, January 9, 1989, as the blessed uprising enters the second month of its second year in order to push it forward and assure its continuation.

Let the uprising continue on the road of *jihad* and liberation until Allah shall bring salvation and give the sign for the conquest [of Palestine] and the clear victory.

"O ye who believe! Endure, outdo all others in endurance, be ready, and observe your duty to Allah, in order that ye may succeed."[4]

Allah is great, praise be to God.

The Islamic Resistance Movement
Hamas
Palestine
14 Rabiʿ al-Thani 1409
Qanun al-Awwal [December] 23, 1988

---

4. Surah of The Family of ʿImran (3), 200.

LEAFLET NO. 39

In the name of Allah the merciful and compassionate

"This is a clear message for mankind in order that they may be warned thereby."[1]

Communiqué No. 39

The second year of the uprising

"The month of Ramadan in which was revealed the Qur'an, a guidance for mankind, and clear proofs of the guidance and the Criterion [of right and wrong]."[2]

The month of Ramadan: a call to the path of righteousness and light, and a call to generosity and to *jihad*.

Praise be to God, Who exalts those who obey Him and humiliates the disobedient, savior of the *mujahidun* and crusher of the tyrants. Prayer and peace unto our master, Muhammad, and unto his family and all the Companions of the Prophet.

Brothers of Islam on the road to liberation,

Celestial lights descend on us with the advent of the month of Ramadan, as we are caught up in the fervor of the confrontation with God's and our enemy, and [the lights] infuse us with energy and bring us hope to continue to defy the soldiers of evil and the aggression against the pure soil of Palestine and our sacred Jerusalem, despite the

---

1. Surah of Abraham (14), 52.
2. Surah of The Cow (2), 185.

precious sacrifices and despite the enemy's barbarous and worsening measures of suppression. Heavenly blessings descend on us with your advent, the good month [the month of Ramadan], and you deepen within us the meaning of beneficence and generosity, and you impel us to step up the effort and the patience in the confrontation with the enemies. You lead us to the brink of a new phase in the stages of resistance to the occupation. As we receive the good month and the blessing, many memories are evoked: the eighth of April, the day on which the *mujahid* ʿAbd al-Qadir al-Husseini fell in the battle for the Qastel, and on the night after his fall the [Jewish] terrorists perpetrated the massacre at Deir Yassin. The sad memories mingle with the memories of the tremendous victories in the month of victories, the month of conquests [Ramadan], and these bind our wounds, are a consolation for bereavements, and regenerate life in the generation of the blessed uprising, the generation of the *takbir*, the generation of the stone, the generation of the liberation and the victory, God willing, for "Allah was predominant in his career, but most of mankind know not."[3]

Sons of Palestine of the *jihad* and the revolution,

The blessed and heroic uprising is advancing with sure steps and steadfast pride in defiance of the continuation of the tyranny, toward its 17th month. The good and blessed fragrances of Ramadan are wafting toward us in order to heighten our generosity and realize the virtues of the first of the *mujahidun* among the God-fearing forefathers, who were horsemen by day and celibates by night, and achieved for this world a prodigious victory, and thus gained the rewards of this world and the next world—truly, an immense triumph. And in their wake, the Islamic Resistance Movement, your movement—Hamas—greets you and salutes the arms of the *mujahidun* who avenged the martyrs who fell in the massacre of the Sheykh Radwan mosque, demonstrating that the blood of our sons is precious and will become a curse that will haunt the occupier until Hamas expels him from our pure soil, and [Hamas] issues the following call:

I. The local level:

1. We greet our people "inside" [the territories] at the outset of the blessed month of Ramadan, and we call on [the people] to make this a month of prayer, fasting, reading the Qurʾan, and wholehearted entreaties to the God of victory and vanquishment.

2. A good return to the precepts of our religion in all spheres, to practice Islam's magnificent inherent virtues and values, and to remove all that is ugly and alien.

---

3. Surah of Joseph (12), 21.

3. Escalation of the confrontations with the enemy so that his army and his Border Police shall be filled with bitterness. Cries of *"Allah akbar"* should be sounded from every locale, for they are the grenades of terror against the enemy of God and your enemy.

4. To strengthen the internal front, to help one another, to support one another, to forgive one another, to tend to the public good, to remove every division and quarrel between all the different currents, and to turn for judgment to [the representatives] of Islamic religious law when resolving disputes.

5. In order to achieve thriftiness, guidance must be provided in consumerism and a boycott imposed on the enemy's products and industry. We also urge those who buy their goods in the enemy's markets inside [Israel] to cease immediately, in order to conserve Muslim money.

6. To see to the sons' education in the houses and the mosques, and to tend to their education in the face of the policy of [inculcating] ignorance introduced by the despised Zionist occupier.

7. Total discipline in driving on the roads and heightened consciousness in traffic, without the necessity to have the police direct traffic.

8. We warn all the opportunists and traitors, enemies of the people, such as thieves, drug dealers, prostitutes, collaborators, and spies who have sold their souls to the devil, that the Islamic Resistance Movement will persecute them everywhere if they do not repent and desist before it is too late.

II. The external domain:

1. At the outset of the month of Ramadan, we greet the Islamic and Arab world and call on them to intensify their response to the blessed uprising. Response in all areas, both moral and material. The Palestinian people inside [the occupied territories] expects more and more from you, for Jerusalem should be on the conscience of every Muslim, no Muslim should be calm and tranquil before its liberation and its purification from the defilement of the usurping Jews.

2. We call on the Palestinian leaders to give their loyalty to God and to take advantage of the fragrances of this month [of Ramadan] to supplicate God for victory, and [seek] understanding not from the West, and not from the East, and not even from America. Let them turn to themselves, as they stand midway on the unknown road of concessions [in the political sphere], and ask themselves sincerely where they are bound, for the day will soon come on which we will hear about a Palestinian move that conceded part of our right, while our enemy did not budge. Until when will this concession continue? What will we gain from it? We warn against falling into the net of American

policy, which is based on gradual and unilateral concession. This is our advice to you.

3. We call on the world Islamic movement to increase its efforts in the information sphere abroad regarding the Islamic Resistance Movement, Hamas, in order to break the barrier of media blackout imposed by the enemy's apparatus and that of the collaborators in the region, about the *jihad* of the Palestinians within the occupied land.

4. The Islamic Resistance Movement supports the establishment of an Islamic state in Afghanistan, and calls on all the Islamic states to recognize and support it. [Hamas] holds out hope for it, and views it as a jumping-off point for Jerusalem, God willing.

5. We call on our brothers in Lebanon to stop the killing that is going on among them and to aim their weapons at the Zionist enemy who is sitting on the soil of Lebanon and the soil of Palestine alike. At the same time, we salute the Islamic Resistance Movement in Lebanon and call on it to step up the escalation against the Zionist enemy.

III. Action plans:

1. To designate the first day of Ramadan as a day of escalation and confrontation marking the onset of the month of conquests and victories.

2. A general strike on Saturday, April 8, 1989—marking the day on which the *mujahid* ʿAbd al-Qadir al-Husseini and his comrades fell in the Battle of the Qastel.

3. A general strike on Sunday, April 9, 1989—marking the advent of the 5th month in the second year of the blessed uprising. The uprising should be escalated to commemorate the massacre at Deir Yassin by the Jewish terrorists.

4. Wednesday, April 12, 1989—A day for calling out *"Allah akbar"* and reading the Qurʾan aloud from the mosques and the roofs of houses to mark the opening of fire at the worshippers in al-Aqsa mosque in 1982.

5. Monday, April 17, 1989—A day of solidarity with the prisoners on the occasion of the Day of the Palestinian Prisoner. On this day there will be an escalation of the confrontation with the occupier and solidarity with the families of the detainees and tending to their family needs.

6. To mark the nights of Ramadan with night prayers, assemblies, reading the Qurʾan and collective meals and to mark the days of Islamic commemoration in the mosques. We wish to remind you that the 6th of Ramadan is the day of the conquest of Amorium in the period of

Muʿtasim,[4] and the 10th of Ramadan is the day on which the Prophet, prayer and peace unto him, set out to conquer Mecca, which was taken on the 20th of Ramadan.

7. The 10th of Ramadan will be marked as the day on which the Egyptian Army crossed the Suez Canal,[5] with cries of *"Allah akbar."* On this day, call out *"Allah akbar"* from the mosques and the roofs of houses.

Let us reiterate our fixed slogan: In the name of Allah, Allah is great, the hour of Khaybar has arrived.

Allah is great, praise be to God.

The Islamic Resistance Movement
Hamas
Shaʿban 29, 1049
Nissan [April] 5, 1989

4. After defeating the Byzantine Emperor Theophilus, the Caliph Muʿtasim took Amorium in Galatia, following a lengthy siege, by the use of treachery, in 837.
5. In the October War of 1973.

LEAFLET NO. 45

In the name of Allah the merciful and compassionate

"Read: In the name of the Lord Who createth."[1]

Communiqué No. 45

The second year of the uprising

Knowledge and study are a sacred right which we shall maintain, and no one does us a favor in this.

Praise be to God, the Sovereign of the universe, prayer and peace to the master of all the created, our master Muhammad, and to his family and his Companions and those who follow him unto the Day of Judgment.

"Say: Are those who know equal with those who know not?"[2]

Our heroic Palestinian people, O sons of the self-sacrifice, the heroism, and the offering, you whose constancy has recorded the most magnificent exploits of heroism and whose patience has recorded the clearest milestones,

O proud Palestinian people,

Despite the Jews' desperate attempts to shatter our will and trample our honor, today they find themselves facing our determination and our constancy, this people's *jihad*, which erupted in the name of Allah, and the sacrifices. Today, they are subdued against their will into partially acknowledging the right of our sons to know and to study, and they are compelled to announce their decision to open the schools, but in a

---

1. Surah of The Clot (96), 1.
2. Surah of The Troops (39), 9.

wretched and bizarre manner, within the framework of their policy, which seeks to inculcate ignorance in our people and to deprive our sons of the right to know and to study.

Our sons the pupils, the beacons of knowledge, the way of integrity and light, the hopes of this nation, its pride and treasure, the school is the firm bastion which we must preserve and whose integrity we must maintain, just as we see to struggling against the occupier and to stoning him, so that [the schools] will continue to be natural hothouses for shaping the generations and building the nation and raising its sons on the basis of the knowledge, the morality, the nobility, and the manliness which God wanted the Islamic nation to possess.

Our magnificent people, our beloved students,

Your movement, the Islamic Resistance Movement, Hamas, understands that the enemy's decision to open the schools is an overt attempt to prettify its severe and ugly face. Despite this, [Hamas] calls on the inhabitants and the students not to belittle this right and not to forgo it, but to preserve it in full, and not to denigrate it. Therefore, your movement, the leading and pioneering Islamic Resistance Movement, Hamas, aware of the essence of the conflict with the Jews, calls on you as follows:

I. In the external domain:

1. We reiterate our call to all the humanitarian institutions in the world to persist with your efforts and to intervene quickly, once again, by exerting pressure for the opening of the universities and the institutes in our beloved Palestine, so that the students will not be deprived of their most basic right.

2. Restricting the duration of studies to a short period (two months, as published) is no more than a media gimmick vis-à-vis the world, in order to conceal the policy of [inculcating] ignorance which the Jews are implementing against our people.

3. We stress to the entire world that dozens of our school pupils are still detained under arbitrary arrest, and therefore we call on the international organizations for cultural affairs to intervene quickly to bring about their immediate and unconditional release.

4. We request that our brethren outside[3] facilitate the process of admitting our students to the universities and press their governments to admit a larger number of Palestinian students.

II. In the internal domain:

1. We call on all the students and teachers to go to the schools this Saturday, July 22, 1989, and to conduct regular classes out of concern for

---

3. Referring to the universities in the Arab states.

the well-being of the educational process. This does not conflict with the general strike which the Islamic Resistance Movement, Hamas, designated in its previous leaflet, a strike which encompasses the workers, public transportation facilities, and businesses.

2. We affirm all the actions noted in leaflet no. 44 of the Islamic Resistance Movement, Hamas.

3. We call on our brother teachers and on our sons, the pupils, to ensure that teacher-pupil relations are relations of friendliness, love, trust, and mutual respect. We express our great esteem to the teachers and pupils who were harmed by the Jews economically and morally, and we view this as [cause for] a *jihad* for the sake of Allah and a *ribat* for His sake.

4. We urge our brother school principals to show consideration for our pupils' mental and economic state and the security conditions. Let us demonstrate patience, wisdom, and a good attitude, and take on ourselves something of the material burden of the destitute pupils.

5. We call on our brother teachers to devote themselves to their work and heighten their efforts to compensate our pupils for the rights they have lost, and may they seek reward from God alone.

6. The families and parents of pupils should assist in school by guiding and training the pupils and encouraging them to assert our right to study.

7. The Islamic Resistance Movement, Hamas, expresses great thanks and gratitude to all those who took part in the education process while the schools were closed.

Knowledge builds indestructible houses, and ignorance destroys houses of magnificence and honor.

Allah is great, praise be to God.

The Islamic Resistance Movement, Hamas
Palestine
Friday, 18 Dhu al-Hijja 1409
Tamuz [July] 21, 1989

LEAFLET NO. 49

In the name of Allah the merciful and compassionate

"This is a clear message for mankind in order that they may be warned thereby."[1]

Communiqué No. 49

The second year of the uprising

The wretched Balfour Declaration proves that the community of unbelievers is one . . .

Praise be to God, Sovereign of the universe, God's prayer on the commander of the *mujahidun*, on his family and on the *sahaba* and the *tabiʿun*,[2] and on those who follow him, the *murabitun* on the soil of the *Isra'*, unto Judgment Day.

O *mujahid* Palestinian people,

Two blessed years of the uprising will soon have passed, which have upset balances, altered strategies, and introduced new factors into global policy. These [developments] were imposed by the blood of the martyrs and the wounded, by our people's patience, fortitude, and determination to continue the *jihad,* and to crush [Israel,] the state of dispossession and despotism, despite all [its] barbaric methods and immoral actions that contradict the most basic human morality.

Two years of glory and pride have been recorded by our heroic Muslim people in defying the undefeated [Israeli] army, the army equipped

1. Sura of Abraham (14), 52.
2. The followers of the *sahaba*.

with American weapons, the army which defeated all the [Arab] collaborationist regimes in six hours, not six days; two years that have restored Palestinian self-confidence, Arab honor, and Muslim hope and longing. Greetings of honor and esteem to all the arms that are engaged in the *jihad,* which are forging the dawn of success for the Palestinian people and all the oppressed peoples in our Arab and Muslim world and for the whole world. Greetings to those who have gained a martyr's death (*shahada*) during the days of escalation which were declared by the Islamic Resistance Movement, Hamas, in Nablus, Maythalun, Jenin, ʿAayda [refugee] camp, Hebron, Gaza, and all the towns, villages, and camps of valiant Palestine.

Our patient Palestinian people,

As the pressure of the uprising increases on the enemy's state and its institutions, there are a growing number of plans which seek to relieve the pressure on [Israel] because of its entanglement—beginning with the Shamir plan, the Mubarak plan, the Baker plan, and many other plans. Here we find ourselves puzzled and ask:

Why were these plans not put forward before the uprising? Why did American imperialism agree to crush the Palestinian people? Is there among all these plans another plan, one which seeks the good of the Palestinian people? We understand that America has activated its people in the region to put forward plans that lead the Palestinian people astray in order to forgo its rights in return for a misleading mirage. Our people has already rejected previously all the plans which harm its rights and grant the usurping enemy [even] one inch of the soil of the blessed soil of *Isra*ʾ, has rejected the partition resolution and the Balfour Declaration, and has given thousands of sacrifices. How, then, shall it assent today to something that is less than those miserable programs?

O heroic Muslim people,

The Islamic Resistance Movement, Hamas, which emerged from the conscience of this people and spoke its language, and around which the Palestinian masses united, believed in its principles and responded to its calls, affirms, as the uprising enters its third year, the third year since the movement's founding, the principles for which it was established, for the implementation of which we are fighting, and around which the masses have united:

1. Palestine from the sea to the river is Islamic soil which must not be conceded and not an inch of which must be given to the enemy.

2. The only method the enemy understands is the method of force, therefore the *jihad* is the only means for restoring the land and liberating the holy places.

3. America and Britain, author of the wretched Balfour Declaration, are full partners of the Jewish entity in all its crimes, and therefore in our eyes are at the same level of hostility.

4. We will not agree to trade in the blood of our martyrs, the torments of our wounded, and the groans of our prisoners. The soul of Palestine and the people of Palestine are not merchandise in the market of cheap commerce.

5. The Palestinian people alone will decide its fate, the people of the uprising are masters of the situation and the defenders of the land.

6. The Islamic Resistance Movement, Hamas, asserts its absolute opposition to all the peace plans being put forward in the region because none of them, including the recent Baker plan, correspond to the goals of the insurgent Palestinian people.

Our *murabit* Muslim people,

Your movement, the Islamic Resistance Movement, Hamas, calls on you, as the third year of the uprising and of the movement's founding draws near, as follows:

I. In the external domain:

1. To aid the uprising with all material and moral means: "Whoever equips one conqueror for God, is himself akin to a conqueror."[3]

2. To denounce the crimes of the Jewish enemy in all the world, Arab, and local media.

3. To hold demonstrations, marches, assemblies, and meetings in support of the uprising.

4. To devote Friday sermons in this period to the uprising and its achievements.

II. In the internal domain:

1. To set up special committees in order to study methods for strengthening the uprising and improving it quantitatively and qualitatively.

2. To warn against the crafty American method that facilitates the procedures for the emigration of Palestinian youth to America, and which has begun to tempt the weak of character.

3. Hamas calls on our Muslim masses to stand up to the Zionist Jews who are called the "Temple Mount Faithful," who wish to lay the cornerstone for the imaginary temple, in place of al-Aqsa. We call on the [Arab] inhabitants of Jerusalem and its surroundings to be prepared to respond to the call of al-Aqsa at any time.

4. To warn against the "planted" leaflets in the name of the Islamic Resistance Movement, Hamas, such as the leaflet attacking the heroic

---

3. A *hadith* ascribed to Muhammad.

inhabitants of Beit Sahur. Hamas movement asserts that this cheap method is far-removed from the way which is familiar to our masses. Likewise, [Hamas] asserts that it is the movement of all the Palestinian masses, Muslims and Christians without distinction, as it follows strictly the way of the Qur'an, which states: "And thou wilt find the nearest of them in affection to those who believe [to be] those who say: Lo! We are Christians. That is because there are among them priests and monks and because they are not proud."[4]

5. To dedicate the general strike on Sunday, October 29, 1989, to the memory of the massacre at Kafr Qassim, and to mark the anniversary of the triple aggression against Egypt, against Arabism, and against Islam.[5]

6. November 2, 1989—A general strike on the anniversary of the wretched Balfour Declaration, as a proclamation by our people of their opposition to solutions that infringe on its rights and [cause them] to lose its land.

7. Prayer for the repose of the souls of the martyrs, on Friday, November 3, 1989.

8. November 9, 1989—A general strike to mark the start of the 24th month of the uprising.

9. November 15, 1989—A day of Palestinian slogans and flags, decorated [with the inscription], There is no God but Allah.

10. November 19, 1989 — A day of escalating the confrontations against the army and the settlers, as the anniversary of the fall of the illustrious religious sage, the *mujahid* 'Izz al-Din al-Qassam, the imam and preacher in the Haifa mosque in 1935.

11. November 22, 1989—A day of a general strike in solidarity with our detainees in the enemy's Nazi prisons.

12. November 24–25, 1989—Two days of escalation of the confrontations against the enemy soldiers and the settlers.

Let the uprising continue: "And Allah was predominant in his career, but most of mankind know not."[6]

Allah is great, praise be to God.

The Islamic Resistance Movement
Hamas
Palestine
Friday, October 27, 1989
27 Rabi' al-Awwal 1410

4. Surah of The Table Spread (5), 82.
5. In the Suez Campaign of 1956.
6. Surah of Joseph (12), 21.

• • •

SPECIAL LEAFLET

In the name of Allah the merciful and compassionate

"Faint not nor grieve, for ye will overcome them if ye are indeed believers."[1]

"Fight them! Allah will chastise them at your hands, and He will lay them low and give you victory over them, and He will heal the breasts of folk who are believers."[2]

Call to the 19th Palestinian National Council [Session]

Our brothers ... the members of the National Council:
The Islamic Resistance Movement, Hamas, has already made it clear that it posits [as a goal] an all-encompassing *jihad* until the liberation of all Palestine, and it took a decision on the eruption of the uprising, on December 8, 1987, in order to realize this goal. All the members of [the people of] Palestine sided, and continue to side, with it. With the help of Allah, the power latent in our people was able to burst forth, making [the people] the paragons of the century when they confronted the usurping Jewish enemy in daily clashes. The enemy tried many times to stop or eradicate the uprising, even [in] coordination with certain sections [of the people] in order to quell it ... But Allah, may He be exalted, blessed the fighting arms of the Palestinian people and thwarted all these plans.
Your people has already proved that it is capable of change and confrontation under the worst conditions of defeat which the nation is

---

1. Surah of The Family of ʿImran (3), 139.
2. Surah of Repentance (9), 14.

experiencing, and leaped forward believing in Allah, certain of victory, and paving the way to the full liberation until you return to your homes and the diaspora shall be ingathered and together we shall build the glorious civilized Palestine with God's help.

In the wake of this substantive reality, we stress to you that we have adopted a strategy of an all-encompassing *jihad* campaign in order to struggle against the occupation until the liberation of all Palestine, no matter how much time and how many victims [this requires] . . . Here is the celestial destiny that confronts you with a fateful choice. We urge you to rise to the occasion. Either you choose the closing of the gates of the *jihad* by recognizing the Zionist entity, or [you choose] the continuation of the all-encompassing *jihad* [as you] find refuge in the Creator and trust in His victory . . .

We all hope that you will stand behind the aspirations of your people, for the people chose the way . . . the way of *jihad*, honor, and sacrifice, finding that for the sake of Allah and the liberation of Palestine, whatever is more precious and more valuable than money, than a son and than the soul, is cheap.

Our brothers, the members of the Palestinian National Council . . . sons of Qibya and Deir Yassin . . .

In this session of your council, there are those who urge agreement on stopping the fighting with the enemy and signing an agreement recognizing him, and an agreement on abandoning the greater part of Palestine . . . Be careful not to be dragged after the exponents of this inclination, which is dangerous and destructive to our cause . . . And let us say to them . . . In whose name are you about to recognize this usurping and false entity? In whose name are you condemning to failure the uprising and delivering a death blow to the achievements of the exemplary and *jihadic* achievements?! Which of the martyrs authorized you?! Which of the wounded solicited you?! Which of the widows has approached you in supplication?! Which of the infants has sought your help to conduct negotiations with the Jews, the enemies of peace and of humanity, the murderers of the prophets?! Is it in the name of the suckling babe into whose eye the Jew was quick to fire a bullet while he was in his mother's arms?! Or in the name of the sheykh whom the Jew kicked in the leg and [then] stepped on his forehead, which worships only Allah?! Or in the name of the mother whose son was robbed from her arms and thrown into the black pits of prison?! Or in the name of the youth whose bones Rabin broke?! Or in the name of the youth upon whom they rained blows and electric stingings [beatings] and who are injected with bacteria at the order of Rabin, Shamir, and Peres?! Or in the name of the family whose home the Jews destroyed, leaving [the family] to live under the open skies?! In whose name, O our gentlemen, will you conduct negotiations?!

O gentlemen:

The defeatist and submissive declarations that were issued by some of those inside occupied Palestine express only the truth of their defeatist stand and their haste [to find] political solutions and the feelings of their submissive heart which hasn't the strength to stand up to the confrontation and is totally unrelated to the uprising. Do not be tempted by statements and voices calling for peace with the murderers who are occupying our land and humiliating our people. We view them as bankrupts who have been spewed out by their people. And if they do not return to common sense, the people and history will ignore them, and the curse of the generations will fall on them.

Members of the National Council . . . sons of our *mujahid* people:

The Islamic Resistance Movement, Hamas, vows to persist on the road of *jihad* until the liberation of all Palestine, and has pledged to the martyrs to punish every traitor as he deserves, and regards whoever recognizes the Jewish entity on even a grain of the soil of Palestine [as doomed] to suffer from the ramifications of that recognition—he will be hounded by the children of the stones with their strong arms wherever he may be!

We in the Hamas movement condemn all the stands calling for a cessation of *jihad* and resistance, or calling for peace with the murderers, or calling for recognition of the Jewish entity over any part of our soil. We warn them that the account of the generations with them will not be light, however long it takes [to settle].

O brothers:

Let us remind you that our people did not sacrifice its blood for seventy years [only so] someone would come and negotiate with the Jews in its name, for the generations preceding us had the ability to do this without the need for all the great sacrifices. All the sacrifices were not [made] for an ugly ministate [which underwent a metamorphosis] as some would like to see. Our people made sacrifices to save the honor and the glory of the nation in order to destroy the cancerous Jewish entity which strives to dominate our whole region. We think that the soil of Palestine is the property of the generations of Muslims until the Day of Judgment, and it or any part of it must not be belittled, and it or any part of it must not be handed over, and no Arab state [whatsoever] nor all the Arab states together have the right to do this. No organization nor all the Palestinian and Arab organizations have this right, because no one has the right to fulfill the role of the generations of Muslims unto Judgment Day, and we consider the handing over of any part of Palestine as forsaking part of the religion!

O gentlemen:

We stress to you that the plan known as a "provisional government," or the "charter of independence," or the "government-in-exile," and whatever includes a plan for a solution, is nothing more than bait with the purpose of sticking a knife in the back of the uprising's achievements, a sword in the back of the children of the stones, and preventing our children from continuing the struggle and [from experiencing] martyrdom. Our struggle with the Zionists is not a campaign for a partition of borders and it is not a dispute over the division of land, it is a campaign over entity and destiny. In this stand we see the hope and aspiration of our people everywhere to arouse in you the spirit of the struggle, the spirit of the outbreak of the revolution of 1965.[3] We call on you to take under your wing the spirit of the children of the stones and the continuation of the armed struggle, no matter what the cost. Our people has often confronted plots, and has made many sacrifices to thwart them. Our people is still possessed with the same readiness to make sacrifice after sacrifice, and it expresses this through this blessed uprising which has been recorded as a phenomenon unexampled in history.

This is your people, this is its hope, this is its readiness and this is its stand. We confront you with your historic responsibility regarding this conflict and regarding this courageous people, so that you will do your duty and offer the most precious sacrifice for Palestine, for the sacred soil, and for its heroic people, in order that your names may be inscribed in golden ink in the histories of this sacred conflict; for you fulfilled your role in foiling the plot and were witnesses to this way, the way of struggle and resistance. You must declare openly and powerfully: no to the Zionist state! Even to a single grain of sand from Palestine. There is no peace with the murderers! No to recognizing the occupier! No to negotiations with the criminals!

Yes to an armed struggle, yes to the uprising, yes to sacrifice no matter how costly, as long as the way takes, and despite all the huge plots!

Our heroic Palestinian people . . . Our sons and brothers the soldiers of the blessed uprising . . . O the *murabitun* on the soil of the *ribat*:

Allah chose you so that you will be the pioneers of the Islamic nation in the confrontation with the Jewish enemy. Did you accept the choice?

---

3. The beginning of Fatah's guerilla warfare against Israel. The mention of this date would seem to indicate the national-Palestinian face of Hamas.

Disperse yourselves in all [parts of] Palestine in order to stand firm in the confrontation with the usurping Jewish enemy, impute to him all the disasters, destroy his institutions and his abhorred entity, so that Sunday, Monday, and Tuesday, November 13, 14, 15, 1988, shall be days of confrontation and resistance, rejection of peace with the murderers in order to thwart all the calls of surrender and in order to stop the capitulators from playing in the conflict and those who are gambling on the enemy's elections.[4]

"Allah is with you, and He will not grudge [the reward of] your actions."[5]

And this is a struggle in the way of Allah until victory or martyrdom.

The Islamic Resistance Movement, Hamas
Palestine
Thursday, 30 Rabi ͨ al-Awwal 1409
Tishrin al-Thani [November] 10, 1988

---

4. The reference is to the Israeli government's plan of 1988 to hold municipal elections in the territories as the first step toward political settlement.

5. Surah of Muhammad (47), 35.

SPECIAL LEAFLET

In the name of Allah the merciful and compassionate

To those of understanding in Palestine

"Allah loveth not the utterance of harsh speech save by one who hath been wronged. Allah is ever Hearer, Knower."[1]

Special Proclamation

The distress of detainees from the Islamic Resistance Movement, Hamas, in the Jewish prisons

Praise be to God, Sovereign of the universe, prayer and peace to the faithful Prophet and his followers, unto the Day of Judgment.
Honorable brother Yasir Arafat, chairman of the Executive Committee of the Palestine Liberation Organization.
Honorable chairman and members of the Palestinian National Council.
Our patient Palestinian people.
Brother supporters of Hamas in the world.
O Muslims everywhere.
Peace unto you and the mercies of Allah, may He be exalted.
We the sons of the Islamic Movement, Hamas, in the Jewish prisons and in the heart of the Jewish detention centers (Juneid, Megiddo, Ramallah, Hebron, al-Dahariya, the Negev, Ashkelon—the police, Bituniya, Jenin, Shatta, and Nafha), send you from behind bars a summary of our situation and of the distress [we encounter] from those who are skin of our skin, members of the Fatah movement. Our slogan during the past years has been patience and not fear, unity and not division, and in preserving unity

1. Surah of the Women (4), 148.

of ranks and the strength of the edifice, we suffered and preferred silence over speech, and pains over division. We constantly deferred being the initiators of harm to anyone, lest the enemy benefit by it ... And the blessed uprising came and our number was doubled, as a result of which the distress began to be felt flagrantly in every location ... And we remained silent, until our silence was taken as weakness.

Our policy was to ensure that the conflict was not shifted to the Palestinian street, out of concern for the national unity which we regard as the first stage toward victory. We relied on the path of forgiveness of the oppressed and on rising above the curses, and therefore we do not curse those who cursed us in their official leaflets and accused us of treachery and [made] other accusations. We made contact with the Fatah command several times, but we found only talk and empty promises. There was no change in the situation of the detainees and in the rest of the distress and in the exploitation on the part of those who are closest. And we had no choice but to reveal to the world the consequences of the situation in which we find ourselves, and which we shall sum up as follows—and Allah is witness to what we shall say:

1. Contempt for the sanctity of Islam on the part of some of the leaders and their aides. This took the form of curses against the Godhead itself and curses against the faith, shouts during prayer, and they are not silent during the call [to prayer], and sometimes they prevent the call, for example the dawn call ... And violating the sanctity of the month of Ramadan by eating openly, and behavior that runs contrary to courtesy and the religion, and they turn up the volume of their radios when immoral songs are played ... and so on and so forth.

2. Preventing many Hamas members from taking part [in Hamas activity in the prisons] when they arrive for classification in the detention centers (before the General National Committee), which is composed of PLO groups. They claim that Hamas does not [exist] in this detention center, and they force the lion-cub detainees (*al-ashbal*) to belong to Fatah, and then threaten them with blows and accuse them of collaboration if they wish to be in the Islamic Movement ... And there are many more examples.

3. Vigorous blows and teasing [with the use of] various expressions. Some of the brothers had hands, legs, and teeth broken. Some were wounded in the head or were slashed on the hands with razors. Some had the hairs of their beard plucked out ... No consideration is given to age or status or education. The elderly and the young, the imam and the religion official, the teacher and the pupil ... all are equal in the face of the torture and suffering.

4. Slanders against us and against our movement [which are voiced] winkingly and implicitly, publicly and indirectly, in our ears and behind our backs, to the point where [such calumnies] appear in writing as basic and systematic material in the pamphlets according to which the units [i.e., the groups of prisoners] are educated day and night. In addition, they say that we are collaborators and have contacts with the [Israeli] authorities, and that the Jews stand behind Hamas so that its leaders will be an alternative to the organization [the PLO].

5. Voicing ongoing threats against us inside the prisons and pledging [that this will continue] on the outside.

6. Depriving the members of the Islamic Movement in the detention centers of all their rights, while at the same time all the PLO branches enjoy their full rights, even if the prison contains only one detainee [from a PLO wing]. These rights include, among others, [activity within the framework of] the national, educational, sports, and other committees, and even the services committees.

7. Preventing the Islamic Movement from receiving separate rooms in many of the detention centers and prisons, where they can carry out their administrative and educational and other activities, like the rest of the Palestinian organizations. Hamas young people are scattered in a large number of rooms and strong pressures are brought to bear on them.

8. Prohibiting some of the Muslim young people from delivering the Friday *khutba*[2] in certain detention centers. They [the Fatah members] assume exclusivity over the *khutba*, even though some of the preachers [of the *khutba*] are not worshippers, so the *khutba* is turned into a political manifesto.

9. Denying the sons of the Islamic Movement access to the "special canteen," which is the money the authorities permit to be brought in from the families in order to purchase vital necessities. Our personal money is confiscated and added to the "general canteen," with most of it earmarked for the purchase of tea, coffee, and cigarettes, whereas we, by our nature, do not smoke and we have no part in anything. What the normal smoker takes in one day would suffice us for two weeks and more, if we had the explicit right to make use of our money.

10. The members of the Islamic Movement are denied winter clothing such as sweaters and overcoats, on the claim that they were purchased at the expense of the organization [the PLO] and Hamas has no

2. *Khutba*—sermon.

right to them. Likewise, we are deprived of writing utensils which we require for education and studies.

O honorable brothers: These are some of the measures which are implemented against us by our people who have blocked every road of debate and understanding, and which has led us to appeal to you. Do we not suffer enough from the enemies of Islam and the enemies of mankind, the grandsons of the apes and the pigs who delight in inflicting various types of physical and mental pain against us and against our people in the imprisoned homeland??!! Their happiness grows when they witness our schisms and the differences between us.

O brothers, we expect of you, each in his place, to take on himself all the measures [required in order to] put a stop to this distress and to the types of mental and physical intimidation being conducted against us, and God will help us enough.

Peace unto you and the mercies of Allah and His blessings.

Sons of the Islamic Resistance Movement, Hamas
in the Jewish prisons and detention centers
April 1990

LEAFLET NO. 71

In the name of Allah the merciful and compassionate

"This is a clear message for mankind, in order that they may be warned thereby."[1]

Communiqué No. 71

The fourth year of the uprising

"Do not slacken, therefore, nor grieve; you will have the upper hand, if you continue firm in the faith."[2]

Praise be to God, prayer and peace to the leader of the *mujahidun* and the members of his household and his Companions and all those who followed him, unto the Day of Judgment.

O our suffering Palestinian people, O [you] who are clashing with all your strength against the enemies of God and your enemy. You who trust [first] in God, and only then in yourselves, in a period in which the enmity against our Arab and Islamic nation is intensifying on every side. Look how you provoke the Zionist enemy despite the suppression, the deportations, the arrests, and the curfew everywhere in our beloved homeland. This gives expression to your will that our people's blessed Intifada shall continue with head held high and with supreme sacrifice and with an iron will, with the aim of clashing with the occupying enemy until the liberation and the establishment of our Islamic state on all our Palestinian soil.

O masses of our *mujahid* people, it was God's wish that the blessed month of Ramadan should fall in critical circumstances and in a period

---

1. Surah of Ibrahim (14), 52.
2. Surah of The Family of ʿImran (3), 140.

of a dangerous shift which is befalling our nation, when the Jewish-Crusader offensive is becoming more intense. Its intention is to despoil the treasures [of our nation] and erode its strength, to break its morale and occupy unjustly its lands, become the master of its fate and perpetuate a situation of dependence causing our nation to remain frightened, subjugated, and helpless—God forbid.

The month of Ramadan has arrived, and the Zionist enemy is still perched on the soil of *al-Isra' wal-Mi'raj*, [a fact] which causes our Palestinian people great suffering. [The Zionist enemy] is pushing ahead with his expansionist plans, taking advantage of the situation created by the Gulf War, and the American-Crusader aggression against our brothers in Iraq.

The Islamic Resistance Movement, Hamas, which is renewing its covenant with God and with the people in order to follow the road toward the liberation of Palestine, all Palestine, calls on our people to draw inspiration from the great heritage of our forefathers in the blessed month of Ramadan, making this the springboard for the nation's revival and awakening in order to achieve cultural independence, release from the cycle of emulating others, and expulsion of the aggressive invaders from its soil.

O masses of our Islamic nation, Kuwait is now being returned to its inhabitants. We would have expected this return to be the result of an Iraqi desire or a response to the call of Hamas and similar initiatives to ensure that the solution would be an Arab-Islamic one. But because of what happened, we call on our brothers in Kuwait to show understanding because the ties with the Iraqi people are ties of faith, blood, and neighborliness. All of us must demonstrate a capacity for restraint and rise to a level of belief and brotherhood. We must not allow the infidels to remain among us and foment discord. We also wish to remind our brothers in Kuwait of the faith, fraternity, and affinity with the Palestinian people. Let them not heed the rumor-mongers who sow strife [*fitna*] and discord between the Kuwaitis and the Palestinian community. It must be explained to America, the leader of the Crusader-Zionist coalition, that it is not the guardian of our nation's interest but the true enemy which implements the Jews' programs.

"Incline not towards those who do wrong lest the Fire should afflict you, and then you will have no friend beside Allah."[3]

O *mujahid* Palestinian people, your movement, the Islamic Resistance Movement, Hamas, calls on you as follows:

I. The external domain

---

3. Surah of Hud (11), 113.

1. We greet our *mujahid* Palestinian people and our Arab Islamic nation which is about to usher in the blessed month of Ramadan. We call on them to take advantage of this event to renew the covenant with God, to draw near to Him through fasting, charitable works, visiting relatives, honest cooperation, and the fear of God.

2. The Islamic Resistance Movement, Hamas, calls on the Arab Islamic governments to act toward their people according to God's will as this is [given expression] in the sacred book [the Qur'an] and in the *sunna*[4] of the Prophet, and to conduct their lives according to the law of the *shura*[5] so that the [Arab and Islamic] peoples can enjoy freedom of will and freedom of decision.

3. The Islamic Resistance Movement, Hamas, calls on the masses of our Arab and Islamic nation to stand adamantly, resolutely, and courageously in the face of the arrogance of America, leader of the Crusader-Zionist coalition. Hamas calls for the withdrawal of the Crusader fleets and armies from Iraq, from the Arab Peninsula, and from the entire region.

4. The Islamic Resistance Movement, Hamas, calls on the Arab and Islamic peoples and governments to reject the new world order which America, the leader of the Crusader-Zionist coalition, is trying to foist on our region with the aim of perpetuating its dependence and depleting its resources.

5. The Islamic Resistance Movement, Hamas, calls on the Arab and Islamic states and on all the Arab and Islamic peoples to reject the U.N. resolutions pertaining to Palestine. [These resolutions] seek to grant legitimacy to the aggressive Jewish entity on every part of our blessed Palestinian soil, even though it is a sacred land and a trust to be shouldered by every Muslim and Arab.

II. The local level

1. The Islamic Resistance Movement, Hamas, strengthens the hands of our people's masses whose morale and whose determination to follow the ways of God were not affected by the latest arrests. May [God] bless them together with the masses of our *mujahid* Palestinian people.

2. The Islamic Resistance Movement, Hamas, places responsibility for the death of the martyr Wa'il Tawfiq Sawalma, from the Balata [refugee] camp, on the Israeli intelligence bodies. He died as a result of torture, shortly after his release from detention. Hamas also emphasizes that the blood of the martyrs is not shed in vain.

---

4. *Sunna*—traditions and customs which together comprise Muslim law of the Orthodox stream.
5. *Shura*—Islamic canonic consultation.

3. The Islamic Resistance Movement, Hamas, calls on the masses of the Palestinian people to maintain relations of mutual help, particularly in the light of the economic crisis being suffered by our people.

4. The Islamic Resistance Movement, Hamas, requests that the month of Ramadan be a month of fulfilling precepts and drawing close to God by reading the Qur'an and preaching for charity.

III. Action plans

1. Saturday, March 9, 1991, a general strike marking the start of the fortieth month of the Intifada.

2. Thursday, March 21, 1991, escalation on the occasion of Karameh Battle Day.

3. Ramadan 17, marking the Battle of Badr.

4. Saturday, March 30, 1991, a general strike on the occasion of Land Day.

5. The nights of Ramadan should be utilized to call out "There is no God but Allah" and for *takbir* ["Allah the greatest"] cries, and for writing slogans on fences and hoisting flags of Palestine under the slogan "There is no God but Allah."

Let the uprising continue until victory.

Allah is great, praise be to God.

The Islamic Resistance Movement
Hamas
Ramadan 1411
March 1991

• • •

LEAFLET NO. 74

In the name of Allah the merciful and compassionate

"This is a clear message for mankind, in order that they may be warned thereby."[1]

Communiqué No. 74

The fourth year of the uprising

"Then sue not for peace because of your slackness, for you will certainly have the upper hand."[2]

Praise be to God, beloved of the believers, helper of the *mujahidun,* victor over tyrants, bringer of disgrace upon the hypocrites, prayer and peace unto the leader of the *mujahidun,* paragon of the creation, Muhammad, may he rest in peace.

O our *mujahid* Palestinian people, O those who continue the blessed Intifada with pride, exultation of spirit, and nobility. [O those] who make the greatest sacrifices despite the Jews' suppression operations, the mass arrests, demolition of houses, land expropriations, deportation of the defenseless, the murder of women, the elderly, and infants, [and despite] the curfew which the enemy imposes on the towns and villages even on holy days. You thereby serve as exemplars in the *jihad,* the steadfastness, and the sacrifice, especially in this period of *jihad,* which means unbounded giving and sacrifice.

The plot against your sacred cause has been going on since the Balfour Declaration because the hypocrites and the cowards from

---

1. Surah of Abraham (14), 52.
2. Surah of Muhammad (47), 35.

among our people aided our enemies and convinced the *mujahidun* to believe the declarations and promises of the allies and their friends and thus to neglect the *jihad* and lay down their arms and to be persuaded that we have common interests with the Jewish enemy. The result is that these fools believed in that and were afraid, and called for peace with the murderers and the Jews. These allies persisted with their plans and thus we arrived at the situation we see today. Today, the enemies play the same tune again, in the same style, concerning the program of the "imaginary peace" and the common interests between the victim-people and the Jewish enemy who had not abandoned one iota of his programs.

We see that [U.S. Secretary of State James] Baker has returned to his shuttle missions, adopting the programs of our [Jewish] enemies and trying to convince the Arab parties [to adopt] the Jews' viewpoint. He tells the Arabs: Today, you are weaker than ever before, and the Jews are stronger than you. You must accept what Israel proposes lest you forgo this opportunity [of a political settlement].

What hurts most is that Baker did not [have to] confront a [united] Arab Islamic stand, but encountered disputes, concessions, and slackness, as though the Palestinian problem is a regional issue which concerns only the Palestinian people. Baker thus perpetuates the Jews' stand which holds that there is an Arab-Israeli conflict and a Palestinian-Israeli conflict, and the problem which has priority in this shuttle mission, from the standpoint of Baker and of the Jews, is resolution of the Arab-Israeli conflict and the establishment of normal relations between Jews and Arabs. Only afterward comes the Palestinian-Israeli conflict. Some Arabs buckle and also make concessions to the point where they [the Arabs] have nothing more over which to negotiate.

We in Hamas are the pioneers and your *mujahidun* who regard the Palestine problem as a problem of belief and religion, and not one of land and earth. To us, it [Palestine] is the most sacred place on earth after Mecca and al-Madina. To forgo even one grain of it is to forgo the faith of the nation and of Islam, [it is] a betrayal of the Prophet [Muhammad] and of the blood of the martyrs, the Companions of the Prophet [*sahaba*], and those who came after them [*tabiʿun*], and those who fell on the soil of the Muslims until our own time.

We call on our *mujahid* people to beware of conceding a single grain of soil from the land of Palestine. We call on the hypocrites and the defeatists and the pimps of the enemy: stop the concessions and the deterioration because there can be no peace with murderers and there is no chance that we will accept these programs.

We say to Baker: go back to your president because our sacred land is not a subject for negotiations, and our people's blood, shed by your bullets and your weapons, shall not come cheap as long as life goes on.

O our suffering Palestinian people, we, with God's help, will continue the *jihad* despite the constraints, the obstacles, and the suppression until the liberation of Palestine, all Palestine, and we stress the following matters:

I. The external domain

1. We request that the governments and peoples of the Arab and Islamic world view the Palestine problem as one of the whole nation and not abandon it or part of it under any circumstances.

2. The Islamic Resistance Movement, Hamas, calls on its supporters everywhere to found a world front [in order to] repulse the plot to eliminate the Palestinian issue.

3. The Islamic Resistance Movement, Hamas, calls on its supporters to publicize the style of the Jewish enemy and his murderous actions in Palestine such as desecrating the holy [places], demolishing mosques and arresting ʿ*ulamaʾ*,[3] and preventing Muslims from reaching the al-Aqsa mosque and ripping up sacred Qurʾans.

II. At the local level

1. We call on the teachers to devote their maximum attention to education, to try to raise it to a scientific level and to invest maximum efforts in education in order to thwart the enemy's endeavors to leave our sons in a state of ignorance.

2. We call on our students to respect their teachers and the schools, to safeguard them, and to be diligent in the educational process.

3. We call on all our people to beware of rumors disseminated by the enemy and his agents regarding strikes. We emphasize that the [only] reliable source in this connection is the leaflet.

4. We call on our brothers in Fatah and the other groups to respect the "Covenant of Honor"[4] and to attain a level of respect for the word and respect for the sacred cause and not to give the enemy the opportunity to widen the dispute between us. We must honor the agreement between us and carry out what it calls for by channeling our efforts into fighting the enemy. We are all the sons of a single homeland, and we are all a common target for our enemy.

3. ʿ*Ulamaʾ*—clergy, those who studied Islamic doctrine and law.
4. "Covenant of Honor"—a joint Hamas-UNC document that was published and circulated in the occupied territories in September 1990. Its purpose was to bring about coordination between the two central streams—the religious and the national—and reduce the friction between them.

5. We call on the merchants to undertake to boycott Israeli goods, and we call on our [fighting] arms who are everywhere to impose [the boycott] forcibly.

III. Action plans

1. Sunday, May 5, 1991, a day of escalating the protest against the policy of expropriating land and establishing settlements.

2. May 9, 1991, a general strike marking the start of the forty-second month of the Intifada.

3. Wednesday, May 15, 1991, a general strike marking the creation of the despicable Jewish state in 1948.

4. Monday, May 20, 1991, a day of escalation on the first anniversary of the massacre at ʿUyun Qara-Rishon Letzion[5] perpetrated by the Zionists.

5. May 27–31 will be days for writing Islamic slogans such as: Islam will punish the murderers, or: Islamic Palestine from the [Mediterranean] sea to the [Jordan] river. The Islamic slogans will fly everywhere.

Praise and honor and glory to the ʿulamaʾ and to our leaders who led the people in the blessed Intifada and are now suffering behind bars.

Praise to all the fathers and mothers who took leave of their martyred sons with calls of "There is no God but Allah," "Allah akbar," and God helps us and is our prop.

Praise to the suffering wives and to the sisters who took leave of their loved ones heroically and steadfastly, and who uphold the pledge to raise a generation imbued with faith and with the spirit of *jihad*, in order to continue the mission.

Praise to all the members of our *mujahidun* Palestinian people for their sacrifice. To them, we say that God is with them and will not abandon them.

Let the uprising continue until victory.

The Islamic Resistance Movement
Hamas
19 Shaʿban 1411
Friday, May 3, 1991

---

5. See UNC leaflet no. 70, n. 6.

THE UNITED NATIONAL COMMAND AND HAMAS
A Comparative View

DURING THE FIRST FIVE YEARS of the Intifada the UNC and Hamas have remained the two most influential bodies among the Palestinian population in the West Bank and the Gaza Strip. Both continue to enjoy significant popularity, both demonstrate an ability to ensure a considerable degree of obedience to their directives, and both obtained broad compliance from the population.

Yet the achievements of both movements reflected different strategies of struggle against Israel, emphasizing different approaches toward institution building and mass mobilization.

The following table summarizes the similarities and differences between the UNC and Hamas according to twenty-nine key issues appearing in the leaflets of one or both bodies.

A careful look at Table 5 shows:

1. Eight issues gained considerable attention from both movements. These included: education, symbolic acts, Palestinian national symbolic figures and events, Muslim symbolic figures and events, Palestinian view of Israeli policy, Israeli and Jewish images, Israeli settlements and settlers in the occupied territories, and attitudes toward peace initiatives.

2. Eight issues received a high degree of attention by the UNC and to a lesser degree by Hamas. These issues revolved around general strikes, forms of violence, boycott against Israeli merchandise, mutual help, Palestinian internal affairs, Palestinian-Arab relations, USA policy and images, Palestinian prisoners, and detainees in Israeli jails.

3. The remaining thirteen issues appeared frequently in the UNC leaflets, while Hamas almost ignored them. These issues related to sit-down strikes, demonstrations and rallies, resignations, civil disobedience, communal economic activities, status of women, Palestinian

TABLE 5

UNC and Hamas Leaflets: A Summary Presentation

UNC

Issues \ Leaflets	1	2	3	6	10	11	12	14	15	16	18	19	21	23	24	25	26	27	28	29	30	36
Education										X	X	X		X	X	X	X	X	X	X	X	X
Symbolic Acts			X	X				X	X	X					X					X		X
National Symbolic figures, events		X				X	X	X	X							X		X	X			X
Muslim Symbolic figures, events		X	X				X							X	X	X			X			
Palestinian view of Israeli policy	X	X			X	X	X					X		X	X	X	X			X		
Israeli & Jewish Images		X			X	X				X	X	X	X	X	X			X	X			
Settlements & settlers		X	X												X	X	X					
Peace Initiatives				X	X		X	X	X		X	X	X			X				X		
General Strikes	X	X	X	X				X	X	X	X	X		X	X		X	X	X	X	X	X
Forms of Violence				X	X	X		X		X	X			X	X					X		
Boycott		X		X	X			X	X	X	X			X						X	X	X
Mutual help				X		X	X	X		X				X		X	X	X	X			
Palestinian Internal affairs				X				X	X			X	X	X	X		X	X	X	X		
Palestinian-Arab states relations				X	X			X	X	X	X	X	X	X	X			X	X			X
USA policy & images				X		X										X	X			X	X	X
Prisoners & detainees	X	X					X				X	X	X	X	X					X	X	X
Sit-down Strikes				X	X	X									X			X				X
Demonstrations & rallies		X		X	X			X	X	X	X							X				X
Resignations				X	X	X	X			X	X	X	X									X
Civil Disobediance				X	X	X	X	X		X	X	X	X	X			X					X
Communal Economic activities						X	X	X	X		X	X	X		X					X		X
Women status & activities		X			X									X						X		
Collaborators		X					X			X	X	X	X			X	X			X	X	
Popular Committees	X					X		X	X	X	X	X	X	X	X	X	X	X		X	X	X
Professionals	X	X	X			X				X		X	X	X				X				X
Workers & Merchants	X	X	X		X	X	X		X					X		X	X	X	X	X	X	
National institutions & unions								X				X				X		X				
Appeals to International organiz.							X	X						X	X	X	X	X	X	X	X	
European & USSR policy/images							X					X	X			X	X	X			X	

Hamas

41	45	48	55	68	70	1	2	4	6	7	8	11	13	14	16	18	21	22	28	30	31	32	33	39	45	49	SL	SL	71	74
X	X	X		X							X	X	X				X			X	X		X	X	X					X
X	X	X	X					X	X	X	X		X									X	X		X				X	X
	X		X				X						X						X	X	X	X	X		X	X		X		
	X	X	X			X		X	X		X		X	X	X		X	X	X		X									
X	X		X	X							X		X		X					X	X	X		X	X		X	X		X
X	X	X		X		X	X	X	X	X		X	X			X				X	X	X			X			X	X	X
X		X	X		X		X	X						X	X	X									X					X
X		X		X	X	X	X		X		X		X		X		X	X							X	X				X
X	X	X	X	X	X					X				X	X		X	X		X	X	X	X		X				X	
	X					X		X					X												X	X				
	X	X		X						X	X		X																	X
X	X	X	X								X			X						X	X			X	X				X	
X	X	X	X	X	X		X													X					X	X	X			X
X		X	X	X	X		X			X									X		X		X	X					X	X
X	X	X		X	X				X	X											X		X	X					X	X
X	X	X	X										X	X						X			X	X	X		X			
X		X	X	X																					X					
X		X	X	X						X											X				X	X	X			X
X		X	X	X			X				X												X	X	X				X	X
X	X	X		X	X					X	X												X	X					X	X
X	X	X	X										X	X						X			X	X	X			X		
X		X	X	X																					X					
X		X	X	X										X											X					
X																														
	X	X	X															X												
X		X																												
	X	X		X																					X					
X	X	X			X																			X						
X	X	X																					X							
	X																						X							X
X	X	X		X																	X									X
	X	X										X											X							
	X	X		X																			X							
		X		X	X																	X								

collaborators with Israel, popular committees, professionals, workers and merchants, building of national institutions and labor unions, appeals to international organizations, and attitudes toward European and USSR policy.

The priorities given by the UNC and Hamas to various issues reflect the character of each movement and their approach to the Intifada. Hamas, in comparison to the UNC, appears as a more populist movement with less sectorial awareness and worldwide perception. Hamas prefers direct appeals to the Palestinian population to follow its directives, while the UNC leans toward mediating bodies such as popular committees and professional and labor unions. Contrary to the UNC, Hamas, as a religious grass-roots movement, pays more attention to issues related to the Arab and the Muslim world rather than to the international arena.

The peace negotiations between the Palestinians and Israel that began in October 1991 in Madrid and the Israeli-PLO agreement of September 1993 to establish a Palestinian Interim Self-Government Authority in the West Bank and the Gaza Strip would affect the status and the strength of the UNC and Hamas among the Palestinian population. An Israeli withdrawal from the territories would be followed by a replacement of the pro-PLO UNC by the PLO itself. Rapid progress in the peace negotiations with clear-cut territorial, institutional, and economic achievements for the Palestinian side would increase the chances of the PLO to gain wider support from the Palestinian community in the occupied territories. Under these circumstances, Hamas would adhere to its extreme ideology, maintaining its organization. Yet, pragmatic considerations would probably lead Hamas to some cooperation with the PLO on a day-to-day level. On the other hand, stagnation or setback in the peace process would increase frustration. It would pave the road for radicalization of the Palestinian public and for an increase in the influence of Hamas and other extremist movements.

· · ·

GLOSSARY

SELECTED BIBLIOGRAPHY

INDEX

GLOSSARY

ahzab	clans
al-Buraq	the Western (Wailing) Wall in the Old City of Jerusalem
fasaʾil	factions; units
fatwa	Islamic legal opinion
fellahin	peasants
fidaʾi	one who sacrifices himself for the sake of Islam
hadith	recollections of what the Prophet, his companions, and his followers said
hajj	pilgrimage to Mecca
al-Haram	holy place; the mosques in Mecca and al-Aqsa in Jerusalem
ʿId al-Fitr	holiday celebrated at the end of the annual month of fasting
ijmaʿ	unanimous consent
jihad	holy war
khutba	sermon
muʾazzin	herald who calls the Muslims for prayer
mujahid (pl. *mujahidun*)	a fighter of Islamic holy war
mukhtar	local leader
murabit (pl. *murabitun*)	a Muslim settler of the frontier
nakba	defeat, disaster
al-Quds	Jerusalem

Ramadan	the month of fasting
ribat	fortress; frontier of the Islamic land
sahaba	companions of the Prophet Muhammad
shabiba	youth
sahwa	religious awakening
shahada	the affirmation of the faith
shahid	martyr
shura	canonic consultation
sunna	traditions and customs comprising Muslim law of the Orthodox stream
surah	chapter of the Qurʾan
tabiʿun	followers of the Prophet
takbir	"Allah the greatest," an order of the commander-in-chief of the Islamic army, which launches the fighting
ʿulamaʾ	clergy, those who studied Islamic law
ussul-al-fiqh	roots of Islamic jurisprudence
waqf	properties dedicated to religious purposes

SELECTED BIBLIOGRAPHY

English

Abu ʿAmr, Ziad. *The Intifada: Causes and Factors of Continuity.* Jerusalem: Passia-Palestinian Academic Society for the Study of International Affairs, 1989.

Abed-Rabbo, Samir, and Doris Safie, eds. *The Palestinian Uprising.* Belmont, Mass.: Association of Arab-American University Graduates, 1990.

Arian, Asher, and Ventura Raphael. *Public Opinion in Israel and the Intifada: Changes in Security Attitudes, 1987–1988.* Tel Aviv: Jaffee Center for Strategic Studies, Tel Aviv University, 1989.

Aronson, Geoffrey. *Israel, Palestinians, and the Intifada: Creating Facts on the West Bank.* London: Kegan Paul International, 1990.

Ayyad, Walid ʿAbd al-Hadi. *The Palestinian Uprising of 1987–1988 and Its Implications for War and Peace in the Middle East.* Ann Arbor, Mich.: U.M.I., 1991.

Bennis, Phyllis. *From Stones to Statehood: The Palestinian Uprising.* Brooklyn, N.Y.: Olive Branch, 1990.

Brynen, Rex, ed. *Echoes of the Intifada: Regional Repercussions of the Palestinian-Israeli Conflict.* Boulder, Colo.: Westview, 1991.

Drury, Richard Toshiyuki. *Plowshares and Swords: The Economics of Occupation in the West Bank.* Boston: Beacon, 1992.

Ellis, Marc H., and Rosemary Radford, eds. *Beyond Occupation: American Jewish, Christian, and Palestinian Voices for Peace.* Boston: Beacon, 1990.

Emerson, Gloria. *A Year in the Intifada: A Personal Account from an Occupied Land.* New York: Atlantic Monthly, 1991.

Goldberg, Giora, Gad Barzilai, and Efraim Inbar. *The Impact of Intercommunal Conflict: The Intifada and Israeli Public Opinion.* Jerusalem: Leonard Davis Institute, 1991.

Heller, Mark, and Sari Nusseibeh. *No Trumpets, No Drums.* New York: Hill & Wang, 1991.

Hilterman, Joost R. *Behind the Intifada: Labor and Women's Movements in the Occupied Territories.* Princeton: Princeton Univ. Press, 1991.

Hudson, Michael C., ed. *The Palestinians: New Directions.* Washington, D.C.: Center for Contemporary Arab Studies, Georgetown Univ., 1990.

Hunter, F. Robert. *The Palestinian Uprising: A War by Other Means*. Berkeley: Univ. of California Press, 1991.
Lederman, Jim. *Battle Lines: The American Media and the Intifada*. New York: Holt, 1992.
Lockman, Zachary, and Joel Beinin, eds. *The Palestinian Uprising Against Israeli Occupation*. Boston, Mass.: South End, 1989.
Marshall, Phil. *Intifada: Zionism, Imperialism, and the Palestinian Resistance*. London: Bookmarks, 1989.
McDowall, David. *Palestine and Israel: The Uprising and Beyond*. Berkeley: Univ. of California Press, 1989.
Melman, Yossi, and Dan Raviv. *Beyond the Uprising: Israelis, Jordanians, and Palestinians*. Westport, Conn.: Greenwood, 1989.
Mosley Lesch, Ann, and Mark Tessler, eds. *Israel, Egypt and the Palestinians: From Camp David to Intifada*. Bloomington: Indiana Univ. Press, 1989.
Nassar, Jamal R., and Roger Heacock, eds. *Intifada: Palestine at the Crossroads*. New York: Praeger, 1990.
Peretz, Don. *Intifada: The Palestinian Uprising*. Boulder, Colo.: Westview, 1990.
Punishing a Nation: Human Rights Violations During the Palestinian Uprising, December 1987–December 1988. Ramallah, West Bank: Al-Haq—Law in the Service of Man, 1988.
Rigby, Andrew. *Living the Intifada*. London: Zed, 1991.
Schiff, Ze'ev, and Ehud Ya'ari. *Intifada: The Palestine Uprising—Israel's Third Front*. New York: Simon and Schuster, 1990.
Shalev, Aryeh. *The Intifada: Causes and Effects*. Boulder, Colo.: Westview, 1991.
Steinberg, Paul. *The Graffiti of the Intifada: A Brief Survey*. Jerusalem: Passia—Palestinian Academic Society for the Study of International Affairs, 1990.
Strum, Philippa. *The Women Are Marching: The Second Sex and the Palestinian Revolution*. Chicago: Lawrence Hill, 1992.
White, Patrick. *Let Us Be Free: A Narrative Before and During the Intifada*. Clifton, N.J.: Kingston, 1989.
Winternitz, Helen. *A Season of Stones: Living in a Palestinian Village*. New York: Atlantic Monthly, 1991.

Arabic

'Abd Allah, Ghassan. *al-Intifadah wa-Isra'il: ta'thir al-Intifadah 'ala Isra'il*. Acre: Dar al-Aswar, 1990.
'Abd al-Hadi, 'Izzat. *al-Intifadah wa-ba'd qadaya al-tanmiyah al-sha'biyah*. Ramalla: S.N., 1992.
'Abd al-Majid, Wahid. *Intifadat al-Daffah wa al-Qita' wa-tatawur al-harakah al-wataniyah al-filastiniyah*. Jerusalem: S.N., 1988.
Abu 'Amr, Ziyad. *al-Intifadah: asbabuha wa-'awamil istimraruha*. Jerusalem: al-Jam'iyah al-Filastiniyah al-Akadimiyah, 1989.
Abu Salih, Ziyad. *al-Intifadah fi nazar al-Isra'iliyyin*. Jerusalem: Manshurat al-'Arab li al-Sihafah, 1990–1991.

Abu Shamalah, Fayiz. *al-Intifadah fi qawaʿid al-lughah al-ʿarabiyah*. Jerusalem: Ittihhad al-Kuttab al-Filastiniyyin, 1990.

ʿAriqat, Saʾib. *al-Intifadah wa al-taghyirat: Dirasah fi athar al-intifada ʿala al-hayakal al-iqtisadiyah wa al-ijtimaʿiyah wa al-siyasiyah wa al-diniyah fi al-mujtamaʿ al-filastini dakhil al-aradi al-filastiniyah al-muhtallah*. Jerusalem: Dar al-ʿAwdah, 1990.

al-Dajani, Ahmad Sidqi. *al-Intifada al-filastiniyah wa al-sahwa al-ʿarabiyah*. Cairo: Dar al-Mustaqbal al-ʿArabi, 1988.

Hajj Yahya, Amin. *al-ʿAmal al-ijtimaʿi fi dhill al-Intifada*. Jerusalem: Markaz al-Irshad al-ʿArabi, 1988.

Hasanayn, Suhayl. *al-Intifadah: al-siraʿ bayn sulutat al-ihtilal wa al-filastiniyyin fi dawʾ ʿilm al-ijram*. Jerusalem: al-Jamʿiyah al-Filastiniyah al-Akadimiyah, 1991.

Hassassian, Manuel S. *Al-Intifada: jabha thalitha li-Israʾil*. Jerusalem: Markaz al-Quds li al-Abhath, 1990.

Jamʿiyyat al-Dirasat al-ʿArabiyah. *al-Intifadah fi al-sahafah al-ʿarabiyah*. Jerusalem: Markaz al-Maʿlumat wa al-Tawthiq, 1989.

al-Jarbawi, ʿAli. *al-Intifadah wa al-qiyadat al-siyasiyah fi al-Daffah al-Gharbiyah wa-Qitaʿ Ghazza*. Beirut: Dar al-Taliʿah, 1989.

Jebarah, Taysir. *al-Intifadah al-shaʿbiyah al-filastiniyah*. Nablus: Jamiʿat al-Najah al-Wataniyah, 1989.

al-Khalili, ʿAli. *al-Intifadah wa al-sahafah al-mahaliyah*. Jerusalem: al-Jamʿiyah al-Filastiniyah al-Akadimiya, 1989.

al-Khuli, Lutfi. *al-Intifadah wa al-dawlah al-filastiniyah*. Jerusalem: Wekalat Abu ʿArafah, 1989.

al-Khuri, Jiryis. *Intifadat al-samaʾ wa-Intifadat al-ard*. Nazareth: Matbaʿat al-Hakim, 1990.

Lagnat al-Dirasat al-Nisawiyah. *al-Intifadah wa baʿd qadaya al-marʾah al-ijtimaʿiyah*. Jerusalem: Markaz Bisan, 1991.

al-Madhun, Rabiʿi. *al-Intifadah al-filastiniyah: al-haykal al-tanzimi*. Acre: Dar al-Aswar, 1989.

Rigbi, Andrew. *al-Intifadah min ajl al-taʿallum*. Jerusalem: al-Jamʿiyah al-Filastiniyah al-Akadimiyah, 1989.

Shaʿban, Ibrahim Muhammad. *al-Intifadah al-filastiniyah fi ʿamiha al-awwal*. Jerusalem: S.N., 1989.

Hebrew

Benvenisti, Meron. *Machol ha-charadot: Intifada, milchemet ha-mifrats, ve-tahalikh ha-shalom*. Jerusalem: Keter, 1992.

Gal, Reuven, ed. *ha-Milchamah ha-shviʿit: hashpaʿot ha-Intifada ʿal ha-chevrah be-Yisraʾel*. Tel Aviv: Hakibbutz Hameuchad, 1990.

Ghanim, Asʿad, and Sarah Ozacky. *Kav yarok, kavim adumim: ʿarviye-Yisraʾel nokhach ha-Intifada*. Givat Haviva: Hamakhon Lelimudim ʿArviyim, 1990.

Gilbar, Gad, and Asher Susser, eds. *be-ʿEin ha-sikhsukh: ha-Intifada*. Tel Aviv: Hakibbutz Hameuchad, 1992.

Golan, Dafna. ʿAtsurim be-lo mishpat: maʿtsarim minhaliyim ba-shtachim me-techilat ha-Intifada. Jerusalem: B'tselem—The Israeli Information Center for Human Rights in the Occupied Territories, 1992.

Golan, Dafna, and Stanley Cohen. Chakirat falastinim be-tqufat ha-Intifada. Jerusalem: B'tselem, 1991.

Inbari, Pinhas. ha-Optsyah ha-falastinit: Ashaf mul ha-etgar ha-tsiyoni. Jerusalem: Carmel, 1989.

Klein, Menachem. Ashaf ve ha-Intifada: me-hitromemut ruach le-metsuqah. Tel Aviv: Dayan Center, Tel Aviv Univ., 1991.

Lazar, Hadara. Maʿrechet ha-misuyi ba-Gadah ha-Maʿravit ve be-Retsuʿat ʿAzah ke-machshir le-akhifat ha-shilton be-tqufat ha-hitqomemut. Jerusalem: B'tselem, 1990.

Mishal, Shaul, and Reuben Aharoni. Avanim zeh lo hakol: ha-Intifada ve-neshek ha-kruzim. Tel Aviv: Hakibbutz Hameuchad and Avivim, 1989.

Pappe, Ilan, ed. Islam ve-shalom: gishot islamiyot le-shalom ba-ʿolam ha-ʿaravi ben zmanenu. Givat Haviva: Hamachon Lecheqer Hashalom (IPR), 1992.

Paz, Reuben. ha-Amana ha-islamit ve-mashmaʿutah: ʿiyun rishoni ve-targum. Tel Aviv: Dayan Center, Tel Aviv Univ., 1988.

Rozen, Roli and Hamerman Ilana. Meshorerim lo yikhtevu shirim. Tel Aviv: Am Oved, 1990.

Swirski, Shlomo, and Ilan Pappe', eds. ha-Intifada: mabat mi-bifnim. Tel Aviv: Mifras, 1992.

INDEX

ᶜAar, 127
ᶜAayda (refugee camp), 266
Abraham, Tomb of, 137
Abu ᶜAmmar. *See* Arafat, Yasir
Abu Dis (college), 3
Abu Jihad, 88, 147, 251; as martyr, 82–83, 85–86, 99, 141, 150, 155
Abu Musa, 109
Abu Ramadan, Kheyri, 95
Abu Sharar, 55
Abu Shilbaya, Muhammad, 12
Abu Talib, Jaᶜfar Ibn, 32, 223
Abu ᶜUbayda Ibn al-Jarrah, 208, 223
Accountants, 160, 167
Acre, 218, 239
Afghanistan, 235, 239, 260
Agents. *See* Israeli agents
Agrexco, 116
Agriculture, 38, 110, 112, 121, 133, 138, 196, 245–46, 247; local, 70, 84, 116, 127, 167
Aid, 46; mutual, 110, 177, 183, 247, 287
Algeria, 68, 88, 95, 191n. 3
Alignment. *See* Labor Alignment
All-Palestine Government, 129
al-Amᶜari (refugee camp), 56, 117, 121
al-ᶜAmla, Jamil, 19
Amman Agreement, 21–22
Amorium, 260–61
ᶜAnabta, 16, 132, 140
Ansar 2, 57
Ansar 3, 57, 117, 119, 129, 150, 160, 161, 166, 224
al-Aqsa Mosque Day, 111, 117
al-Aqsa mosque, 111, 117, 179, 204, 217, 239, 249–50, 267

Arabism, 244, 247
Arab-Israeli conflict, 283
Arab-Israeli War (1967), 189, 251
Arab-Israeli War (1973). *See* October War
Arab Liberation Front, 164, 197
Arab Nationalists, 12
Arab revolt, 55
Arabs, 85, 177–78, 287
Arab states, 65n. 2, 154, 191, 237–38; UNC appeals to, 111, 114, 177–78. *See also states by name*
Arab summit, 8, 68, 73, 99, 108–9; UNC on, 78–79, 104, 113. *See also* Baghdad summit; Rabat summit; Uprising summit
Arafat, Yasir, 10, 20, 21, 88, 129, 130, 136, 141, 196, 274; and United Nations, 124, 143, 150, 154
Arens, Moshe, 19
Army, 29, 47n. 13, 129, 132, 137, 179; Israeli, 109, 265–66; opposition to, 57–58, 74, 109
al-ᶜArub, 121
al-Asad, Hafiz, 73, 88
Ashkelon, 274
ᶜAskar (refugee camp), 56
Assassinations, 22, 88, 251
Associations, 46, 126–27
ᶜAtlit, 105
Autonomy, 163–64
ᶜAyn Jalut, Battle of, 32
ᶜAyn Yabrud, 185
al-Azhar University, 3, 202
al-ᶜAziz, Ahmad ᶜAbd, 240
ᶜAzun, 117, 121

299

Badr, Battle of, 227, 281
Baghdad, 251
Baghdad summit, 9
Baker, James, 176, 194, 266, 267, 283, 284
Balata (refugee camp), 56, 121, 280
Balfour, Arthur James, 246
Balfour Declaration, 144, 245, 246, 266, 267, 268, 282–83
Bani Naʿim, 121
Banks, 38
Banu Nadir, 246
Baʿth, 12
Baybars Al-Zahir Baybars, 32, 202
Beit Furiq, 115, 185
Beit Hanina, 3
Beit Jala, 16, 117, 121
Beit Saffa, 177
Beit Sahur, 117, 121, 176, 178, 184, 268
Bethlehem, 110, 117, 121, 196
Bethlehem University, 3
Bidya, 127
al-Bira, 3, 12, 15, 18, 22
Bir Zeit University, 2–3, 18, 22
Bittin, 60
Bituniya, 274
Black September, 124–25, 129, 173
Blockades, 62–63
Border Police, 159
Boycotts, 104, 107, 114, 128, 133, 171, 287; of Israeli goods, 38, 43, 70, 74, 96, 100, 110, 121–22, 153, 160, 177, 179, 197, 219, 226; work, 84, 89–90, 167
British Mandate, 25, 57n. 4, 137
al-Buraq revolt, 122
Burj al-Barajneh (refugee camp), 112
al-Bureij (refugee camp), 56, 117
Burka, 121
Bush, George, 154
Businesses, 56–57
Businessmen, 45. *See also* Merchants

Camp David accords, 14, 103, 163, 189, 190, 234; opposition to, 16, 201–2, 205, 223

Camps. *See* Refugee camps
Charitable societies, 16, 126–27
Chartered Accountants Association, 167
Children, 101, 187
Chile, 115
Christians, 32, 33, 156
Civil Administration, 18, 29, 45, 107, 133, 167; resignations from, 38, 69, 74, 85, 95, 104, 110, 160
Civil disobedience, 12, 176–77, 287; directives for, 38, 39, 58, 73–74, 91, 100–101, 115
Collaborators, 65n. 1, 100, 127, 133, 184, 251, 290; opposition to, 70, 149, 171, 191
Colleges, 2–3, 116
Committees, 46, 100, 110, 115, 128, 179; of National Solidarity, 12; neighborhood, 182, 183, 186; roles of, 97, 101, 117, 132; and UNC, 56, 91, 105, 166, 182, 290. *See also* Popular committees
Confrontation, 91, 122; Hamas's calls for, 214–15, 242–43, 267; UNC calls for, 162, 173, 179
Council for Higher Education, 116, 138, 153, 162
Curfews, 58, 125n. 1, 139, 205, 208, 227; in Gaza Strip, 72, 79, 95, 119

al-Dahariya, 105, 119, 121, 156, 274. *See also* Ansar 3
Dawud, Bishara, 16
Dayan, Moshe, 15, 18
Day of the Palestinian Prisoner, 226, 260
Declaration of Human Rights, 127
Defense Regulations. *See* Emergency Laws
Deir al-Balah, 90, 127
Deir Yassin massacre, 81, 125, 223, 258, 260, 270
Democratic Front for the Liberation of Palestine (DFLP), 25
Demonstrations, 13, 16, 66, 74, 91, 101–2, 287

Deportation, deportees, 158, 179; opposition to, 57, 85, 118, 119, 122, 124, 132, 149, 206
Deportees Day, 85, 186
Detainees, 57, 96, 118, 122, 132, 137, 159, 206, 256, 274, 287; UNC support for, 105, 115, 117, 129, 150, 152, 156, 160, 161, 178, 179
Detention centers, 34, 105, 109, 129, 159, 160, 166, 179, 224; Hamas members in, 274, 275, 276–77
DFLP. *See* Democratic Front for the Liberation of Palestine (DFLP)
Doctors, 62, 116, 138
Dudin, Mustafa, 19
al-Duheisha (refugee camp), 117, 121
Dumas, Roland, 196
Duweima, 125

Economy, 46–47, 57, 114, 116, 287; home-based, 38, 66, 74, 110; in West Bank and Gaza Strip, 1, 3, 41–42, 44, 132
Education, 1, 2–4, 161, 162, 247, 287; importance of, 38–39, 57, 74–75, 91, 96, 106, 111, 121, 127, 133, 137–38, 143–44, 155, 171–72, 179, 187, 197, 220, 221–22, 233, 243, 255, 259, 262–64; shutdown of, 61–62, 116
Egypt, 17, 129n. 2; Hamas references to, 201–2, 244, 247
Eighteenth Palestinian National Council, 22
Elections, 4, 10, 15, 16, 57, 132, 144, 250, 273
Emergency Laws, 57, 132
Emigration, 3, 161, 247, 267
Employment, 3–4, 15, 38, 79–80, 227
Etzion Bloc, 14
Europe, 16, 154, 290
European Common Market, 116
European Community, 159, 191
European Parliament, 129, 130, 178

Factory owners, 110, 133, 196
al-Farʿah, 57, 105
al-Faruqi, Hamdi al-Taji, 12
Fatah, 4, 5, 25, 27, 82n. 1, 164, 272n. 3, 275, 276, 284
al-Fawar, 121
France, 196, 244n. 4, 247

Galilee, 69
Gaza Strip, 3, 5, 9, 10, 26, 29, 69, 74, 75, 90, 101, 105, 109, 110, 119, 121, 125, 128, 132, 133, 162, 176–77, 214, 218, 266, 287, 290; curfews in, 72, 79; demography of, 1–2; Israeli policy and, 14–23; refugee camps in, 95, 116–17, 235; UNC and, 159, 160, 166, 167, 185
General Assembly Resolution 181. *See* Partition Resolution
General Union of Students, 186
Geneva Conventions, 99, 124, 127, 132
Golan Heights, 85, 251
Gorbachev, Mikhail, 101, 103, 154
Great Britain, 144, 244n. 4, 246, 247, 251, 267. *See also* British Mandate
Green Line, 90, 120, 133
Gulf War, 114, 188–89, 190–91, 194, 278–79. *See also* Iran-Iraq War

Habib, Philip, 65
Haifa, 218, 239
Halhul, 11, 15
Hamas, 26, 27, 30–33, 38n. 9, 42–43, 44, 45–46, 48, 197, 217–18, 287; on agriculture, 245–46; on Arab states, 237–38; on Balfour Declaration, 282–83; on confrontation, 214–15, 242–43; directives of, 39–41, 219–20, 235–36, 239–40, 243–44, 247–48, 252, 255–56, 258–61, 266–68, 275–77, 280–81, 284–85; on education, 221–22, 262–64; on Egypt, 201–2; on Gulf War, 278–79; on Jews, 218–19, 246–47; on *jihad*, 265–66, 269–73; leaflets

Hamas (continued)
 of, 28, 29; on nationalism, 238–39; on oppression, 227–28, 234–35, 241–42; on partitioning, 250–51; and PLO, 274, 275–77; on prisoners, 225–26; proclamations of, 202–10, 223–24, 230–33, 253–55, 257–58, 283–84; on Temple Mount, 216–17, 249–50; and UNC, 35–37, 125–26; on United States, 211–13
Hamdallah, Wahid, 16
Hanun, Hilmi, 15–16
Harakat al-muqawama al-Islamiyya. See Hamas
al-Haram. See Temple Mount
al-Haramayn, 217
al-Hasan, Hani, 7
Health services, 62, 80
Hebron, 11, 12, 15, 22, 127, 266, 274
Hebron University, 3
Hittin, Battle of, 32
Holy places, 115, 117. See also Shrines
House demolitions, 13, 115, 132, 158, 227, 271
Hukumat ʿummum Filastin. See All-Palestine Government
Hussan, 117
Hussein, King, 20, 21, 131
Hussein Bin Ali, 246
al-Husseini, ʿAbd al-Qadir, 33, 77, 78, 80, 125, 253, 256, 258, 260

Identity cards, 90, 101, 105, 227, 246
ʿIdna, 117
Imperialism: American, 64–65, 73, 89, 131, 143, 191, 266; Israeli, 163, 189
Independence Day, 144, 149, 178–79
Industry, 66, 219
Institutions, 290; educational, 2–3, 38, 57, 126–27, 247. See also Schools; Universities
Intelligence. See Israeli intelligence
Intelligentsia, 12
Internal front, 133–34, 138
International Committee of the Red Cross, 85, 224
Iran, 114

Iran-Iraq War, 114, 239
Iraq, 16, 114, 181, 251; and Gulf War, 188–89, 190, 191, 194, 279
Islam, 244, 247; figures and symbols of, 32, 287; fundamentalism and, 4, 5; Hamas's views of, 216–18, 255, 280
Islamic Association. See al-Mujammaʿ al-Islami
Islamic Bloc, 26
Islamic Jihad, 22, 26, 27, 28–29
Islamic Movement, 251
Islamic Resistance Movement. See Hamas
Islamic University, 3, 5
Islamic Young Women's Society, 26
Israel, 7, 12, 13, 34, 43, 116, 131–32, 178, 244n. 4, 247, 250, 251, 287; economic break with, 38, 41–42, 44, 47; and Hamas, 31–33; as imperialist, 163, 188, 189; and Lebanon, 95, 101, 143; and local leadership, 14–23; negotiation with, 21–22, 191, 251, 290
Israeli agents, 105, 110
Israeli Communist party, 111
Israeli intelligence, 105, 154, 242, 280
al-Istiqlal mosque, 239

Jabal al-Nar. See Nablus
Jabalya (refugee camp), 22, 56, 60, 95, 117, 127
al-Jaʿbari, Muhammad ʿAli, 12
Jails. See Prisons, prisoners
al-Jalazun (refugee camp), 117, 121, 185
Jamʿiyyat al-shabbat al-Muslimat, 26
al-Jazzar mosque, 239
Jedid, Chedli Ben, 73
Jenin, 117, 127, 133, 144, 266, 274
Jericho, 110
Jerusalem, 12, 33, 110, 113, 115, 117, 122n. 1, 127, 131, 168, 177, 180, 185; Hamas's view of, 216–17, 259
Jerusalem Day, 117, 155, 185
Jews: images of, 32–33, 217, 245–46, 287
al-Jiddi, Muhammad, 95
Jihad, 26, 30; of Hamas, 32–33, 204, 226, 227, 228, 235, 238, 255, 260, 264, 265, 269–73, 285

Index

al-Jihad al-Islami. *See* Islamic Jihad
John Paul II, 178
Jordan, 17, 20, 70, 113, 114, 120, 131, 191n. 3, 218; and local leadership, 10–14, 15, 16; and PLO, 6–10, 19, 21–22, 125
Jordanian Communist party, 12
Jordan Rift Valley, 14, 110, 167
Journalists, 117, 119
Judiciary, 168
Juneid, 274

Kafr Malik, 121, 132, 185
Kafr Nueʿima, 60
Kafr Qassim, 125, 139, 241, 244, 247
Kanafani, Ghassan, 33, 55
Karameh, Battle of, 71
Karameh Day, 157, 162, 192, 281
Karameh, Battle of, 157–58, 159–60
Khalaf, Karim, 11, 15, 16
Khalid Ibn al-Walid, 32, 212, 214, 234
Khalid al-Islambuli, 251
Khaldi Nazzal, 55
al-Khalil al-Rahman, 137
Khan Yunis, 56, 95, 134, 140, 185
al-Khatib, Yusuf, 19
Khaybar, Battle of, 32, 212, 215, 242
Kifl Kharith, 166
Killing, internal, 183–84
Kissinger, Henry, 67, 71, 211
al-Kutla al-Islamiyya, 26
Kuwait, 189, 195, 279

Labor, 161
Labor Alignment, 14, 15, 18
Land, 13, 57, 161, 247, 283–84
Land Day, 72, 75, 77, 192, 281
Lawyers, 96, 139, 161
Leadership: and Israeli policy, 14–23; local, 6, 10–14, 45; pamphlet, 29–30
Leaflets, 25; distribution of, 27–28, 121, 172; false, 148–49, 210, 252, 267–68; impact of, 47–48; wording of, 26–27, 31, 33, 34–36, 38
Lebanon, 20, 89, 95, 101, 109, 260; Palestinians in, 142–43, 195–96, 218, 251

Lebanon War, 19, 189
Levinger, Moshe, 137
Libya, 88, 95, 181
Lijan al-shabiba lil-ʿamal al-ijtimaʿi. *See* Shabiba Movement
Likud, 14, 15, 18
London Conference, 251

Maʿad Bin Jabal, 208
al-Madina, 217
al-Maghazi (refugee camp), 56
Mandela, Nelson, 115
Mansur, Tahsin, 19
al-Maqdes, 111
Marches, 66, 116, 125; UNC calls for, 91, 101, 173, 179, 186
Martyrs: commemoration of, 144, 151, 155, 166, 178, 187, 206, 240, 243–44, 258; Intifada, 111–12, 119, 122, 140, 141, 150, 266, 280
al-Masri, Hikmat, 20
Massacres, 111; commemorations of, 81, 124–25, 129, 139, 241, 247, 258, 260, 285
Matussian, Mardus, 184
May Day, 89–90, 186, 196, 198
Mayors, 11
Maythalun, 266
Media, 110, 119, 252
Medical treatment, 121, 122
Megiddo, 105, 274
Merchants, 45, 116, 121–22, 167, 177, 246, 290; participation by, 6, 79, 105, 128, 132–33, 138
Middle class, 45
Milhim, Muhammad, 11, 15, 16
Military Government, 13, 15–16, 18, 114
Mitterrand, François, 178
Money changers, 128, 161
Mordechai, Yitzhak, 170
Moscow summit, 99
Mosques, 241–42, 258; destruction and closing of, 111, 117, 179, 204, 217, 239. *See also* mosques by name
Mubarak, Husni, 65, 266
Mujahidun, 32, 208
al-Mujammaʿ al-Islami, 5, 25, 26, 27, 48–49, 121

Murabitun, 32, 201, 230–31
Murders, 158, 196, 198
Murphy, Richard, 65, 114
Muslim Brothers, 5, 25, 26, 27, 40–41, 48–49
Mu`tah, Battle of, 32, 223
Mu`tasim, 261

Nablus, 16, 22, 110, 116, 117, 121, 125, 132, 133, 159–60, 162, 176, 266; leadership in, 11, 12, 15, 18
Nafha Prison, 112, 274
Nahalin, 166
al-Nahar (newspaper), 104
al-Najah University, 3
Namibia, 115, 119
al-Nasser, Gamal `Abd, 189
al-Nassir, Amin, 16
Nassir, Muhammad, 19
National consciousness, 4–5, 111
National Guidance Committee (NGC), 11, 16, 18
Nationalism, 25, 238–39
Nazareth, 69, 111
Negev, 69, 105, 109, 112, 274
Newspapers, 18, 65, 104
NGC. *See* National Guidance Committee

October War, 8, 189, 261
Officials: noncooperating, 90, 95
Oppression, 141; Hamas on, 227–28, 234–35, 241–42
Organization of Islamic States, 111

Palestine, 69, 88, 122n. 1, 239, 287; independence of, 89, 93, 99, 106, 108, 113, 115, 137, 146–48, 152–53, 164, 175–76, 178, 194; as Islamic state, 26, 30–31, 40, 255; partitioning of, 36, 246, 250–51, 266; recognition of, 154–55; as sacred, 283–84; and United Nations, 171, 280

Palestine Liberation Organization (PLO), 4, 20–21, 37, 41, 59, 60, 83, 130, 143, 152, 190, 290; activities of, 25–26; and Hamas, 274, 275–77; and Israel, 16–18; and Jordan, 6–10, 19, 21–22, 125; leadership of, 48–49, 105, 114–15, 124; as legitimate representative, 73, 78–79, 93, 99, 100, 113–14, 148, 154, 158, 191, 194; and local leadership, 10–14, 15–16, 17; and peace negotiations, 21–22, 195; and resignees, 84–85; and Syria, 73, 88–89, 94–95, 178; and UNC, 27, 34, 56, 65, 66, 68, 147, 164, 171, 173
Palestinian Central Council, 114, 176, 190, 195
Palestinian Communist party (PCP), 25, 164, 210
Palestinian Declaration of Independence, 144, 147, 148, 175–76
Palestinian Interim Self-Government Authority, 290
Palestinian-Israeli conflict, 283
Palestinian Left, 4
Palestinian Liberation Front, 164
Palestinian National Council (PNC), 36, 114–15, 136, 147, 149, 152, 164, 176, 190, 270, 271; goals of, 142, 154, 159; meetings of, 89, 125, 140–41
Palestinians, 16, 25, 30, 32, 49, 85, 251, 287, 290; identity of, 120–21, 168; in Lebanon, 142–43, 195–96; national rights of, 88, 98–99, 114, 116, 131; and PLO, 14, 100, 124; self-determination of, 21, 106, 108–9, 115, 132, 142, 148, 164, 176, 178, 194
Palestinian Teachers Day, 155
Partition Resolution, 36, 251, 253
Pax Americana, 194
PCP. *See* Palestinian Communist party
Peace: as goal, 34–35, 142, 154
Peace initiatives, 21–22, 195, 287, 290
Peddlers, 161
Peel Commission, 250–51
Péres, Shimon, 15, 34, 47n. 12, 60, 270
Perez de Cuellar, Javier, 124
PFLP. *See* Popular Front for the Liberation of Palestine

Index   305

PLO. *See* Palestine Liberation
  Organization
PNC. *See* Palestinian National Council
Police, 127, 159, 274
Popular committees, 46, 74, 95, 118, 119,
  123, 127; calls for, 69, 91; roles of,
  48–49, 101, 112, 132, 138, 143, 144,
  149, 166, 172, 173
Popular Front for the Liberation of
  Palestine (PFLP), 25, 153, 155, 164
Population growth, 1–2
Prices, 70, 167, 179
Prisons, prisoners, 39, 57, 100, 112, 139,
  159, 166, 187, 227, 274, 287; Hamas
  support for, 225–26, 256, 260; UNC
  support for, 119–20, 152, 155, 161,
  198
Professionals, 6, 74, 290
Property, 110. *See also* Land
Public services, 38

Qabatya, 117, 121, 127
Qalandya, 56, 121
Qalqilya, 16, 60, 117, 132, 134, 166
al-Qassam, ʿIzz al-Din, 33, 55, 60, 77,
  125, 144, 179, 245, 247, 268
al-Qassim, ʿUmar, 166
Qastel, 33, 78, 258
Qastel Battle Day, 80–81
Qawasima, Fahd, 11, 15, 16
al-Qawmiyyun al-ʿArab, 12
Qibya, 125, 139, 241, 243, 270
al-Qiyada al-wataniyya al-muwahada. *See*
  United National Command
al-Quds. *See* Jerusalem
Qutuz, 202
QWM. *See* United National Command
  (UNC)

Rabat summit, 8–9, 10, 14
Rabin, Yitzhak, 19, 34; references to, 72,
  104, 118, 119, 134, 159, 163, 164, 270
Racism, 114, 119, 165
Radicalism, 1, 6, 12–14, 45
Radio, 71

Rafah, 56, 60, 140, 185
Raids, 135–36, 142
Rallies, 106, 129, 287
Ramallah, 11, 12, 15, 18, 22, 79, 274
Reagan, Ronald, 101, 103, 154, 164, 189
Red Cross. *See* International Committee
  of the Red Cross
Refugee camps, 22–23; references to, 56,
  60, 90, 95, 116–17, 121, 142, 162, 196,
  205, 218, 235
Religion, 32–33, 250. *See also* Islam
Rent, 128, 219
Resignations, 66, 100, 287; calls for, 74,
  95, 105, 107, 115; from Civil
  Administration, 38, 69, 104, 110, 160;
  support for, 79, 84–85
Rights: human, 79, 120, 137, 165;
  national, 88, 98–99, 114, 116, 131,
  136–37; of self-determination, 21, 33,
  106, 109, 113, 115, 132, 142, 148, 164,
  176, 178, 194
Riots, 22, 47n. 13, 122n. 1. *See also*
  Confrontation; Demonstrations
Rishon Letzion, 198, 285
Rogers, William, 211
Russian Compound, 119

Sabra (refugee camp), 124–25, 129, 173
Sadat, Anwar, 16, 189, 251
Salah al-Din al-Ayyubi, 32, 202, 208,
  212, 214, 218, 234, 239
Salim, 185
Saudi Arabia, 16
Sawalma, Waʾil Tawfiq, 280
Schools, 172, 235, 243; shut down of,
  61–62, 74–75; UNC support for, 91,
  111, 144
Security, 14, 29, 154
Security Council, 124, 126, 127, 142,
  195, 212; resolutions of, 21, 88, 114,
  132, 147, 153
Security Council Resolution: No. 242,
  21, 147, 153; No. 338, 21, 147; No.
  598, 114; No. 605, 88, 132
Self-determination, 21, 33, 106, 109, 113,
  115, 132, 142, 148, 164, 176, 178, 194
Services, 42, 95

Settlements, 13, 14–15, 65, 131, 287; opposition to, 57, 132, 181, 209; work boycotts in, 84, 85, 89–90, 100, 104, 167
Shabiba Movement, 5, 79, 119
al-Shakʿa, Bassam, 11, 15, 16
Shamir, Yitzhak, 35, 60, 67, 68, 128, 130, 158, 163, 164, 176, 189, 270
Shamir Plan, 189–90, 266
Sharon, Ariel, 18, 19, 34, 57, 60, 128
al-Shati (refugee camp), 56, 90, 95, 117, 235
Shatila (refugee camp), 109, 112, 124–25, 129, 173
Shatta, 274
al-Shawwa, Rashad, 20
Shehada, ʿAziz, 12
Sheykh Radwan mosque, 60, 258
Shock squads, 69, 116, 125, 127, 132, 162; role of, 37–38, 46, 48–49, 54, 70, 91–92, 95–96, 106, 110, 112, 122, 143, 144, 166, 173, 183, 184–85
Shomron, Dan, 47, 124
Shrines, 110, 111
Shultz, George, 154; plan of, 67, 68, 78–79, 80, 89, 99, 100, 101, 103, 211–12, 223, 234, 235
Sinai, 251
Sinjil, 133, 166
Societies. *See* Charitable societies
Soviet Union, 84, 88, 104, 178, 235, 251, 290
Strikes, 13, 16, 35, 39, 44, 46–47, 56, 110, 121, 122, 172, 197, 287; Hamas calls for, 126, 236, 239, 243, 244, 247, 252, 256, 260, 268, 281; UNC calls for, 53–54, 60–61, 62, 65, 71, 75, 80, 85, 91, 96, 97, 101, 105–6, 107, 111–12, 115, 117, 122, 129, 133, 134, 139, 144, 149, 150, 155, 156, 168, 173, 174, 179–80, 183, 185, 186, 187, 191, 198
Strike units. *See* Shock squads
Student associations, 16, 21
Students, 3, 5, 62, 75, 202, 243; associations and councils of, 4, 16, 21; Hamas appeals to, 222, 263–64;

UNC appeals to, 106, 111, 161, 162, 167, 186
Supreme Students Council, 167
Symbolic acts, 287
Syria, 16, 109; and Palestine Liberation Organization, 22, 73, 88–89, 94–95, 178

Taba, 218
Tamir, Avraham, 124
Tamun, 166
Tawil, Ibrahim, 15, 16
Taxation, taxes, 13, 116, 181, 227; nonpayment of, 39, 73–74, 79, 84, 96, 100, 104, 128, 133; opposition to, 56, 57, 70, 117, 160, 167, 233
Teachers, 235; Hamas appeals to, 222, 263–64; UNC appeals to, 96, 111, 161, 162, 197
Teaching days, 74–75
al-Tell, 121
Temple Mount, 115, 179, 216–17, 249–50
"Temple Mount Faithful," 267
Triangle, 69
Tulkarm, 16, 56, 117, 121, 132, 140
Tunis, 251

ʾUhud, Battle of, 232–33
ʿUmar Ibn al-Khattab, 217
UNC. *See* United National Command
UNESCO, 127, 137–38, 161, 179
"Union Plan," 251
Unions, 16, 79, 110, 126–27, 290
United National Command (UNC), 45–46, 47, 93, 123–24, 287–90; on Abu Jihad, 82–83, 85–86; on Arab summit, 78–79, 113–14; on autonomy, 163–64; on blockades, 62–63; directives of, 38–42, 43, 67–71, 84–85, 90–92, 95–97, 100–102, 106–7, 110–12, 115–17, 121–22, 129, 132–34, 143–45, 149–50, 155–56, 159–62, 166–68, 171–74,

176–80, 182–87, 197–98; on education, 61–62; on elections, 189–90; goals of, 30, 33–35, 44, 77–78, 141–42; on government raids, 135–36; on Gulf War, 188–91; and Hamas, 35–37, 125–26; on independence, 146–49, 175–76; on Karameh Day, 157–58; on Land Day, 72–75; leaflets of, 26, 27–28, 29, 48; on Lebanon, 142–43; on national rights, 98–99, 136–37; on May Day, 89–90; and PLO, 114–15, 140–41; proclamations of, 59–60, 76–78, 80–81, 87–88, 103–6, 108–10, 118–21, 126–28, 130–32, 151–55, 164–65, 169–71, 181–82, 193–97; shock squads of, 37–38; strike calls by, 53–54, 56, 60–61, 62; on Syria, 88–89, 94–95; on United States, 64–65, 158–59

United Nations, 109, 124, 154, 171, 255; on partitioning, 251; resolutions of, 21, 36, 88, 114, 193–94, 251, 280; UNC appeals to, 111, 126, 131–32, 136, 143, 147–48, 150, 178

United Nations Relief and Works Agency (UNRWA), 3, 75, 85, 90, 172–73

United States, 16, 17, 88, 154, 168, 178, 250, 251; and Gulf War, 188, 190–91, 279; Hamas opposition to, 211–13, 267, 280; as imperialist, 64–65, 73, 89, 131, 143, 266; policies of, 171, 176, 194, 259–60, 287; UNC opposition to, 78–79, 80, 99, 100, 101, 103–4, 114, 154, 158–59

U.S. Navy, 114
Universities, 2–3, 116, 153, 202
UNRWA. *See* United Nations Relief and Works Agency
Uprising Summit, 99, 104, 108–9, 114
USSR. *See* Soviet Union
ʿUyun Qara, 198, 285

Vatican, 111
Vendors, 128
Village Leagues, 18–19
Villages, 60, 66, 90, 185–86. *See also villages by name*
Violence, 21, 22–23, 35, 230, 287; calls for, 39–40, 41, 42–43, 67–68, 160
Voice of the Revolution, 71
Voluntary work camp, 111

Weizman, Ezer, 15, 16
West Bank, 1, 5, 12, 17, 23, 69, 74, 109, 160, 218, 287, 290; education in, 2–4; Israeli policy and, 15–23; Jordan and, 113, 120; Palestine Liberation Organization and, 8, 9, 10, 20–21, 25; radicalism on, 13–14; settlement on, 14–15; UNRWA and, 172–73
White-collar workers. *See* Professionals
Women, 2, 16, 96, 115, 117, 287
Work, 38, 43–44, 65, 80; boycotts of, 84, 89–90, 100, 104, 167
Workers, 149, 165, 172–73, 198, 290; support for, 79–80, 85, 186; UNC appeals to, 74, 100, 133, 196
World Children's Day, 101
World Health Day, 80
World Women's Day, 191
World Workers' Day, 89
Yaʿbed, 144
Yarmuk, Battle of the, 32
Yatta, 127, 133
Youth, 5, 45, 91–92
Youth Committees for Social Activity. *See* Shabiba Movement
Youth organizations, 4, 21

Zionism, 34, 65n. 2, 90, 165, 225

Contemporary Issues in the Middle East

This well-established series continues to focus primarily on twentieth-century developments that have current impact and significance throughout the entire region, from North Africa to the borders of Central Asia.

Recent titles in the series include:

Arab Women in the Field: Studying Your Own Society. Soraya Altorki and Camillia Fawzi El-Solh, eds.
The Communist Movement in Egypt, 1920–1988. Tareq Y. Ismael and Rifa'at El Sa'id
The Crystallization of the Arab State System, 1945–1954. Bruce Maddy-Weitzman
Egypt's Other Wars: Epidemics and the Politics of Public Health. Nancy Elizabeth Gallagher
Extremist Shiites: The Ghulat Sects. Matti Moosa
Family in Contemporary Egypt. Andrea B. Rugh
International Relations of the Contemporary Middle East: A Study in World Politics. Tareq Y. Ismael
The Iranian Revolution and the Islamic Republic. Nikki R. Keddie and Eric Hoogland, eds.
Iraq and Iran: Roots of Conflict. Tareq Y. Ismael
Islam and Politics. Third Edition. John L. Esposito
Khul-Khaal: Five Egyptian Women Tell Their Stories. Nayra Atiya
Law of Desire: Temporary Marriage in Shi'i Iran. Shahla Haeri
The Middle East from the Iran-Contra Affair to the Intifada. Robert O. Freedman, ed.
Muslim Hausa Women in Nigeria: Tradition and Change. Barbara J. Callaway
Naguib Mahfouz: From Regional Fame to Global Recognition. Michael Beard and Adnan Haydar, eds.
Oil, Power, and Principle: Iran's Oil Nationalization and Its Aftermath. Mostafa Elm
The Politics of Social Transformation in Afghanistan, Iran, and Pakistan. Myron Weiner and Ali Banuazizi, eds.
Reveal and Conceal: Dress in Contemporary Egypt. Andrea B. Rugh
The Rise of Egyptian Communism, 1939–1970. Selma Botman
The Roots of Separatism in Palestine: British Economic Policy, 1920–1929. Barbara J. Smith
The Rushdie File. Lisa Appignanesi and Sara Maitland, eds.
Toward an Islamic Reformation: Civil Liberties, Human Rights, and International Law. Abdullahi Ahmed An-Na'im
Veils and Words: The Emerging Voices of Iranian Women Writers. Farzaneh Milani
Women Farmers in Africa: Rural Development in Mali and the Sahel. Lucy E. Creevey, ed.
Women in Egyptian Public Life. Earl L. Sullivan
Women in Muslim Family Law. John L. Esposito